The Catholic Concept of Love and Marriage

Other Anthologies

EDITED BY RALPH L. WOODS

A TREASURY OF CATHOLIC THINKING
THE CONSOLATIONS OF CATHOLICISM
THE CATHOLIC COMPANION TO THE BIBLE

The Catholic Concept of
LOVE
and
MARRIAGE

As Explored and Explained in
Moving and Searching Writings by
Prominent Contemporaries and
Famous Earlier Catholics

COMPILED AND EDITED BY
Ralph L. Woods

J. B. LIPPINCOTT COMPANY
Philadelphia and New York

Copyright © 1958 by Ralph L. Woods
First Edition
Printed in the United States of America
Library of Congress Catalog Card Number 58-11125

NIHIL OBSTAT:
The Rt. Rev. Msgr. Joseph H. Brady, S.T.D.
Censor Librorum

IMPRIMATUR:
The Most Reverend Thomas A. Boland, S.T.D.
Archbishop of Newark

Newark, New Jersey
June 16, 1958

Acknowledgments

It is a pleasure for the publisher and editor to acknowledge with thanks the cooperation of the following publishers, authors and copyright owners in granting permission to include material from the works indicated:

APPLETON-CENTURY-CROFTS, INC.: Fulton J. Sheen, *Three to Get Married*, copyright 1951 by Fulton J. Sheen, reprinted by permission of the publishers Appleton-Century-Crofts, Inc.

AVE MARIA MAGAZINE: "A Wife's Prayer," Anonymous, May 25, 1957; "A Mother's Prayer," Anonymous, July 6, 1957; Ed Willock, "A Catholic Approach to Dating," April 20, 1957; Forrest Macken, C.P., "Must a Wife Obey Her Husband?" November 16, 1957.

AVE MARIA PRESS: paper by Eileen Nutting in *It's a Woman's World*, copyright 1951 by The Ave Maria Press.

ACKNOWLEDGMENTS

BENZIGER BROTHERS, INC.: St. Thomas Aquinas, *Summa Theologia*, translated by Fathers of the English Dominican Province, reprinted with permission of Benziger Brothers, Inc., publishers and copyright owners; Vincent J. McNabb, O.P., *The Wayside: A Priest's Gleanings*.

BLACKFRIARS PUBLICATIONS, London, England: Gerald Vann, O.P., *Eve and the Gryphon*, copyright 1946.

THE BRUCE PUBLISHING COMPANY: Joseph A. Breig, *A Halo For Father*, copyright 1954 by The Bruce Publishing Co.

CATHOLIC TRUTH SOCIETY, London, England: Bede Jarrett, O.P., *Meditations For Layfolk*, copyright 1915.

DR. ALPHONSE H. CLEMENS; from his *Marriage and the Family*, copyright 1957 by Prentice-Hall, Inc.

COLUMBIA MAGAZINE: John C. Knott, "More Miracles at Cana," June, 1957.

THE CONFRATERNITY OF CHRISTIAN DOCTRINE: Edwin V. O'Hara, in *Teaching Honesty in the Home, The Parent-Educator*, New Series, vol. IV, copyright 1943 by Confraternity of Christian Doctrine; J. Francis Moroney, in *Teaching Citizenship in the Home, The Parent-Educator*, New Series, vol. V, copyright 1944 by Confraternity of Christian Doctrine.

JOHN C. CORT, and GRAIL MAGAZINE: issue of August, 1957.

CHARLES HUGO DOYLE and GRAIL MAGAZINE: issue of September, 1957.

FARRAR, STRAUS AND CUDAHY, INC.: Francois Mauriac, *The Woman of the Pharisees*, translated by Gerard Hopkins.

EILEEN FARRELL and GRAIL MAGAZINE: issue of September, 1956.

FIDES PUBLISHERS: R. de Montjamot, in MARRIAGE IS HOLY, ed. by H. C. Caffarel, translated by Bernard G. Murchland, C.S.C., copyright 1957 by Fides Publishers.

EUGENE S. GEISSLER and GRAIL MAGAZINE: in issue of

December, 1956, and later in author's book *Father of the Family*, 1957.

GRAIL PUBLICATIONS, St. Meinrad, Indiana: papers from *The Child and Problems of Today*, symposium sponsored by Family Life Bureau of N.C.W.C., copyright 1944 by St. Meinrad Archabbey, Inc.; papers from *The Mother the Heart of the Home*, symposium sponsored by Family Life Bureau of N.C.W.C., copyright 1955 by St. Meinrad Archabbey, Inc.

HARPER AND BROTHERS: Alexis Carrel, *Man the Unknown*, copyright 1935 by Harper and Brothers.

P. J. KENNEDY AND SONS: *The Law of Love: The Spiritual Teachings of Francis Devas, S.J.*, edited by Philip Caraman, S.J., copyright 1954 by P. J. Kennedy and Sons.

LEO J. KINSELLA: *The Wife Desired*, copyright 1953 by Leo J. Kinsella, distributed by Divine Word Missionary Publications, Techny, Ill.

ALFRED A. KNOPF, INC.: Mlle. De Beauvoir, *The Second Sex*, quoted in passage from Lucius F. Cervantes, S.J.

THE LITURGICAL PRESS, St. John's Abbey, Collegeville, Minn.: Dr. Karl Adam, *Holy Marriage*, copyright 1956.

LIVERIGHT PUBLISHING CO.: Bertrand Russell, *Marriage and Morals*, copyright 1956 by Bertrand Russell, quoted in passage from Lucius F. Cervantes, S.J.

LONGMANS, GREEN AND CO.: Gerald Vann, O.P., *The Heart of Man*, copyright 1945 by Gerald Vann, O.P.; T. G. Wayne, *Morals and Marriage*, copyright 1936.

LONGMANS, GREEN AND CO. LTD.: P. J. Gannon, S.J., *Holy Matrimony*, copyright 1923.

PHYLLIS McGINLEY and CURTIS BROWN, LTD.: "Unchastity Is a Sin (What Shall I Tell My Daughters?)" copyright 1954 by The Hearst Corporation.

FORREST MACKEN, C.P. and AVE MARIA MAGAZINE: issue of November 16, 1957.

THE MACMILLAN COMPANY: Canon Jacques Leclercq,

ACKNOWLEDGMENTS

Marriage: A Great Sacrament, translated by the Earl of Wicklow.

NATIONAL CATHOLIC WELFARE COUNCIL, Family Life Bureau: from papers in *The Father, the Head of the Home*, 1953.

NATIONAL COUNCIL OF CATHOLIC MEN: and The Catholic Hour and NBC as co-producers, from radio sermon by Ignatius Smith, O.P., April, 1932.

OXFORD UNIVERSITY PRESS: *St. Thomas Aquinas Philosophical Texts*, selected and translated by Thomas Gilby, O.P., copyright 1951.

J. S. PALUCH CO. INC.: Mario L. Dittami, O. Carm., *I Thee Wed*, copyright 1952 by J. S. Paluch Co. Inc.; Walter Farrell, O.P., *The Looking Glass*, copyright 1951 by J. S. Paluch Co. Inc.

PRENTICE-HALL, INC.: Dr. Alphonse H. Clemens, *Marriage and the Family*, copyright 1957 by Prentice-Hall, Inc., Englewood Cliffs, N. J.

FREDERICK PUSTET CO., INC.: *Christ in the Home*, by Raoul Plus, S.J., a translation from the French, translator not named, copyright 1951 by Frederick Pustet Co., Inc.

THE QUEEN'S WORK: Daniel A. Lord, S.J., *Love's All That Matters*, copyright 1948 by The Queen's Work, St. Louis, Mo.

RANDOM HOUSE, INC.: Modern Library edition of *Introduction to St. Thomas Aquinas*, edited and translated by Anton C. Pegis, copyright 1948 by Random House, Inc.

REDEMPTORISTS FATHERS: Donald F. Miller, C.SS.R., *For Wives and Husbands Only*, copyright 1957 The Liguorian, Liguóri, Mo.

HENRY REGNERY CO.: C. C. Zimmerman and L. F. Cervantes, S.J., *Marriage and the Family, A Text for Moderns*, copyright 1956 by Henry Regnery Co.

CHARLES SCRIBNER'S SONS: Jacques Maritain, *Reflections on America*, copyright 1958 by Jacques Maritain, reprinted by permission of Charles Scribner's Sons.

SHEED AND WARD, INC.: G. K. Chesterton, *What's Wrong with the World* in the *New World*, by Chesterton; Wingfield-

Hope, *Life Together*, copyright 1943 by Sheed and Ward, Inc., New York; Maisie Ward, *Be Not Solicitous*, copyright 1953 by Sheed and Ward, Inc., New York; F. J. Sheed, *Society and Sanity*, copyright 1953 by Sheed and Ward, Inc., New York.

SIMON AND SCHUSTER, INC.: Ernest Dimnet, *What We Live By*, copyright 1932 by Simon and Schuster, Inc.

SOCIETY OF THE LITTLE FLOWER: Albert H. Dolan, O.Carm., *Happiness in Marriage*, copyright 1940 by The Carmelite Press, Englewood, N. J.

JOHN L. THOMAS, S.J. and GRAIL MAGAZINE: issue of March, 1956.

JOSEPH F. WAGNER, INC.: *Catechism of the Council of Trent for Parish Priests*, edited and translated by John A. McHugh, O.P. and Charles J. Callan, O.P., copyright 1937 by Joseph F. Wagner, Inc.

A. P. WATT AND SON, and MISS D. E. COLLINS: G. K. Chesterton, *What's Wrong With the World*, copyright 1910, 1938 Dodd, Mead and Co. Inc.

ED WILLOCK and AVE MARIA MAGAZINE: issue of April 20, 1957.

Miss Rita Keckeissen, of St. Peter's Catholic Lending Library, New York, N. Y., always knowledgeable and helpful, referred me to a number of valuable works I might otherwise have overlooked. I am grateful to both the Rev. Claude Burns, O.F.M.Cap., and Miss Tay Hohoff, of the J. B. Lippincott Company, who almost simultaneously gave me the idea for this collection and urged me to compile it. Miss Hohoff subsequently gave me valuable editorial counsel. Finally, I want to thank the Rt. Rev. Msgr. Irving A. DeBlanc for writing so helpful an introduction to the volume.

RALPH L. WOODS

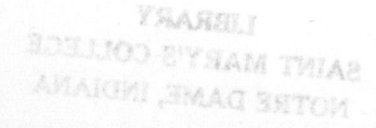

It is indeed of the most utmost importance that the faithful should be well instructed concerning matrimony; both by word of mouth and by the written word, not cursorily but often and fully, by means of plain and weighty arguments, so that these truths will strike the intellect and will be deeply engraved on their hearts.

Pope Pius XI
CASTI CONNUBII, 1930

Contents

Introduction BY THE RT. REV. MSGR. IRVING A. DEBLANC 17
Foreword BY ALPHONSE H. CLEMENS 21

·One

LOVE AND MARRIAGE

Love and Marriage Implanted by God from the Beginning, ST. JOHN CHRYSOSTOM 27
The Profound Significance of Love, COVENTRY PATMORE 29
"Love Is the Wealth of the Soul," W. BERNARD ULLATHORNE 30
Reason and Love, BLAISE PASCAL 31
Love Needs God as an Accomplice, JEAN BAPTISTE LACORDAIRE 32
Romantic Love and Marriage, JACQUES MARITAIN 33
Inordinate Love, FRANCOIS MAURIAC 35
Innate Characteristics of Love, JEAN BAPTISTE LACORDAIRE 36
Supernatural Love, RAOUL PLUS, S.J. 37
Stages of Love, T. G. WAYNE 38
True Love versus Lust, ERNEST DIMNET 40
When Romance Is Exaggerated, DANIEL A. LORD, S.J. 43

Love and the Poets, FRANCIS THOMPSON	44
The True Dowry, JEAN BAPTISTE LACORDAIRE	46
Choosing a Partner, PIUS XI	47
The Council of Trent Cites Acceptable Reasons for Marrying	48
Dangers in Mixed Marriages, PIUS XI	49
Three Fundamentals, PIUS XII	50
On Celebrating the Marriage, ST. JOHN CHRYSOSTOM	50
Marriage and the Liturgy, VINCENT MCNABB, O.P.	51
"For Better—For Worse," P. J. GANNON, S.J.	53
The Ancient Ritual of Blessing the Nuptial Bed	59
The Proper Use of the Power to Pass on Life, FRANCIS DEVAS, S.J.	59
The Origin and Corruption of Marriage, and Its Restoration by Christ and His Church, LEO XIII	61
Natural Reason Supports Matrimony, ST. THOMAS AQUINAS	65
Synodical Letter of the Council of Gangra Defending Marriage	66
"A Seed Sown in the Soul," JACQUES LECLERCQ	67
True Marriage, ST. THOMAS AQUINAS	68
The Moral Guidance of the Church, PIUS XI	69
Marriage Must Be a Free Act, PIUS XI	70
Decisions by the Council of Trent	71
"A Perpetual and Indissoluble Bond," PIUS XI	72
The Catholic Matrimonial Courts, M. J. BROWNE	73
The Catholic Interpretation of the Scriptural Passage Many Non-Catholics Quote to Justify Divorce and Remarriage, LUCIUS F. CERVANTES, S.J.	77
Legitimately Contracted Marriage Always Sacred, PIUS XII	79
Modern Enemies of Christian Marriage, LUCIUS F. CERVANTES, S.J.	80

Fundamental Differences between Man and Woman,
   ALEXIS CARREL   85
Marriage: A Part of the Divine Plan of Society, FATHER
   CUTHBERT, O.S.F.C.   86
Marriage and Celibacy Compared, FRANCIS DEVAS, S.J.   91
Total Unity in Marriage, R. DE MONTJAMOT   93
The Pledge to Christian Marriage   99

Two
HUSBAND AND WIFE

The Triumph of Subjection, WINGFIELD HOPE   103
The Priest's Customary Address to the Bride and Groom   105
Counsel for Newlyweds, PIUS XII   107
Quotation, TOBIAS   108
Reverence between Husband and Wife, F. J. SHEED   108
The Payment of the Marriage Debt, CHARLES HUGH
   DOYLE   110
The Splendor of Sex, F. J. SHEED   112
The Marriage Act, ST. THOMAS AQUINAS   116
Restraint, PIUS XI   117
Chastity, ST. THOMAS AQUINAS   118
Gentleness in Love, GERALD VANN, O.P.   118
"Collaborators of God," PIUS XII   122
Sexual Moderation, PIUS XII   122
Married People Need Chastity, ST. FRANCIS DE SALES   125
Unnatural Birth Control, PIUS XI   126
The Natural Law, ST. THOMAS AQUINAS   127
When the Natural Law Is "Blotted Out," ST. THOMAS
   AQUINAS   128
*Families Are Not Required To Have as Many Children
   as Biologically Possible*, THURSTON DAVIS, S.J.   128
The Use of Rhythm, PIUS XII   129

14   The Catholic Concept of Love and Marriage

The Morality of Rhythm, DONALD F. MILLER, C.SS.R.	131
The Mother or the Child? PIUS XII	134
Must the Sterile Seek Medical Attention? DONALD F. MILLER, C.SS.R.	136
Artificial Insemination, PIUS XII	137
When Love Falters, Transfigure It, FULTON J. SHEEN	138
Counsel for Husbands, ST. JOHN CHRYSOSTOM	141
True Married Love, PIUS XI	142
"The Obedience Woman Owes to Man," PIUS XI	144
Must a Wife Obey Her Husband? FORREST MACKEN, C.P.	145
The Vocation of Women in the World, GERALD VANN, O.P.	150
Love Creates Domestic Harmony, ST. JOHN CHRYSOSTOM	155
Pope St. Gregory the Great Instructs the Clergy How to Counsel Husbands and Wives	156
The Husband's Contribution to Happiness, PIUS XII	158
A Wife's Prayer, ANONYMOUS	159
Should a Wife Ever Permit a Divorce? DONALD F. MILLER, C.SS.R.	159
Avoiding Family Fights, LEO J. KINSELLA	161
If Love Dies, ALBERT H. DOLAN, O.CARM.	164
"The Child Is a Sort of Bridge," ST. JOHN CHRYSOSTOM	165

Three

PARENTS AND CHILDREN

The Parents' Obligations as Educators, as Stated in the Code of Canon Law	169
Love for Children, ST. JOHN CHRYSOSTOM	169
An Ancient Legend	170
"A Paternity Like to That of God," JEAN BAPTISTE LACORDAIRE	171
To Fathers, LEO XIII AND PIUS XII	172

CONTENTS 15

The Romance of Fatherhood, JOSEPH A. BREIG	173
Provider for the Family, EUGENE GEISSLER	175
The Father—an Important Factor in the Development of the Child, ROBERT P. ODENWALD, M.D.	177
The Mother's Sacred Ministry, JEAN BAPTISTE LACORDAIRE	181
A Mother's Prayer, ANONYMOUS	182
Duties and Responsibilities of Mothers, PIUS XII	183
Parents' Duty to Children, ST. AUGUSTINE	187
Papal Pronouncements on the Education and Training of Children, PIUS XI, PIUS XII, LEO XIII	188
Religious Instructions for Children, ST. JOHN CHRYSOSTOM	192
The Child: Citizen of Two Worlds, CATHOLIC BISHOPS OF THE UNITED STATES	193
St. Thomas More Instructs the Tutor of His Children	196
Present-Day Errors in Child Training, ROBERT P. ODENWALD, M.D.	197
A Lesson from the Eagle, SISTER M. TERESA GERTRUDE, O.S.B.	201
There Is No Substitute for Parents, JOHN L. THOMAS, S.J.	202
The Role of the Father in the Christian Home, GREGORY SMITH, O.CARM.	205
Teaching Children to Love Their Neighbor, EILEEN NUTTING	207
Teaching Honesty in the Home, EDWIN V. O'HARA	209
Teaching Citizenship in the Home, J. FRANCIS MORONEY	210
The Young Patriarchs, JOSEPH A. BREIG	213
The Parents' Part in Sex Education, ALEXANDER A. SCHNEIDERS	216
What Shall I Tell My Daughters?, PHYLLIS MCGINLEY	221
A Catholic Approach to Dating, ED WILLOCK	226
Mothers-in-Law and Others-in-Law, MARIO L. DITTAMI, O.CARM.	231

Four
THE FAMILY

Notable Statements on the Family by Pius XII	241
The Christian Family, KARL ADAM	243
The Inspiration of Christ at Home, IGNATIUS SMITH, O.P.	243
The Christian Family, CATHOLIC BISHOPS OF THE UNITED STATES	246
Love When Divinely Protected, BEDE JARRETT, O.P.	249
Woman: Peacemaker and Homemaker, WALTER FARRELL, O.P.	251
The Emancipation of Domesticity, G. K. CHESTERTON	255
Economic Principles for the Christian Family, SISTER MARY ANSELM O'BRIEN, C.S.J.	258
We Didn't Pray Alone, EILEEN FARRELL	261
More Miracles at Cana, JOHN C. KNOTT	264
Wanted: Married Saints!, JOHN C. CORT	268
A Plea for the Family, MAISIE WARD	272
Index of Authors with Sources	279

INTRODUCTION

The love between man and woman which is the source of all other human loves, and of life itself, is again going through a tortuous crisis. We seem to be always only one generation away from paganism. Every generation must again and again resell Christian truths. Ralph L. Woods realizes this and has tirelessly and skillfully marshaled into this one volume one of the most impressive arrays of thinkers on the subject of love and marriage that exists today. This anthology will prove invaluable and indispensable for any leader in the field who is looking for big, authoritative ideas which are quickly accessible.

Modern man is overwhelmed with new thinking, new customs, new needs. Much of it is pagan. Like an overstuffed stomach, his mind cannot digest what it is fed. He finds it very difficult to adapt his interior life to his exterior life. He can hardly respond with his whole being to anything. He responds with that part of himself which first reacts; it may be his emotions or his brains, but it is rarely his whole life. He is in a world of abstraction and of distraction and the two go together. Events, ideas have only a surface and a superficial entry. Ideas either reach his head and remain there in a stratosphere of inactivity or he is like a cork on the river of fashion. His heart, his gestures, react and respond to every change of the current. Man is thus divided into body or soul, into stomach or brain. Love is either chemical, glandular, imaginary, or dreamlike. The soul is no longer considered to be a principle of unity for man is split into two. His love is anonymous, materialistic, sportive.

A phantom is thus being created which is often adored as an idol. This phantom has many of the elements of love. It lacks one main thing: it doesn't exist. It is only imagined; it is a body without soul, a soul without body. This monster takes on godlike proportions. Love becomes a religion. It becomes its own law, its own justification, its own end. It lives in itself and of itself. It is a god. The worshippers of this god share its divinity and that is why two lovers seem to adore each other. "I adore you" is such an easy cry, if said only with the body or a romantic imagination. The word "adore" requires no follow-up. "I love you," however is more difficult to say for it demands action, a gift of one's self.

In the present crisis of conjugal love children are being thought of more frequently, but often not because of religious convictions or because of some enduring reason. Children came as a reaction against the depersonalization of society or because of prosperity, or because of the loneliness of city life or because they represent a sense of social achievements. A third child is often just an intruder. "The greatest enemy of the child is love." Mr. Woods offers proof that it should be otherwise.

With over one thousand divorces a day in the United States, it is obvious that many who marry do not use reason or religion or tradition, but whims, emotions, a thirst for wild pleasure, the idolatry of love.

Christian marriage has always had problems which menaced it, such as drinking, quarreling, adultery, economics, and so on. But there was once a time when individuals could not upset Matrimony itself. There was once a time when there was a collective, a community love which preceded individual love in time and in importance. Lovers today, however, have often no other guarantee of fidelity than the intensity and duration of their own passions.

Our greatest concern is that love is separating itself more and more from our religious climate. Almost every civilization believed that married love was not just a social institution but primarily a divine institution. As love parts from religion it begins to degenerate. Love is never so close to profanity as when instead of consecrating itself in a sacred vow it pretends to replace sacredness. This love is really "free love"; but it is free to do what? To destroy love itself and the two who marry. The idolatrous acts by which two lovers separate themselves from the sacred separate them from each other. It is fatal. The principles involved are suicidal.

A couple thus isolated from the sacred can easily be plunged into abject selfishness. Almost every severe physical or emotional test will break the bonds of that love. To be bound together by flesh alone or by romantic dreams alone is like being bound together by glue.

The Catholic Concept of Love and Marriage is a fortunate timely contribution to the restoration of Christian conjugal love. Ideas will have consequences. Love must again and again be forced into its general context. The very expression, "I love you always," said by young lovers in the ecstasy of a moment can be true only in God. True conjugal love must be placed in the context of having children, of group service, of common ideals, of being protected by the community. To love is not so much to contemplate and to enjoy each other as it is to give one another to realities which surpass one another.

The job of the editor of this book was to shed the illusions of love, to separate the mirage from the oasis, that which is not from that which is. Where love is only a daydream, an awakening must follow. The essence of unity for a couple is not to enjoy each other but to suffer together. Suffering and joy are not two opposites, but two sides of a unity called love. This love must pass from the body to the soul. What was once "desire" must become "offering." Some speak of three aspects of love: digestive, reciprocal, and oblative. Love above all needs the oblative for it is a purification; without it love will die. Passion can only promise; love alone can keep that promise.

Though "love" is the title of this book, it is really concerned with the whole man, for there will be no saving of love unless man himself is saved. May it be as enjoyed as it is needed.

THE RT. REV. MSGR. IRVING A. DEBLANC
Director, Family Life Bureau
National Catholic Welfare Council
Washington, D. C.

Foreword

A foreword is useful when it points up the importance of a particular subject and underlines the necessity or value of carefully exploring it. Precisely this has been done by Professor Alphonse H. Clemens, of The Catholic University of America, in the following passage from his recently published Marriage and the Family, *a comprehensive and notable work. Mr. Clemens and his publisher have generously permitted me to use the passage as a foreword to this volume.*

R.L.W.

Marriage is the oldest natural profession, having started with the human race itself. On the natural level, it is the *noblest* profession; no other has the dignity and privilege of producing and shaping the noblest handiwork of creation—human beings. Artists may produce lasting works on canvas, stone or wood; physicians may treat ailing bodies; lawyers may assist in effecting justice in present human relationships; but parents alone assist in the creation of human beings *who will live for eternity.*

Important as are the other professions, none (except the priesthood or the religious life) can equal marriage. No other natural profession—in fact, not all others combined—have the effect for good or evil upon the race, nation, the Church, and the world. Nor does any other natural profession require the versatility and the broad scope of qualities and knowledge that marriage demands. To attain success in marriage, both as a partner and a parent, implies competency in the art of human relations, knowledge of physical health and care, and an understanding of adult and juvenile human nature, human education, the techniques of homemaking, the earning of a living, the art and science of holiness, and many other accomplishments. This is just one reason why the chores of family living and homemaking, far from being dull, should be stimulating and challenging.

Another fact often escaping our attention is the constant striving for progress and improvement which has brought about the raising of standards in other professions. A century ago, for instance, the young man aspiring to become a physician simply acted as an assistant to some practitioner before engaging in the practice of medicine on his own. Today society thinks the responsibilities of this profession too weighty to permit it to be pursued by any without many years of study, research, and internship. Yet when it comes to preparation for marriage, we still act today as the medical profession did a century ago. . . .

Associated with this failure is another; we have neglected to provide facilities for study, research, and expertness in marriage. Every profession except marriage has had its scholars and experts. The Church has had its theologians; the state has had its political scientists; the world of business and finance has had its economists; the sick body and mind have had doctors of medicine and psychiatry. However, the most important of the natural professions—marriage—has not until quite recently trained experts or specialists to study it, to counsel it, to improve it!

This widespread neglect of preparation for marriage induced Pius XI to write:

"We wish to call your attention in a special manner to the present-day lamentable decline in family education. The offices and professions of a transitory and earthly life, which are certainly of far less importance, are prepared for by long and careful study; whereas for the fundamental duty and obligation of educating their children, many parents have little or no preparation, immersed as they are in temporal cares."

This position was confirmed by Pius XII when he noted:

". . . that whereas no one would dream of suddenly becoming a mechanic or an engineer, a doctor or a lawyer, without an apprenticeship or preparation, yet every day there are numbers of young men and women who marry without having given even an instant's thought to preparing themselves for the arduous work of educating their children which awaits them."

Despite these warnings given by wise counsel, many still persist in refusing to acknowledge the need for better preparation of youth for marriage. Many prefer to believe that in the pioneer days youth was not given such education, yet there was less divorce than today. Such a view fails to grasp the fact that the pioneer home was, in the main, vastly different from the modern home in its training of children, and that the need always remains to raise the standards of marriage just as those of other professions. Perhaps the chief fact neglected by this position is that married life and its duties of rearing children have become more and more complicated as the general environment of the family has grown in complexity. Pioneer parents were not confronted with the neurotic pressures of our age. They had no need for concern about the effect of radio and television on children; they were not faced with the problem of censoring comics, books, periodicals, and movies. In their simple economy, there was little need of the complicated arts of budgeting, buying, insuring, and financing. Attractive wages were not present to allure mothers from the home to the office or factory, and women did not question their role as mothers. Automobiles and commercialized amusements did not threaten the pattern of home recreation. Wild theories of romantic love, freedom of sex, divorce, birth control, and the like were not so prevalent, pulling youth and adults into insane concepts of the meaning of marriage.

The tragic fact cannot be ignored that today our culture and civilization are to a large extent a conspiracy against marriage. The home is basically at fault, especially the city home. Not only is distorted child training giving us increasing amounts of delinquency, but the art of homemaking and the appetite for domesticity are not being imparted to our youth, and sex education has been almost totally ignored or fraught with damaging Puritanism.

Yet all the while this failure to educate aright for marriage has been in evidence, the secular media of education and propaganda have been feverishly active. Irreligious professors, authors, dramatists, producers, and editors have been influencing youth through classroom, lecture platform, radio, press, and television with their secularistic notions of marriage. They did not and do not hesitate to insist that marriage is not God-made but man-made, and that it can be changed to suit our whims, that divorce is a blessing and that children are a curse. . . .

When God, in His Infinite Wisdom, conceived the Divine Plan of marriage, He could have decided to prepare men and women by innate abilities. However, He decided otherwise; He would not have us born with all the traits and knowledge required for success in marriage. Rather would His plan embrace the need for children to *acquire* these through early family education, social environment, the grace of God, the assistance of the church and school. In fact, He would impose this as an obligation upon all agencies responsible for the education of youth; and He would impose it upon the youth themselves. Like other professions, marriage was to attain success only by long, arduous, and careful preparation. . . . This remains the continuing responsibility and challenge of parents, educators, clergy, youth, and married couples. This is that Prudence embodied in the Divine Plan by which we are mandated to employ all available means, natural and supernatural, for the successful attainment of marital goals and purposes.

ALPHONSE H. CLEMENS

One

LOVE AND MARRIAGE

And God created man to his own image: to the image of God he created him: male and female he created them.

And God blessed them, saying: Increase and multiply, and fill the earth, and subdue it, and rule over the fishes of the sea, and the fowls of the air, and all living creatures that move upon the earth.

GENESIS 1:27-28

Love and Marriage Implanted by God from the Beginning

ST. JOHN CHRYSOSTOM

God from the beginning contrived ten thousand ways for implanting *love* in us. Thus, first, He granted one head to all, Adam. For why do we not all spring out of the earth? Why not full grown, as He was? In order that both the birth and the bringing up of children, and the being born of another, might bind us mutually together. For this cause neither made He woman out of the earth; and because the thing of the same substance was not equally sufficient to shame us into unanimity, unless we had also the same progenitor, He provided also for this: since, if now, being only separated by place, we consider ourselves when from one another; much more would this have happened if our race had had two originals. For this cause therefore, as it were from one head, He bound together the whole body of the human race. And because from the beginning they seemed to be in a manner two, see how He fastened them together again, and gathers them into one by marriage. For saith He, "shall a man . . . cleave unto his wife; and they shall be one flesh." And He said not, "the woman," but "the man," because the desire too is stronger in him. Yea, and for this cause He made it also stronger, that it might bow the superior party to the absolute sway of this passion, and might subjugate it to the weaker. And since marriage also must needs be introduced, him from whom she sprang He made husband to the woman. For all things, in the eyes of God are second to love. . . .

Even before the race was increased to a multitude, when the first two only were in being, He bade him govern, and her obey. And in order again that He might not despise her as inferior, and separate from her, see how He honored her, and made them one, even before her creation. For "Let us make man," saith He, "a help meet," implying that she was made for his need, and thereby drawing him unto her who was made for his sake: since to all those things are we more kindly disposed, which are done for our sakes. But that she, on the other hand, might not be elated, as being granted to him for help, nor might burst this bond, He makes her out of his side, signifying that she is a part of the whole body. And that neither might the man be elated therefore, He no longer permits that to belong to him alone which before was his alone, but effected the contrary to this, by bringing in procreation of children, and herein too giving the chief honor unto the man, not however allowing the whole to be his.

Seest thou how many bonds of love God hath wrought? And these indeed by force of nature He hath lodged in us as pledges of concord. For both our being of the same substance leads to this: (for every animal loves his like) and the woman being produced from the man, and again the children from both. Whence also many kinds of affection arise. For one we love as a father, another as a grandfather; one as a mother, another as a nurse; and one as a son, or grandson, or great-grandson again, and another as a daughter, or grand-daughter, and one as a brother, another as a nephew; and one as a sister, another as a niece. And why need one recount all the names of consanguinity? And He devised also another foundation of affection. For having forbidden the marriage of kindred, He led us unto strangers, and drew them again unto us. For since by this natural kindred it was not possible that they should be connected with us, he connected us anew by marriage, uniting together whole families by the single person of the bride, and mingling entire races with races.

(Translated by Talbot W. Chambers)

The Profound Significance of Love
COVENTRY PATMORE

Every man and woman who has not denied or falsified nature knows, or at any rate feels, that love, though the least "serious," is the most significant of all things. The wise do not talk much about this knowledge, for fear of exposing its delicate edge to the stolid resistance of the profligate and unbelieving, and because its light, thought, and for the reason that, it exceeds all other, is deficient in definition. But they see that to this momentary transfiguration of life all that is best in them looks forward or looks back, and that it is for this the race exists, and not this for the race—the seed for the flower, not the flower for the seed. All religions have sanctified this love, and have found in it their one word for and image of their fondest and highest hopes; and the Catholic has exalted it into a "great Sacrament," holding that, with Transubstantiation—which it resembles—it is unreasonable only because it is above reason. "The love which is the best ground of marriage," writes also the Protestant and "judicious" Hooker, "is that which is least able to render a reason for itself." Indeed, the extreme unreasonableness of this passion, which gives cause for so much blaspheming to the foolish, is one of its surest sanctions and a main cause of its inexhaustible interest and power; for who but a "scientist" values greatly or is greatly moved by anything he can understand—that which can be comprehended being necessarily less than we are ourselves? . . .

The world is finding out, as it has often done before, and more or less forgotten, that it cannot do without religion. Love is the first thing to wither under its loss. What love does in transfiguring life, that religion does in transfiguring love: as anyone may see who compares one state or time with another. Love is sure to be something less than human if it is not something more; and the so-called extravagances of the youthful heart, which always claims a character for divinity in its emotions, fall necessarily into sordid, if not shameful, reaction, if those claims are not justified to the understanding by the faith which declares man and woman to be priest and priestess to each other of relations inherent in Divinity itself, and proclaimed in the words, "Let us make man in our own image" and "male and female created he them." Nothing can reconcile the intimacies of love to the higher feelings unless the parties to them are conscious—and true lovers always are—that, for the season at least, they justify the words "I have said, ye are gods." Nuptial love bears the clearest marks of being nothing other than the rehearsal of a communion of a higher nature.

"Love Is the Wealth of the Soul"

THE MOST REV. W. BERNARD ULLATHORNE

What is life without love? Apathy is deadness, enmity is a killing bitterness, love is the wealth of the soul, making her rich with life, and glowing with good in proportion to the goodness of that life to which she devotes her own. What we see instructs us, but what we love works a change in us. Our love is both an active and an attractive force: it draws to us the qualities of the object we love, those qualities change our qualities, and make us like the object that we love. The life we love enters into our life, and changes our spirit and character into something of the goodness, greatness, and dignity of the object to which we give our love. With love our soul expands, and is enlarged with the greater life that attracts our affections, and is purified with its purity, and the soul goes forth out of herself, to live in the object of her love.

Reason and Love

BLAISE PASCAL

If a man be endowed by nature with a sensitive and delicate spirit in the ordinary concerns of existence, it will be the same in love.... This delicacy originates in a pure and elevated degree of intelligence....

The higher qualities of intelligence are not to be acquired by effort; they can only be enlarged and perfected. Thence it is obvious, that refinement is a gift of nature, and cannot be gained by artificial means.

In proportion as the intellect is refined, we become alive to beauty of various kinds; but it is otherwise with the lover—all beauty is to him concentrated in one....

When a person is in love, he seems to himself wholly changed from what he was before; and he fancies that everybody sees him in the same light. This is a great mistake; but reason being obscured by passion, he cannot be convinced, and goes on still under the delusion.... The length and deviousness of an attachment serve only, in a mind of sensibility, to heighten the pleasure.

The first effect of genuine love is, to inspire a profound respect; veneration is ever the fruit of deep attachment. This is as it should be....

I agree with one who holds that in love, fortune, friends, relatives, are all forgotten; this is the tendency of most elevated attachments. A man in love feels, for the time, that he wants nothing but the object of his preference; the mind is filled; there is no room for other care or solicitude. Passion always impels to extremes: thence it is that we become indifferent to the opinion of the world; we satisfy ourselves that we have right on our side, and ought not to be the object of censure....

It has been usual, but without cause, to underrate, and regard, as opposed to reason, the passion of love. Reason and love are, however, consistent with each other. It is a precipitation of mind that thus carries us into partialities and extremes; but it is still reason, and we ought not to wish it to be otherwise. We should, in that case, only prove man to be a very disagreeable machine. Let us not seek to exclude reason from love; for they are inseparable.

(Translated by George Pearce)

Love Needs God as an Accomplice

THE REV. JEAN BAPTISTE LACORDAIRE

Purely human love is a passing effervescence produced by causes which have in themselves but little duration; it is born in the morning, and vanishes in the evening. It is not the act of a man who is master of himself, sure of his will, and carrying the energy of duty even into the intimate enjoyments of the heart. True love is a virtue; it supposes a soul constant and resolute, which, without being insensible to fugitive gifts, penetrates even to the immutable region of the beautiful, and discovers in the very ruins a blooming which touches and retains it. But the Christian soul alone possesses this creating faculty; the others halt on the surface, and see death on all sides. Two young persons approach the altar in that beautiful ceremony of marriage; they bring with them all the joy and all the sincerity of their youth; they vow to each other eternal love. But very soon the joy diminishes; fidelity totters, the eternity of their vows crumbles away little by little. What has happened? Nothing; hour has followed hour; they are what they were, save an hour in addition. But an hour is a great deal without God. God entered not into their vows; He was not an accomplice in their love, and their love ends, because God alone is without end.

(Translated by Henry Langdon)

Romantic Love and Marriage

JACQUES MARITAIN

To my mind "romantic love" is sexual love when it goes beyond the sphere of simple animality (in which it remains rooted), and bursts into full bloom in the properly human sphere, exalting and ravishing everything in the human being—sentiments, thought, creative activity, which are henceforth imbued with and stimulated by the basic passion of desire.

Such a love carries man beyond himself—in imagination—into a kind of poetical paradise, and makes him believe that he is entirely and eternally dedicated to the one he loves, and that he lives and breathes only for this one, while in reality this other human person is so passionately cherished first of all for the sake of sexual desire and possession, which remain the primary essential incentive.

This romantic love might be defined as a total intoxication of the human being by sexual desire taking the loftiest forms and disguised as pure and absolutely disinterested, pure and eternal love of the other.

Now, since sexual attraction and satisfaction remain the essential incentive and the essential aim, it must be said that romantic love—*l'amour passion*—being but a transcendent human expression of the strongest animal instinct, is, by nature: first, deprived of permanence and liable to fade away; second, unfaithful and liable to shift from one object to another; and third, intrinsically torn between the love for another, which it has awakened, and its own basically egoist nature.

Consequently, to found marriage on romantic love, and to think that marriage must be the perfect fulfillment of romantic love is, as I submitted, a great illusion.

Mankind has been so well aware of this fact that for centuries marriage, being considered a merely social affair, was regarded as a thing with which personal inclination and personal love had nothing—or very little—to do. I am thinking of all those marriages which were arranged by parents, for family interests or tribal considerations—even national interests when it was a question of kings and queens. So that sometimes a boy and a girl had never met one another before they were married.

There was some sad, wicked wisdom in this conception, so far as it recognized the fact that romantic love and married love are two quite different things; and that the aim of marriage is not to bring romantic love to perfect fulfillment.

Yet, in proportion as, in the course of history, the human person became more and more aware of his or her own value and own importance, the merely social conception of marriage to which I just alluded appeared more inhuman and more harmful. For, especially in modern times, a result was that in a number of cases men and women looked for mutual personal love, and romantic love (which is an inherent dream of the human being) outside of marriage. Thus people came to realize that if mutual personal love, and even initially an element of romantic love, are not a necessary requirement of the validity of marriage—at least they are a necessary requirement for its intrinsic dignity and welfare.

Finally, the truth of the matter, as I see it, is, first, that love as desire or passion, and romantic love—or at least an element of it —should, as far as possible, be present in marriage as a first incentive and starting point. Otherwise, it would be too difficult for the human being, if and when an opportunity for romantic love outside of marriage should later appear, to resist the temptation; for what makes man most unhappy is to be deprived not of that which he had, but of that which he did not have, and did not really know.

The second point is that far from having as its essential aim to bring romantic love to perfect fulfillment, marriage has to perform in human hearts quite another work—an infinitely deeper and more mysterious, alchemical operation: I mean to say, it has to *transmute* romantic love, or what existed of it at the beginning, into real and indestructible *human* love, and really disinterested love, which does not exclude sex, of course, but which grows more and more independent of sex, and even can be, in its highest forms, completely free from sexual desire and intercourse, because it is essentially spiritual in nature—a complete and irrevocable gift of the one to the other, for the sake of the other.

Thus it is that marriage can be between man and woman a true community of love, built not on sand, but on rock, because it is built on genuinely human, not animal, and genuinely spiritual, genuinely *personal* love—through the hard discipline of self-sacrifice and by dint of renouncements and purifications. Then in a free and unceasing ebb and flow of emotion, feeling, and thought, each one really participates, by virtue of love, in that personal life of the other which is, by nature, the other's incommunicable possession. And then each one may become a sort of guardian Angel for the other—prepared, as guardian Angels have to be, to forgive the other a great deal: for the gospel law of mutual forgiveness expresses, I believe, a fundamental requirement which is valid not only in the supernatural order, but in the terrestrial and temporal order as well, and for basically natural societies like domestic society and even political society. Each one, in other words, may then become really dedicated to the good and salvation of the other.

Inordinate Love

FRANCOIS MAURIAC

If we want to know in what relationship we really stand to God we cannot do better than consider our feelings about other people. This is peculiarly the case when one person, above all others, has touched our affections. If he is seen to be the source of all our happiness and all our pain, if our peace of mind depends on him alone, then, let it be said at once, we are separated as far from God as we can be, short of having committed mortal sin. Not that love of God condemns us to aridity in our human friendships, but it does lay on us the duty of seeing that our affection for other human beings shall not be an end in itself, shall not usurp the place of that utterly complete love which no one can begin to understand who has not felt it.

(Translated by Gerard Hopkins)

Innate Characteristics of Love

THE REV. JEAN BAPTISTE LACORDAIRE

Affection naturally produces indissolubility. Who is the being base enough, when he loves, to calculate the moment when he will love no longer? Who is the being unworthy enough to conceive and to merit affection, who lives with that which he loves as if he should, some day, love it no longer? Which of us, on the contrary—an illusion too often destroyed, but an illusion which honors us—which of us, when he once loves, does not believe, at least in that moment, that he will love always with all the ardor and all the youthfulness of his heart? I admit that very many deceive themselves; but this is not the less the innate character of every serious attachment.

Unity is another of these. We do not love by threes, but by twos. It is impossible to imagine an affection of the same nature and of the same strength, existing between three souls. It is even on this account that we possess so little capacity for loving. Our love is exclusive; when we give ourselves, we give ourselves but to one; and it required all the power of Jesus Christ to communicate breadth to our affections without destroying their energy.

So then, the heart and the Bible say the same thing to us, and on no other point are they more in agreement; they tell us that the relations between man and woman are those of dignity, indissolubility and unity.

(Translated by Henry Langdon)

Supernatural Love

THE REV. RAOUL PLUS, S.J.

Some persons imagine that the endeavor to transform their natural love into supernatural love will make them awkward, make them lose their spontaniety, their naturalness.

Indeed, nothing is farther from the truth, if supernatural love is rightly understood.

What does it really require?

First of all, does it not require us to fulfill the perfections of natural love? Supernatural love, far from supressing natural love, makes it more tender, more attentive, more generous; it intensifies the sentiments of affection, esteem, admiration, gratitude, respect, and devotion which constitute the essence of true love.

Supernatural love takes away one thing only from natural and spontaneous love—selfishness, the arch-enemy of love. It demands that everything, from the greatest obligation to the simplest, be done as perfectly as possible. Then by elevating simple human love to the love of true charity, it ennobles the greatest powers of that love. It suppresses nothing. It enriches everything. Better still, it provides in advance against the danger of a diminution in human love. It pardons weaknesses, deficiencies, faults. Not that it is blind to them, but it does not become agitated by them. It bears with them, handles them tactfully, helps to overcome them. It is capable of bestowing love where all is not lovable. Penetrating beyond the exterior, it can peer into the soul and see the image of God behind a silhouette which has become less pleasing.

That is the whole secret. Supernatural love in us seeks to love in the manner and according to the desire of God; it requires us therefore to love God in those we love and then to love the good qualities He has given them and bear with the absence of those

He has not given or with the characteristics He has permitted them to acquire.

(*Translator anonymous*)

Stages of Love

T. G. WAYNE (*pseudonym*)

Love of another can advance through three stages: desire, devotion, friendship.

Desire (*amor concupiscentiae*) is caused by a need in us, the love of another for our own sake. With sex this springs from a natural attraction of body and soul lying deeper than deliberate choice; a desire for the excitement and rest of coming close together, for the life that only the other can awaken and share; a need to hold and to be held in love. The will must establish control over this impulse and guard its expression if dissipation into lust and waste is to be avoided. Passion should not have full control. Nevertheless, the desires of both will and passion are in themselves quite healthy and caused by God; the natural hunger of every creature to strengthen and comfort its life from outside. The mutual attraction between men and women is certainly not the result of the Fall.

Unruliness, not ardor, is the effect of original sin, through which man is deprived of supernatural life and disorganized in his natural life. Powers which should work in harmony tend to seek their own satisfaction to the detriment of the whole personality. This general disorder is not confined to the field of sex, though here its results are particularly evident. Maturity consists in establishing a central control over many and various desires, of being master of oneself; sexual disorders mark a certain childishness to the theologian as well as to the psychologist.

It must be remarked that sex desire is not merely bodily and animal, a blood-and-muscle movement pointing only to the sensuous satisfaction of male and female intercourse; a relief of tension; an effect of glands. Underlying this necessary stream in sex there should exist a complete love between two human persons which is more than an attraction between bodies, more than male and female desire. The chief quality of the union sought is that it represents the intimacy of two *persons* who are in love with one another. It is not just a man-woman relationship, but essentially the relationship of this man and this woman and no other.

Devotion (*amor benevolentiae*) marks a stage past desire. This disinterested affection wishes and works for and enjoys the happiness of another without much thought of self. Here is wonder and reverence and self-sacrifice.

Beyond desire and devotion, yet including them both, comes friendship (*amor amicitae*), the love by which two people belong, as it were, to one another, sharing in something as equals. The foundation of friendship may be a common occupation or interest, but no foundation is so deep and lasting as a whole life shared in common, the life of marriage that gathers in the everyday joys and worries and humors as well as the greater concerns of love, birth, death, grace. Sex love at its best is such a friendship, including but also surpassing the primary bodily and biological relationship. Mutual desire, mutual devotion, and penetrating these the certainty that each is committed to the other. In their equal dignity as persons made to the image of God, a man and woman give themselves to one another, not for an incident, not for a period, but for a whole life; not only that their bodies may be stirred and satisfied and tended, not only that children may be born from them and cared for and trained, not only that they may interest and support one another, but that two persons, immortal souls animating bodies that will rise again after death, may draw close to one another and in their joys and sorrows shared may be alive and strong together in the eternal life of God. *Two in one flesh;* even more than that.

True Love versus Lust

ABBÉ ERNEST DIMNET

It is not an easy task to speak of love. It has the reputation of unsettling life. Bacon, in one of his essays, the cynical tone of which is not pleasant, and Saint Paul, in a sad tender passage of Corinthians I, take that view. On the other hand, nobody can give the subject a moment's thought without recognizing that love is an evident part of the divine plan and therefore can only be regarded as normal.

But here again there is danger. No word has been treated so unceremoniously by the past three or four generations as love has been. Modern literature in its delight at having broken loose from Puritanic restraint is vociferous in giving it its most technical and consequently its most inadequate meaning. The theatre and the lecture-platform resound with it till one is sick of its implications. . . . Nowhere is use so much in danger of turning to abuse as it is here. . . .

All this comes from the most usual cause of human error, viz., confusion of terms, so that there is nothing more imperative than to remind the human race that love is one thing, lust is another. If modern people would be as frank about this as they pretend to be they would resolutely adopt this vocabulary and cease to apply, to what is whispered about amid unpleasant chuckling, the word which poetry has glorified in a thousand forms. The world would at once be a better world because truth would force upon it realities instead of lies as the language does today. . . .

It must be admitted that even perfect sincerity is often baffled by the complexity of what we call love, that is to say sex-attraction in its most legitimate form. It has a physical aspect which no spiritualization can make other than it is. Without it the world would promptly come to an end, and both Church and State agree that, in its default, marriage is not complete and can be annulled as not answering its specific object. Indeed, the majority of mankind regards it as one kind of magic to which all men have a right, while the strictest moralists recognize in it something higher than mere necessity. . . .

Why should this particular tendency be discussed any more openly than others about which not a word is ever said? One of the most striking characteristics of a man who is really in love, is that his conversation is chaste. He is willing to analyze sentiment, but not sensation. When he begins to do so it is a sign of deterioration. In the second place, it is not true that the relations between the sexes are of the same order with the rest of man's instincts. They have social consequences which place them in a class apart. . . .

Probably the greatest mistake made by our modern world is to speak of love all the time, and to give the impression that love offers itself to everyone all the time. As a matter of fact, attraction is continuous, but love only comes once. Most people learn this as a conclusion of varied experiences. Too late. Few miss the encounter which shows them what their life might have been. . . .

When love is real love, when people's souls go out to their beloved, when they lose their hearts to them, when they act in the unselfish way in which these exquisite Old English phrases denote, a miracle is produced. Without any effort, without the least hypocrisy, men and women only show their best as birds are at their most brilliant in April. It is difficult then to exercise one's critical faculties and not to "buy the cat in a bag," as the French phrase goes. Yet, there is a brief period between attraction and fascination, during which wisdom still has her word to say. Then is the time to remember that the happiness of most people we know is not ruined by great catastrophes or fatal errors, but by the repetition of slowly destructive little things. Trivial pieces of little egoism, a not very obvious but chronic habit of thoughtlessness, unexpected outbursts, an idea that politeness is a superfluity with the people one lives with all the time, result in the same barrenness of feeling that some violent reactions will produce. These warning incidents should be taken notice of and put under the microscope while it is not too late. If, while the May moon shines on the fragrant hay, you are ever so little offended by an "I—I—me—me" attitude, multiply your annoyances by a hundred and decide whether you can endure it in future. Discount sex appeal as much as you can, and try to remember the old saying that one should only let oneself fall in love with the woman who could be made a friend of if she were a man. Otherwise the inward note made by us all the time: "he or she has done this" will gradually change to "he or she *does* this" and inevitably, some day, the final and catastrophic "he or she IS this or that" will mark the end of the spell that love has been.

Such precautions should be elementary. If, instead of attaching so much importance to the so-called technique of love,—so obvious that its simplicity is offensive,—people would give the least attention to the morals or the minor morals of married life, they would be touching instead of so often being laughable in their disappointments, and, above all, their disappointments would be less frequent. But the lesson of experience is that mankind, all the time in quest of recipes for wisdom and happiness, does not see the obvious conditions of wisdom or happiness. The mortal sin of literature is to emphasize the difficulty, instead of the simplicity, of this common-sense view of life. On the other hand the folly of men and women is to imagine, when they read such simple advice, that it is enough to have read it, instead of starting out to live it. A minimum of sense would inevitably ensure that modicum of satisfaction which most humans regard as bliss.

To sum up, love is sure to bring down to solid earth people inclined to soar out of the stratum of realities. Only it should not make them terrestrial. If the higher companionship that love should be does not make men and women nobler, more generous, more ready to sacrifice even their beautiful life for a lofty purpose, there is a suspicion that their love is not love but a combination of egoisms. True love makes our ideal brighter and our purpose stronger. If the word God, with the train of superior thoughts and superior sentiments that it connotes, is only used with an awkward feeling by people who think themselves in love, let them be sure that they miss the best part of love, and not only of romantic love but of simply love.

When Romance Is Exaggerated

THE REV. DANIEL A. LORD, S.J.

Strong, pure, unselfish, stable young love can be a beautiful thing. Mature love grows in dignity and strength. A man and a woman who are consecrated by the sacrament knit their souls through trial and joy, creation and achievement. The old, mellowed love of a man and a woman on their golden wedding day is an amalgam of affection and respect, of dangers known and triumphs shared, of lives that side by side grew into something vast and grand and noble.

But the physical love of a man for a woman or of a woman for a man, the fascination that can spring up between totally unsuited people, is by no means the only kind of love—if it is true love at all.

Let's realize that there are all kinds of emotions that fall under the too easily used word called love. We speak of the love of God and the love of good food, the love of family and of work, the love of friends and of books, the love of scenery and of horses, the love of a hobby and the love of good conversation, the love of prayer and the love of sea and sky, the love of exercise and the love of sport, the love of travel and good wine and ripe tobacco, the love of peace and the love of the saints. . . .

So even the most dignified and most beautiful love of a man and a woman is by no means the whole life. So can the quick fascination or brief infatuation felt by two youngsters be the whole of life? Often a really strong and constructive love seems much like the background for life. It is an atmosphere from which a man moves out to great achievement. It is the shelter in which a woman achieves her more complete development.

No Roman however ardent could possibly spend his entire night seven times a week serenading beneath a Juliet's window. No Juliet could be content to gaze into her husband's eyes each evening and concentrate on his picture while he was off to his business affairs each day.

Love may often be very important—when it is an inspiration that lifts the lover to higher levels and gives him or her new motives for virtue and creative living. But there is something terribly unfair about the writers who make every life story merely a love story that presents the whole of existence as a concentration on that brief period of intense physical love and that presents the great objective of life as the search for and the finding of the right partner for romance.

Life has much more, often very much more to offer. A really perfect marriage is one that opens to both husband and wife long and inviting avenues for exploration and for their individual and joint development. . . .

Life, if it is to be satisfactory, has to be made up of a variety of elements; it has to satisfy the whole human being, body, soul, tastes, habits, possibilities for development, aspirations. Even those of the fairy tales that talked in terms of "bread and cheese and kisses" put the bread and cheese before the kisses. . . .

A wholesome, satisfactory life has in it a lot of hard things—like cash.

A man or a woman need—if they are to attain lasting happiness here and now—a great many elements to satisfy natural cravings and God-given desires. Love cannot long outlast hunger. That hunger may be for God, for peace, for understanding, for success in life, for self-development, for virtue, for grace.

To offer romance and physical fascination as substitutes for all these hungers is to make men and women too, too simple.

Love and the Poets

FRANCIS THOMPSON

The rite of Marriage was to the pagan the goal and attainment of Love—Love which he regarded as a transitory and perishable passion, born of the body and decaying with the body. On the wings of Christianity came the great truth that Love is of the soul, and with the soul coeval.

It was most just and natural that from the Christian poets should come the full development of this truth. To Dante and the followers of Dante we must go for its ripe announcement. Not in marriage, they proclaim, is the fulfillment of Love, though its earthly and temporal fulfillment may be therein; for how can Love which is the desire of soul for soul, attain satisfaction in the conjunction of body with body? Poor, indeed, if this were all the promise which Love unfolded to us—the encountering light of two flames from within their close-shut lanterns. Therefore, sings Dante, and sing all the noble poets after him, that Love in this world is a pilgrim and wanderer, journeying to the New Jerusalem; not here is the consummation of his yearnings, in that mere knocking at the gates of union which we christen marriage, but beyond the pillars of death and the corridors of the grave, in the union of spirit to spirit within the containing Spirit of God.

The distance between Catullus and the *Vita Nuova* [of Dante], between Ovid and the *House of Life*, can be measured only by Christianity. And the lover of poetry owes a double debt to his Creator, who, not content with giving us salvation on the cross, gave us also, at the marriage in Cana of Galilee, Love. For there Love was consecrated, and declared the child of Jehovah, not of Jove; there virtually was inaugurated the whole successive order of those love-poets who have shown the world that passion, in putting on chastity, put on also ten-fold beauty. For purity is the sum of all loveliness, as whiteness is the sum of all colors.

The True Dowry

THE REV. JEAN BAPTISTE LACORDAIRE

Permit me to offer an advice to those who have not yet bound their youthful liberty in the bonds of marriage. Let them understand distinctly to ally themselves with a family is to ally themselves with benedictions or with maledictions, and that the true dowry is not that which the public officer mentions upon paper. The true dowry is known to God alone. But to a certain degree, from the experience of men, you also may know it. Seek not visible gold, but invisible gold; ascertain whether the blood which is about to be mingled with yours contains traditions of human and divine virtues, whether it has long been purified in the sacrifice of duty, whether the hand which you are about to receive has been joined to the other hand in invoking God, whether the knees which are to bend with yours before the altar have been accustomed and happy thus to humble themselves. See whether the soul is rich in God. . . . If the aureola of sanctity is manifestly wanting, flee to the opposite pole, although the resources of the world may be offered to you, and do not confound in an adulterous alliance a long record of benedictions with a long record of maledictions. Alas! if so many wailings stronger than shame issue forth from the bosoms of families, it is because when forming them one day the dower of earth was counted and no reckoning was made of the dower of Heaven.

(Translator Anonymous)

Choosing a Partner

PIUS XI

To the proximate preparation of a good married life belongs very specially the care in choosing a partner; on that depends a great deal whether the forthcoming marriage will be happy or not, since one may be to the other a great help in leading a Christian life, or, a great danger, and hindrance. And so that they may not deplore for the rest of their lives the sorrows arising from an indiscreet marriage, those about to enter into wedlock should carefully deliberate in choosing the person with whom henceforward they must live continually: they should, in so deliberating, keep before their minds the thought first of God and of the true religion of Christ, then of themselves, of their partners, of the children to come, as also of human and civil society, for which wedlock is a fountain head. . . . Lastly, let them not omit to ask the prudent advice of their parents with regard to the partner, and let them regard this advice in no light manner, in order that by their mature knowledge and experience of human affairs they may guard against a disastrous choice, and, on the threshold of matrimony, may receive more abundantly the divine blessing of the fourth commandment: "Honour thy father and thy mother (which is the first commandment with a promise) that it may be well with thee and thou mayest be long-lived upon the earth."

The Council of Trent Cites Acceptable Reasons for Marrying

We have now to explain why man and woman should be joined in marriage. First of all, nature itself by an instinct implanted in both sexes impels them to such companionship, and this is further encouraged by the hope of mutual assistance in bearing more easily the discomforts of life and the infirmities of old age.

A second reason for marriage is the desire of a family. . . . A third reason has been added as a consequence of the fall of our first parents. On account of the loss of original innocence the passions begin to rise in rebellion against right reason; and man, conscious of his own frailty and unwilling to fight the battles of the flesh, is supplied by mariage with an antidote by which to avoid sins of lust. . . .

These are ends, some one of which those who desire to contract marriage piously and religiously, as becomes the children of the Saints, should propose to themselves. If to these we add other causes which induce to contract marriage, and, in choosing a wife, to prefer one person to another, such as the desire of leaving an heir, wealth, beauty, illustrious descent, congeniality of position—such motives, because not inconsistent with the holiness of marriage, are not condemned. We do not find that the Sacred Scriptures condemn the Patriarch Jacob for having chosen Rachel for her beauty, in preference to Lia.

Dangers in Mixed Marriages

PIUS XI

This religious character of marriage . . . evidently requires that those about to marry should show a holy reverence towards it, and zealously endeavor to make their marriage approach as nearly as possible to the archetype of Christ and the Church.

They, therefore, who rashly and heedlessly contract mixed marriages, from which the maternal love and providence of the Church dissuades her children for very sound reasons, fail conspicuously in this respect, sometimes with danger to their eternal salvation. . . . If the Church occasionally on account of circumstances does not refuse to grant a dispensation from these strict laws (provided that the divine law remains intact and the dangers above mentioned are provided against by suitable safeguards), it is unlikely that the Catholic party will not suffer some detriment from such a mariage.

Whence it comes about not unfrequently, as experience shows, that deplorable defections from religion occur among the offspring, or at least a headlong descent into that religious indifference which is closely allied to impiety. . . .

Assuredly, also, will there be wanting that close union of spirit which as it is the sign and mark of the Church of Christ, so also should be the sign of Christian wedlock, its glory and adornment. For, where there exists diversity of mind, truth and feeling, the bond of union of mind and heart is wont to be broken, or at least weakened. From this comes the danger lest the love of man and wife grow cold and the peace and happiness of family life, resting as it does on the union of hearts, be destroyed.

Three Fundamentals

PIUS XII

Faithful Catholics must therefore keep unshaken the following three fundamental points:

They cannot contract a true valid marriage except according to the form prescribed by the Church.

Marriage validly contracted between baptized persons is by that very fact a Sacrament.

This valid marriage between baptized persons, once consummated, cannot for any cause be dissolved by any human authority, by any power on earth, but only by death.

On Celebrating the Marriage

ST. JOHN CHRYSOSTOM

When thou makes a marriage, go not round from house to house borrowing mirrors and dresses; for the matter is not one of display, nor dost thou lead thy daughter to a pageant; but decking out thine house with what is in it, invite thy neighbors, and friends, and kindred. As many as thou knowest to be of good character, those invite, and bid them be content with what there is. Let no one from the orchestra be present, for such expense is superfluous, and unbecoming. Before all the rest, invite Christ. . . . Adorn the bride not with ornaments made of gold, but with gentleness and modesty, and the customary robes. . . . The dinners and suppers, let them not be full of drunkenness, but of abundance and pleasure. See how many good things will result, whenever we see such marriages as those.

(Oxford translation revised by John A. Broadus)

Marriage and the Liturgy

THE REV. VINCENT MCNABB, O.P.

It has been left to modern times to evolve a marriage with ceremonies of only the most meagre fare. The nineteenth century is thus responsible for secularizing and uncrowning a social rite which has its roots far beyond the Christian era. There is hardly a people, civilized or uncivilized, that has not surrounded the wedding of their young with a wealth of ceremony. Indeed, the liturgy of even Pagan wedlock belongs to the poetry of social institutions. Where a nation's topmost note of song has not been a *Te Deum*, it has been for the most part an Epitholamium.

Nowhere was the instinct of Christianity truer and wiser than in the preservation of all that was best and most human in pre-Christian wedlock. Her attitude is symbolized in the miracle of Cana, whereby the water was not cast out into the street, but was changed into wine at the wedding feast. The "natural love" which is such a feature of the giving and taking of two trustful hearts is looked upon as the clear water, dyed into wine by the spilt blood of Jesus crucified.

This attitude toward the *naturalis amor* and *naturalis contractus*, the natural love and bond of marriage, has led the Church to take over from Paganism such characteristic ceremonies as the giving of the wedding ring. The clasping and unclasping of the hand was a rite of the Romans, may even have had its rise in the Teutonic respect for women and wedlock. The giving of gold and silver is even more linked with Teutonic ceremonial. . . .

The chief change made by the Church was characteristic. She linked the wedding ceremony, as indeed she linked almost everything, with the mystic offering of Christ's death. Every one of the Sacraments was more or less closely joined to Holy Mass. Even Baptism was but an interlude in the Sacred liturgy.

So early as the first decade of the third century, Tertullian (who died about 220 A.D.), uses the phrase "marriage which the Church accepts and the Sacrifice strengthens." The Leonine, the Gelgasian, and the Gregorian Sacramentaries contain the Nuptial Mass, with our present prayers. (A special *Hanc Igitur* and *Preface*.) The Gelgasian Sacramentary, which is not later than the seventh century, and may be as early as the fourth, contains the blessing now said after the *Ita Missa Est*. . . .

The present rite of marriage, as found in the *Rituale Romanum*, received its authoritative setting at the Council of Trent, in the last memorable phase of the Council, some seventeen years since it had begun. Protestantism had already wrought out to their conclusion some of the specious untruths which it had propagated as principles. . . . Elizabeth's government had set the foot of Protestantism firmly upon English life. Too many errors about marriage were abroad in Europe to be tolerated. . . . The duty of the Council was, on the one hand, to condemn such errors as polygamy, the denial that matrimony is a sacrament, the rejection of the Church's power to make impediments, the right to divorce, the evil of virginity. On the other hand, the Church's duty was not to reject, but to foster those local customs which had been the national conscience adorning a great human institution. For this reason the best feature of the famous Council may perhaps be found in the quiet adjunct to the form of marriage, "juxta receptum uniusuijusque provinciae ritum"—according to the received rite of each province. It was a broad statesmanlike recognition of local varieties of home rule, which had been, not a decadent, but a fruitful principle in liturgy. This phrase of the Council was expanded in the *Rituale Romanum* into the ampler form, "If, however, in any provinces other laudable customs and ceremonies are in use besides the foregoing in the celebration of the Sacrament of Matrimony, the Holy Council of Trent desires that they should be retained." . . .

The Mystical Mass, as we have seen, followed the actual ceremony and Sacrament of Marriage. We have seen, too, that allusions to it are found as early as the third century. By the seventh, or perhaps the fourth, a Nuptial Mass, with special variants of the *Preface* and *Hanc Igitur* are in use in Rome and Gaul. . . .

As it stands, the whole wedding ceremony is one calculated to stir up those feelings which should be the accompaniment of a mutual love covenanting to be stronger than death. Not one of the simple ceremonies has less than a nation's history, or holds less than the Master's power to teach. The whole atmosphere of human love is charged during the Holy Sacrifice with that uncreated love which carried self-sacrifice to self-immolation. . . . Marriage becomes not a mere mating of two chance acquaintances, but the tragedy of two hearts daring to promise each an eternity of love.

"For Better—For Worse"

THE REV. P. J. GANNON, S.J.

It has always seemed to me that a peculiarly sad significance attaches to the word "worse" of the marriage ceremony. Right at what is supposed to be the crowning moment of two young lives . . . when joy is in their hearts and the love-light in their eyes; when their hopes reach dazzling heights of expectancy, and they look forward to a future of unclouded happiness, the very ritual of the Church breaks in upon their dreams with a note of warning. It hints at a possibility which must, to them in their present mood, seem almost blasphemy to contemplate. "For worse." But how can it be for worse, that two hearts, which love as never human hearts loved before or shall again—for it is always thus—should be united before God and man? Are these two not made for one another? Does not he find the sun's rays somehow brighter when they shine upon her hair? And she deems the moonlight and the stars alone romantic when his arm is linked with hers?. . . . Why, then, does the Church, in this cold-blooded and inhuman way, break in upon the harmony with a discordant note, suggesting possibilities of disaster? Is it, perchance, a touch of priestly cynicism, the sarcasm of celibates at the state they have abjured?

Ah, no, the Church is not cynical, and certainly would not choose such a moment for the manifestation of this unlovely trait. Nor will any priest feel anything but sympathy with the two young voyagers setting out upon the Great Adventure. It is not with any sense of mockery or triumph that he hints at the difficulties and dangers of the rose-strewn path opening up before their feet. But the Church knows that roses grow among thorns, and that under the orange-blossoms pitfalls may lurk; that the road is likely to be long, and to traverse not only smiling fields and pleasant places, but arid stretches of scrub and sand or very dark defiles. She knows—sad admission against which humanity has struggled since Eden!—that love, that even love, is vain, or at least that there is only one love which will never waver and never disappoint. She has learned, from long experience, that human hearts are wayward and human wills fickle, and that the chances and changes of life are utterly incalculable. She has seen many millions of such couples kneel radiant at her altars, and, later, creep broken-hearted to her tabernacles, seeking some consolation amid the ruins of their edifice of dreams. . . . And so she says: "Even now I want you to face every contingency, with your wills firmly set upon your great purpose of steadfast and unwavering fidelity till death brings the pang of parting, or—the joy of release. You are not embarking on a fairy voyage through enchanted seas. Rather you are entering into a serious and irrevocable engagement to share another being's multi-colored existence, to rejoice in its joys, grieve in its sorrows, take part in its fights with adverse circumstances—nay, more, put up with its weaknesses, limitations and defects, greater perhaps than as yet you can imagine. Do you realize all this, and yet say 'Yes'? You do? Bravo! you do well. But now look to it that you honor your engagement. God is witness to it, and seals it with His sacramental grace. He will watch over your fulfillment of it, and your judgment at His hands will largely turn on that fulfillment." . . .

Let us not be too hard on human infirmity, or expect too lofty ideals from the generality of mankind. Let us admit that they are fully entitled to look for happiness in and through marriage.

Let us even admit that they would be extremely foolish to enter on this state without fair prospects of such happiness. Only let us remind them that marriage was not instituted for their happiness, nor sexual instinct implanted for its own sake alone. Rather Nature baits the trap with a romantic allurement to induce men and women to fulfill the purpose it has in view—the continuation of life on earth, the preservation of the species. And should felicity not result, even still they must endure the consequences of their choice. They have to carry their cross, and far be it for me to say that it is not a heavy cross. . . .

Let us suppose the choice made, and wisely made, what next by way of advice? Well, it is strange and may appear paradoxical, but it seems to me quite sound. Do not look for happiness and you may find it. "What?" I can hear some say, "This is jesting with us, and besides, contradicts what has been said before." In appearance only. What I mean is this: The golden rule of life for married or unmarried alike is not to expect too much from it. Then they need not fear disappointment. For what is the source of all our feverish longings and regrets? Is it not that we pitch our hopes too high, asking more from life than it can give, and from fallen human nature than it can accomplish even with the aid of grace? We think in Springtime that the birds will sing the livelong year and the forget-me-nots bloom into December. . . . Or, again, we see others suffer shipwrecks; but we refuse to contemplate the possibility that our vessel may founder in the storms. Nay, we are so prone to foolish confidence in our own exceptional importance in the eyes of Providence that we neglect the precaution of having lifeboats or lifebelts on board. We say, as St. Peter said, "Even if all others, yet not I," and pay, like him, the price of our presumption. Time, the great reaper, reaps our April hopes, and leaves us with an armful of withered grasses, which we preserve as mournful mementos of departed joys, or burn in disgust, seeking in cynicism, if not in revolt against Providence, some relief from the pangs of regret which consume us. But neither is of much avail.

What if we started with a plainer and saner realization of the facts of life? The first of these is vouched for by the Holy Spirit Himself: "We have not here a lasting city, but seek one that is to come." It is because we forget this—because we seek here and now the perfect peace which Christ has warned us the world cannot give—and it is for this reason we are always deceived. And we must be forever deceived, until we realize that even our home is but an oasis on a desert journey, a mating place on a road to more ultimate things. . . .

The secret of not being disappointed with your partner in life is not to expect too much from him or her. The cause of much domestic misery is the absurd atmosphere of romance created by the mass fiction on which the imagination of youth is fed. For tell me, my dear reader, did you ever see in the flesh anybody remotely resembling the heroine of a love-novel? With star-like eyes, ruby lips and pearly teeth, cheeks white as the snowdrop where not red as the carnation, hair gleaming like gold, and, finally, in intellect as wise as the Ancient Sibyl and as witty as a dialogue by Bernard Shaw? Or, on the other hand, if you search the city with lamps, like the old Cynic philosopher, will you find a man like the hero, as brave and handsome as Cuchulain or Conall Cearnach, uniting the muscles of a Milo to the chivalry of Bayard and the devotion of Sir Bedivere? When the youth is looking for the former in some ordinary daughter of Eve, is he not likely to get a rude awakening some day? When the maiden is dreaming of the latter, is she not steering straight for disillusionment? If he started with eyes that were not blinded, the scales would not fall off later on. If she had not invested some quite decent and respectable, but normal, male biped with qualities no man could possibly combine, she would not in a few years be wondering what she had seen in this husband of hers, who is cross if the dinner is cold, and would run away from a barking terrier, not to speak of a roaring lion.

For my part, I have seen but one proposal in fiction which had the ring of sense about it. It is found in a work by Mr. Chesterton, that admirable philosopher in motley, who has uttered very many wise things to the jingling of his bells. The scene is a London boarding-house. A new arrival proposes to one of the lady lodgers within twenty-four hours. Then a certain Irishman, named Michael, catches the infection and proposes to another, with whom he had been on good terms for some time. She demurs and dwells upon the evils of "imprudent marriages."

"Imprudent marriages," roared Michael. "And pray! where on earth or in heaven are there any prudent marriages: Might as well talk of prudent suicides. You and I have dawdled round each other long enough, and are we any safer than Smith and Mary Gray who met last night? You never know a husband till you marry him. Unhappy! Of course you'll be unhappy. Who are you that you shouldn't be unhappy like the mother that bore you? Disappointed! Of course, you'll be disappointed. I, for one, do not expect till I die to be so good a man as at this minute; for just now I'm fifty thousand feet high—a tower with all the trumpets shouting."

"You see all this," said Rosamund, with a grand sincerity in her solid face, "and do you really want to marry me?"

"My darling, what else is there to do?" roared the Irishman. "What other occupation is there for an active man on this earth except to marry you? What's the alternative to marriage, barring sleep? It's not liberty, Rosamund. Unless you marry God, as our nuns do in Ireland, you must marry Man—that is, me. The only third thing is to marry yourself—to live with yourself, yourself, yourself—the only companion that is never satisfied and never satisfactory."

"Michael," said Miss Hunt is a very soft voice, "if you won't talk so much I'll marry you."

I think that couple never came within sight of the divorce court. You see she started with the realization that he talked too much. And it has been well said: "Women have to learn to bear the stories of the men they love. It is the curse of Eve." . . . Similarly, if Michael recognized her face as solid, it was much better than writing sugary sonnets on her eyebrows. Further, he must have felt that she accepted him to put an end to his shouting. Hence he was likely to make some allowance, if later on her patience gave way when he could not check the exuberance of his Irish eloquence. All solid contentment must be based on truth. If based on falsehood, exaggeration, or make-believe it cannot last. . . . Why, ah why, cannot even enamored mortals be got to understand that no one, man or woman, is always good company? Even the wise are occasionally otherwise; even the witty are sometimes dull as stagnant pools. . . .

So I say to the husband who is beginning to feel the company of his wife dull—the little patch of cloud upon the horizon which heralds the storm—"What about yourself? Are you never wearisome to her? Never out of sorts—moody, silent, irritable? Do you keep smiling when things go ill, and uncomplaining when the head aches, or the liver is torpid, or indigestion punishes your prandial excesses? If not, bear with her human infirmities?"

And to you, madam, who are growing restless, I say: "If he gets upon your nerves, pray tell me have you a monopoly of that universal excuse? Perhaps his nerves, too, prick and tingle; perhaps he is smarting under a reprimand from his superiors, or an insult from his equals, or insolence from his inferiors. Perhaps he has difficulties with the banker, which he wishes to spare you till you must know. Yet you go on nagging at him because he is not quite as thoughtful, quite as observant of the little amenities, as he was in the early days, when all around the woodlands of life rang with the songs of Spring. Be a little patient, and you will find out all—of course you will, being a woman—and then you will both put both heads together and solve the problem, and he will wonder at your wisdom, and will take you into his confidence earlier next time."

To both I say: "Please remember you have espoused a human soul inhabiting so many stones of human flesh—both suffering from the result of that Original Sin for which the two sexes share responsibility. Get rid of the angel in the flesh theory. Angels do not dwell in flesh. Cut out the Apollo Belvidere conception. Apollo was a myth, and the statue a block of marble; and no woman wants to imitate Pygmalion, who fell in love with the marble he had chiselled into a human form. But if you both want a consort of flesh and blood, do not expect too much from any being bearing around the weight of our mortality."

The Ancient Ritual of Blessing the Nuptial Bed

Bless, O Lord, and look down upon this chamber, O thou who sleepest not. Thou who watchest over Israel, protect thy servants who sleep in this bed, from all deceitful illusions of the wicked one. Keep them while they watch, that they may meditate upon thy precepts, and while they sleep, that they may find thee in their slumbers, and that both here and everywhere they may be defended by thy assistance. Through Jesus Christ our Lord. Amen.

The Proper Use of the Power to Pass on Life

THE REV. FRANCIS DEVAS, S.J.

When we speak of sex the association of ideas is with physical actions, and purity becomes a difficult thing to think or speak about. It means for us: "I must not commit certain sins or think about them, because they are sins." The difficulty with this virtue is precisely that the things which we are forbidden to do are not bad in themselves. Purity is connected with that great gift of God to us—life. God has given us control over our own life, and the power of passing on that life to others. Because we share that gift with animals, we are tempted to look upon it as something bestial. But it is not the power of passing on life which is the important thing. They merely pass on animal life, but we pass on life that is valuable, because for every single living person God became man, that they might have supernatural life, eternal life. God by His revelation has hedged about the use of this power in a way which He has not done with any other power. This power is immensely more important than our other powers. All our other powers—the power of the mind, and so on—we can use at our discretion for the purpose for which they were given. Here is the one exception. In one way, and one way only, have we permission to use this power, and using it in that way gives Him greater glory—we are sharing with Him in His wonderful prerogative of Creator. We pass on life to human beings who have souls. The dignity of parenthood, therefore, is enormous. There is a tendency to think of sex as something degrading; it is not, it is magnificent, an enormous privilege, but, because of that, the rules are tremendously strict and severe, and "better is the man who rules his spirit than he that taketh cities." To govern one's spirit in this particular matter is to give God continual witness of our service to Him. It is easy to serve God in most other ways, but it is not so easy here. The enemy is our own nature, which desires the free use of these powers.

What should be our motive for not giving way? Nothing natural. It is revealed to us that it is against God's will that we should use this power except in marriage; that is the one and only motive, but the less we think of God, the weaker that motive becomes. The good nature that God has given us rises up in rebellion against God. Besides our nature, we know the temptations that come from others, from the spirit of the world. It is here that you show real courage, when you persevere in fighting against self, and pray for grace to do what you do not want to do. Here is a virile, active life, a way of immense sanctity open to you, but it means constant effort and a humility which depends on the strength of God. That is one side, and the most obvious side, of purity; but there is another side. It is not an inactive virtue; it does not merely consist in not committing certain sins. It means using your life in the way God wants, exercising constant restraint. All nature seems to show us the enormous importance of restraint. Take rivers, electricity—all the strong agencies of nature. What is essential? The storing up of energy, a governed repression, and release at the chosen time—by will, not by accident. That is shown in all our conquests of nature, and it must be the same in ourselves. Self-restraint gives us something indescribable. A man who has no self-restraint, no self-control, is useless; he has no character. But where a man has self-control—not from self-regard or from the love of others, but from the desire to serve God in the most generous way—there you have the virtue of courage helping to control self for God's sake. We are not meant by God to stifle our life; we are dead-and-alive persons if we have tried to kill the life within us. God wants us to have the power strongly, but under control; to be the master.

There is the ideal that God puts before us.

The Origin and Corruption of Marriage, and Its Restoration by Christ and His Church

LEO XIII

God, on the sixth day of creation, having made man from the slime of the earth, and having breathed into his face the breath of life, gave him a companion, whom He miraculously took from the side of Adam when he was locked in sleep. God thus, in His most far-reaching foresight, decreed that this husband and wife should be the natural beginning of the human race, from whom it might be propagated and preserved by an unfailing fruitfulness throughout all futurity of time.

And this union of man and woman, that it might answer more fittingly to the infinite wise counsels of God, even from the beginning manifested chiefly two most excellent properties—deeply sealed, as it were, and signed upon it—namely, unity and perpetuity. From the Gospel we see clearly that this doctrine was declared and openly confirmed by the divine authority of Jesus Christ. . . .

This form of marriage, however, so excellent and so preeminent, began to be corrupted and to disappear among the heathen; and became even among the Jewish race clouded in a measure and obscured. . . . All nations seem, more or less, to have forgotten the true notion and origin of marriage; and thus everywhere laws were enacted with reference to marriage, prompted to all appearance by State reasons, but not such as nature required. Solemn rites, invented at will of the lawgivers, brought about that women should, as might be, bear either the honorable name of wife or the disgraceful name of concubine; and things came to such a pitch that permission to marry, or the refusal of the permission, depended on the will of the heads of the State, whose laws were greatly against equity or even to the highest degree unjust. Moreover, plurality of wives and husbands, the abounding source of divorces, caused the nuptial bond to be relaxed exceedingly. . . .

Nothing could be more piteous than the wife, sunk so low as to be all but reckoned as a means for the gratification of passion, or for the production of offspring. Without any feeling of shame marriageable girls were bought and sold, just like so much merchandise; and power was sometimes given to the father and to the husband to inflict capital punishment on the wife. Of necessity the offspring of such marriages as these were either reckoned among the stock in trade of the commonwealth or held to be the property of the father of the family; and the law permitted him to make and unmake the marriages of his children at his mere will, and even to exercise against them the monstrous power of life and death.

So manifold being the vices and so great the ignominies with which marriage was defiled, an alleviation and a remedy were at length bestowed from on high. Jesus Christ, who restored our human dignity and who perfected the Mosaic law, applied early in His ministry no little solicitude to the question of marriage. He ennobled the marriage in Cana of Galilee by His presence, and made it memorable by the first of the miracles which He wrought; and for this reason, even from that day forth, it seemed as if the beginning of new holiness had been conferred on human marriages. Later on He brought back matrimony to the nobility of its primeval origin, by condemning the customs of the Jews in their abuse of the plurality of wives and of the power of giving bills of divorce; and still more by commanding most strictly that no one should dare to dissolve that union which God Himself had sanctioned by a bond perpetual. . . .

What was decreed and constituted in respect to marriage by the authority of God, has been more fully and more clearly handed down to us, by tradition and the written Word, through the Apostles, those heralds of the laws of God. To the Apostles, indeed, as our masters, are to be referred the doctrines which *our holy Fathers, the Councils, and the Tradition of the Universal Church have always taught,* namely, that Christ our Lord raised marriage to the dignity of a sacrament; that to husband and wife, guarded and strengthened by the heavenly grace which His merits gained for them, He gave power to attain holiness in the married state; and that, in a wondrous way, making marriage an example of the mystical union between Himself and His Church, He not only perfected that love which is according to nature, but also made the natural union of one man with one woman far more perfect through the bond of heavenly love. . . .

Christ, therefore, having renewed marriage to such and so great excellence, commended and entrusted all the discipline bearing upon these matters to His Church. . . .

A law of marriage just to all, and the same for all, was enacted by the abolition of the old distinction between slaves and free-born men and women; and thus the rights of husbands and wives were made equal: for, as St. Jerome says, "with us that which is unlawful for women is unlawful for men also, and the same restraint is imposed on equal conditions." The self-same rights also were firmly established for reciprocal affection and for the interchange of duties; the dignity of the woman was asserted and assured; and it was forbidden to the man to inflict capital punishment for adultery, or lustfully and shamelessly to violate his plighted faith.

It is also a great blessing that the Church has limited, so far as is needful, the power of fathers of families, so that sons and daughters, wishing to marry, are not in any way deprived of their rightful freedom; that, for the purpose of spreading more widely the supernatural love of husbands and wives, she has decreed marriages within certain degrees of consanguinity or affinity to be null and void; that she has taken the greatest pains to safeguard marriage, as much as is possible, from error and violence and deceit; that she has always wished to preserve the holy chasteness of the marriage bed, personal rights, the honor of husband and wife, and the security of religion. . . .

In Christian marriage the contract is inseparable from the sacrament; and for this reason, the contract cannot be true and legitimate without being a sacrament as well. For Christ our Lord added to marriage the dignity of a sacrament; but marriage is the contract itself, whenever that contract is lawfully concluded. . . .

Now those who deny that marriage is holy, and who relegate it, stripped of all holiness, among the class of common things, uproot thereby the foundations of nature, not only resisting the designs of Providence, but, so far as they can, destroying the order that God has ordained. . . .

When the Christian religion is rejected and repudiated, marriage sinks of necessity into the slavery of man's vicious nature and vile passions, and finds but little protection in the help of natural goodness. A very torrent of evil has flowed from this source, not only into private families, but also into States. For the salutary fear of God being removed, and there being no longer that refreshment in toil which is nowhere more abounding than in the Christian religion, it very often happens, as from facts is evident, that the mutual services and duties of marriage seem almost unbearable; and thus very many yearn for the loosening of the tie which they believe to be woven by human law and of their own will, whenever incompatibility of temper, or quarrels, or the violation of the marriage vow, or mutual consent, or other reasons induce them to think that it would be well to be set free. . . .

It must consequently be acknowledged that the Church has deserved exceedingly well of all nations by her ever-watchful care in guarding the sanctity and the indissolubility of marriage.

Natural Reason Supports Matrimony

ST. THOMAS AQUINAS

That is said to be natural to which nature inclines, although it comes to pass through the intervention of the free-will; thus acts of virtue and the virtues themselves are called natural; and in this way matrimony is natural, because natural reason inclines thereto in two ways. First, in relation to the principal end of matrimony, namely the good of offspring. For nature intends not only the begetting of offspring, but also its education and development until it reaches the perfect state of virtue. Hence . . . we derive three things from our parents, namely *existence, nourishment* and *education*. Now a child cannot be brought up and instructed unless it have certain and definite parents, and this would not be the case unless there were ties between the man and a definite woman, and it is in this that matrimony consists. Secondly, in relation to the secondary end of matrimony, which is the natural services which married persons render one another in household matters. For first as natural reason dictates that men should live together, since one is not self-sufficient in all things concerning life, for which reason man is described as being naturally inclined to political society, so too among those works that are necessary for human life some are becoming to men, others to women. Wherefore nature inculcates that society of man and woman which consists in matrimony.

(Translator Anonymous)

Synodical Letter of the Council of Gangra Defending Marriage

(PROBABLY 343, A.D.)

Forasmuch as the most Holy Synod of Bishops, assembled on account of certain necessary matters of ecclesiastical business in the Church at Gangra, on inquiring also into the matters which concern Eustathius, found that many things had been unlawfully done by these very men who are partisans of Eustathius, which it was compelled to make definitions, which it has hastened to make known to all, for the removal of whatever has by him been done amiss. For, from their utter abhorrence of marriage, and from their adoption of the proposition that no one living in a state of marriage has any hope towards God, many misguided married women have forsaken their husbands, and husbands their wives; then, afterwards, not being able to contain, they have fallen into adultery; and so, through such a principle as this, have come to shame. . . .

Wherefore, the Holy Synod present in Gangra, was compelled on these accounts, to condemn them, and to set forth definitions declaring them to be cast out of the Church; but that if they should repent and anathematize every one of these false doctrines, then they should be capable of restoration. . . . If any one will not submit to the said decrees, he shall be anathematized as a heretic, and excommunicated, and cast out of the Church. . . .

Canon I. If any one shall condemn marriage and condemn a woman who is a believer and devout, and sleeps with her own husband, as though she could not enter the Kingdom [of heaven], let him be anathema. . . .

Canon IX. If any one shall remain virgin, or observe continence, abstaining from marriage because he abhors it, and not on account of the beauty and holiness of virginity itself, let him be anathema.

Canon X. If any one of those who are living a virgin life for the Lord's sake shall treat arrogantly the married, let him be anathema. . . .

Canon XIV. If any woman shall forsake her husband, and resolve to depart from him because she abhors marriage, let her be anathema.

Canon XV. If any one shall forsake his own children and shall not nurture them, nor so far as in him lies, rear them in becoming piety, but shall neglect them, under pretense of asceticism, let him be anathema.

(Translated by Henry R. Percival)

"A Seed Sown in the Soul"

CANON JACQUES LECLERCQ

Marriage is the only sacrament which transforms a human institution into an instrument of the divine action, using a human act which up to then had been used for a natural end; it is the only human institution, the only essential act of the natural life which has been raised to that dignity. . . . The sacrament of marriage is the imprint of God on the souls of the married couple, not merely in order to deify their life in general, but in order to deify their union. It is towards their conjugal life that the sacramental act is aimed. . . . The sacrament of marriage is thus not merely a religious act sanctifying a human one; it is a seed sown in the soul and bearing fruit through the whole of married life, giving life to all its acts and sentiments; the sacrament of marriage exerts an influence on husband and wife to make them supernaturalize their married life; it is a predisposition to holiness placed in their souls by God on the day of their wedding. By the sacrament of marriage God becomes as it were a third party in the intimacy of married life. Man and wife are united in God; this last expression can be interpreted in a very strict sense, for the action of the sacrament being a unique divine action in the souls of each of them, and sacramental grace being a reality in their souls, one can truly state that they have something in their souls which really unites them, which constitutes a principle of unity, and that this unifying reality is a divine action. The sacrament of marriage is thus in a sense a deifying of the conjugal union, a means of translating into action the unity and the divine character which God imposes in the sacrament.

(Translated by the Earl of Wicklow)

True Marriage

ST. THOMAS AQUINAS

Marriage is called true when it achieves its proper perfection. The perfection of anything is twofold, primary and secondary. The first consists in a thing's form, which constitutes it as a thing of a definite kind. The second consists in the activity through which in some manner it reaches its end. The form of marriage lies in an inseparable union of minds by which either is unalterably plighted to serve the other loyally. The end of marriage is the begetting and rearing of children.

(Translated by Thomas Gilby)

The Moral Guidance of the Church
PIUS XI

In order, therefore, to restore due order in this matter of marriage, it is necessary that all should bear in mind what is the divine plan and strive to conform to it.

Wherefore, since the chief obstacle to this study is the power of unbridled lust, which indeed is the most potent cause of sinning against the sacred laws of matrimony, and since man cannot hold in check his passions, unless he first subject himself to God, this must be his primary endeavour, in accordance with the plan divinely ordained. . . .

Consequently, as the onslaughts of these uncontrolled passions cannot in any way be lessened, unless the spirit first shows a humble compliance of duty and reverence towards its Maker, it is above all and before all needful that those who are joined in the bond of sacred wedlock should be wholly imbued with a profound and genuine sense of duty towards God, which will shape their whole lives, and fill their minds and wills with a very deep reverence for the majesty of God. . . .

But everyone can see to how many fallacies an avenue would be opened up and how many errors would become mixed with the truth, if it were left solely to the light of reason of each to find it out, or if it were to be discovered by the private interpretation of the truth which is revealed. . . .

In order that no falsification or corruption of the divine law but a true genuine knowledge of it may enlighten the minds of men and guide their conduct, it is necessary that a filial and humble obedience towards the Church should be combined with devotedness to God and the desire of submitting to Him. For Christ Himself made the Church the teacher of truth in those things also which concern the right regulation of moral conduct, even though some knowledge of the same is not beyond human reason. . . .

Wherefore, let the faithful also be on their guard against the overrated independence of private judgment and that false autonomy of human reason. For it is quite foreign to everyone bearing the name of a Christian to trust his own mental powers with such pride as to agree only with those things which he can examine from their inner nature, and to imagine that the Church, sent by God to teach and guide all nations, is not conversant with present affairs and circumstances; or even that they must obey only in those matters which she has decreed by solemn definition as though her other decisions might be presumed to be false or putting forward insufficient motive for truth and honesty. Quite to the contrary, a characteristic of all true followers of Christ, lettered or unlettered, is to suffer themselves to be guided and led in all things that touch upon faith or morals by the Holy Church of God through its Supreme Pastor the Roman Pontiff, who is himself guided by Jesus Christ Our Lord.

Marriage Must Be a Free Act

PIUS XI

For each individual marriage, inasmuch as it is a conjugal union of a particular man and woman, arises only from the free consent of each of the spouses; and this free act of the will, by which each party hands over and accepts those rights proper to the state of marriage, is so necessary to constitute true marriage that it cannot be supplied by any human power. This freedom, however, regards only the question whether the contracting parties really wish to enter upon matrimony or to marry this particular person; but the nature of matrimony is entirely independent of the free will of man, so that if one has once contracted matrimony he is thereby subject to its divinely made laws and its essential properties. . . .

By matrimony, therefore, the souls of the contracting parties are joined and knit together more directly and more intimately than are their bodies, and that not by any passing affection of sense or spirit, but by a deliberate and firm act of the will; and from this union of souls by God's decree, a sacred and inviolable bond arises. . . .

Therefore the sacred partnership of true marriage is constituted both by the will of God and the will of man. From God comes the very institution of marriage, the ends for which it was instituted, the laws that govern it, the blessings that flow from it; while man, through generous surrender of his own person made to another for the whole span of life, becomes, with the help and cooperation of God, the author of each particular marriage, with the duties and blessings annexed thereto from divine institution.

Decisions by the Council of Trent
(1563)

The first parent of the human race, under the influence of the divine Spirit, pronounced the bond of matrimony perpetual and indissoluble when he said, "This now is bone of my bone, and flesh of my flesh. Wherefore a man shall leave father and mother, and shall cleave to his wife, and they shall be two in one flesh." But, that by this bond two only are united and joined together, Our Lord taught more plainly when, repeating those last words, as having been uttered by God, He said: "therefore now they are not two, but one flesh"; and straight-way confirmed the firmness of that bond, proclaimed so long ago by Adam, in these words: "What, therefore, God hath joined together, let no man put asunder."

If any one saith that the Church hath erred in that she hath taught and doth teach . . . that the bond of matrimony cannot be dissolved on account of the adultery of one of the married parties . . . let him be anathema.

"A Perpetual and Indissoluble Bond"

PIUS XI

Our predecessor Pius VI of happy memory, writing to the Bishop of Agria, most wisely said: "It is clear that marriage even in the state of nature, and certainly long before it was raised to the dignity of a sacrament, was divinely instituted in such a way that it should carry with it a perpetual and indissoluble bond which cannot therefore be dissolved by any civil law. Therefore although the sacramental element may be absent from a marriage as is the case among unbelievers, still in such a marriage, inasmuch as it is a true marriage there must remain and indeed there does remain that perpetual bond which by divine right is so bound up with matrimony from its first institution that it is not subject to any civil power. And so, whatever marriage is said to be contracted, either it is so contracted that it is really a true marriage, in which case it carries with it that enduring bond which by divine right is inherent in every true marriage; or it is thought to be contracted without that perpetual bond, and in that case there is no marriage, but an illicit union opposed of its very nature to the divine law, which therefore cannot be entered into or maintained." . . .

Indeed, how many and how important are the benefits which flow from the indissolubility of matrimony cannot escape anyone who gives even a brief consideration either to the good of the married parties and the offspring or to the welfare of human society. First of all, both husband and wife possess a positive guarantee of the endurance of this stability which that generous yielding of their persons and the intimate fellowship of their hearts by their nature strongly require, since true love never falls away. Besides, a strong bulwark is set up in defence of a loyal chastity against incitements to infidelity, should any be encountered either from within or from without; any anxious fear lest in adversity or old age the other spouse would prove unfaithful is precluded and in its place there reigns a calm sense of security. Moreover, the dignity of both man and wife is maintained and mutual aid is most satisfactorily assured, while through the indissoluble bond, always enduring, the spouses are warned continuously that not for the sake of perishable things nor that they may serve their passions, but that they may procure one for the other high and lasting good have they entered into the nuptial partnership, to be dissolved only by death. In the training and education of children, which must extend over a period of many years, it plays a great part, since the grave and long enduring burdens of this office are best borne by the united efforts of the parents. Nor do lesser benefits accrue to human society as a whole. For experience has taught that unassailable stability in matrimony is a fruitful source of virtuous life and of habits of integrity. Where this order of things obtains, the happiness and well being of the nation is safely guarded; what the families and individuals are, so also is the State, for a body is determined by its parts. Wherefore, both for the private good of husband, wife and children, as likewise for the public good of human society, they indeed deserve well who strenuously defend the inviolable stability of matrimony.

The Catholic Matrimonial Courts

THE REV. M. J. BROWNE

If a question is raised whether a particular marriage is valid and binding, the Church must answer that question herself. She cannot hand it over to the State, and at the same time hold that marriage is a sacrament. She is, therefore, bound to provide a tribunal to decide that question fully and formally, according to the written law of Christian marriage. Otherwise she would be false to the divine teaching that the marriage of Christians is a sacrament and false to her duty to Christians.

The decision of matrimonial cases is, therefore, for the Church the discharge of a duty. The only cases which are considered by an ecclesiastical court are cases of nullity, those in which it is contended that the marriage was from the beginning null and void because of the absence of some of the conditions required for marriage; and in which the decision sought is a declaration of that nullity.* Thus one of the obvious conditions required for a valid marriage is that each of the contracting parties be sane: lunatics cannot contract marriage. Now if a question be raised about a particular marriage, and if it be proved that one of the parties was insane at the time of the ceremony, the Court will give a declaration of nullity. It does not dissolve the marriage: it merely gives an official recognition of a fact that there was no marriage there from the beginning. Decisions of nullity do not affect the sanctity or indissolubility of the marriage bond: they do not break, lessen, or weaken that bond: they are not opposed to the doctrine of the indissolubility of marriage, for they are concerned only with the preliminary question whether a valid marriage had been contracted at all.

They are totally distinct in law and in practice from divorce cases. In law a divorce case is one in which the marriage is admitted by both parties to have been valid, but for some reason which has supervened since the marriage, a dissolution or breaking of the bond is sought. In these cases the Court does not merely recognize a fact; it claims and exercises a power, to make what has been good and binding no longer of any effect. Sentences of divorce are contrary to the indissolubility of marriage: they are directly opposed to, and destructive of, the teaching that a valid marriage cannot for any cause be dissolved.

That there is a world of difference between divorce cases and cases of nullity is quite clear to any person who reflects. The difference is of vast theoretical and practical importance. Divorce in theory is based on a denial of the sacredness of the marriage tie: in practice whenever it has been introduced it has led to the breaking up of countless marriages and homes, and to a general

---

* This statement is true only in a limited and technical sense. Actually, an ecclesiastical court, by common Church law, handles cases not connected at all with marriage, and, by special commission of the bishop, matrimonial cases other than those of nullity.—R.L.W.

lowering of public moral standards. Neither of these objections attach to cases of nullity: they do not impugn the binding force of the marriage, and they are of their nature so rare and infrequent that they cannot by any stretch of imagination lead to abuse. . . .

The Catholic Church does not recognize or admit divorce. Once a marriage has been validly contracted there is no release till death. Hence she is particularly careful to see that marriages are validly contracted. Hence, too, she is also careful not to impose the obligations of marriage on any but a valid marriage. One of the conditions she requires for a valid marriage is full freedom of the contracting parties from violence and intimidation. Marriage means a bond that will end only with death: it involves obligations and restraints of a most serious personal nature. Every individual has an inalienable right to decide freely for himself whether he will marry or not. He has a right to decide to whom he will get married. . . . If, therefore, a case occurs in which intimidation is alleged, the Church must be prepared to examine it fully and judicially. If intimidation is proved, she must be as firm in denying any force to that invalid ceremony as she is in upholding the sanctity of a free, valid marriage.

Hostile critics of the Church pretend that the requirement of conditions for validity of marriage provides a loophole or pretext by means of which a great number of marriages are rendered invalid, so that afterwards if need arise they can be impugned. They forget—or pretend to forget—that even the State requires such conditions and that there *must* be conditions. How could there be such a thing as marriage, if it were not made up of certain essential elements? How could we define it, or distinguish it from such an act as that of engaging a housekeeper? Conditions there must be in the absence of which the act is not a marriage; and they must be defined in detail. . . .

Now let us suppose that for some reason or other a Catholic believes that his marriage was invalid and wishes to have it declared invalid. He has a serious proposition before him, a long and difficult road to travel. In the first place he has to *prove* that the marriage was invalid. The burden of proof rests on him. It is a maxim of Canon Law that "marriage enjoys the favour of the law: wherefore in case of doubt the validity of the marriage must be upheld until the contrary be proved." Hence, if the plaintiff does not prove his case to the hilt, the decision of the Court will be *Non constat de matrimonii invaliditate in casu*—The invalidity of the marriage has not been established. It is not necessary in an ecclesiastical court to say any more: the case has failed.

In the second place the plaintiff will have to deal with the Defender of the Bond. Matrimonial proceedings in which he has not been cited or appeared are null and void. His function is to defend at all costs the validity of the marriage and to prevent fraudulent or collusive proceedings.

Even if the other party does not defend the case, the Defender of the Bond will, and *must* by law, undertake the work. He will be present at the examination of witnesses and have them closely questioned: he will produce witnesses and evidence for the defence, will submit pleadings and counter pleadings. Finally, if the decision be given that the marriage is invalid, he will immediately appeal to the higher court. When for the first time sentence is given for the nullity of the marriage, he is in fact *bound* to appeal and if he fails, will be compelled to do so. . . .

These are very serious legal obstacles for the Catholic who wishes to contest the validity of his marriage. But there is one handicap under which he will not lie, *viz.*, poverty. The fact that he has little of the world's goods will not debar a Catholic from prosecuting his claims at the Courts of the Church. . . .

The rights of the poor are carefully safeguarded in theory and in practice. It is laid down in Canon Law (Canon 1914) that those who are quite unable to bear the expenses of their case *have a right* to entire release from costs: those who are partially unable, have a right to a reduction of the costs. It is not a question of a favor or condescension, but a strict right conferred by law, which the judge is bound to respect, once the litigant supplies proof of his financial condition. The judge must also appoint one of the advocates of the Court to undertake the defense of the poor person's case and the advocate so appointed must faithfully discharge the trust under penalty of suspension from the Roll if the judge so decree. These regulations bind on all ecclesiastical courts from the highest to the lowest. In the case of the Roman Rota we have precise statistics of the number of cases in which it was availed of. In 1927 of the sixty-one cases which were decided, in twenty-five the proceedings were gratuitous.

This was in no way exceptional. Thus for six years the percentage of cases which were decided free of costs and with the free services of an advocate was 30 per cent—one out of every three. Such statistics speak for themselves. . . .

It is the only international tribunal that is in permanent session and that functions daily. Yet it is independent not merely of individual states but of all of them. It is a striking visible symbol of two outstanding qualities of the Church, its universality and its independence.

The Catholic Interpretation of the Scriptural Passage Many Non-Catholics Quote to Justify Divorce and Remarriage

THE REV. LUCIUS F. CERVANTES, S.J.*

And there came to him some Pharisees, testing him, and saying "Is it lawful for a man to put away his wife for any cause?" But he answered and said to them, "Have you not read that the Creator, from the beginning made them male and female, and said, 'For this cause a man shall leave his father and mother, and cleave to his wife, and the two shall become one flesh?' Therefore now they are no longer two, but one flesh. What therefore God has joined together, let no man put asunder." They said to him, "Why then did Moses command to give a written notice of dismissal, and to put her away?" He said to them. "Because Moses, by reason of the hardness of your heart, permitted you to put away your wives; but it was not so from the beginning. And I say to you, that whoever puts away his

* From Marriage and the Family, A Text for Moderns, Carl C. Zimmerman and Lucius Cervantes, S.J.; Copyright, 1956, Henry Regnery Co.

wife, except for immorality, and marries another, commits adultery; and he who marries a woman who has been put away commits adultery." His disciples said to him: "If the case of a man with his wife is so, it is not expedient to marry."

(St. Matthew 19:3-11)

The writer has heard an extremely competent student of marriage literature say: "In this passage Jesus contradicts himself; in other passages of the New Testament Jesus outlaws divorce; here he permits it." It is true that if Jesus' words, "Whoever puts away his wife, except for immorality, and marries another, commits adultery" were isolated and had neither a remote or proximate field of reference, it might be assumed that where adultery is committed the innocent party might claim not merely permanent or temporary separation but an absolute divorce with the right of remarriage. However it can be shown, even prescinding from the constant teaching of the historical Church, of the Greek Church until the sixth century, of the fathers of the Church, and even of the rest of Scripture, that the context of the words prohibit remarriage. Unless the words are understood as prohibiting remarriage even in the case of unfaithfulness Jesus' replies lose all coherence with the immediate words themselves and with all the rest of the New Testament, whereas, if they bear the sense of an imperfect divorce, or separation a *thoro et mensa*, then their consistency is perfect. . . . Such has been the historical Christian interpretation based ultimately on the authority of the teaching Church but proximately on the following cogent reasons. The clause "except for impurity" implies no right to remarriage and the absolute dissolution of the marriage bond because:

1) Otherwise Christ straightaway cancels his own appeal to the original institution of God: "What God has joined together let no man put asunder."

2) Otherwise Christ would be immediately sanctioning a permission He has just discountenanced: "Moses, by reason of the hardness of your hearts, permitted you to put away your wives; but it was not so from the beginning."

3) Otherwise Christ would be contradicting his own previous

teaching as recorded by the same evangelist on the Mount of the Beatitudes (Matthew 5:31-32).

4) He would be misinterpreted by His own Apostles, who were present, and who immediately questioned him on that very matter.

5) It would make nonsensical His own disciples' later exclamation at the severity of the doctrine: "If the case of a man with his wife is so, it is not expedient to marry." His pronouncement is evidently a shock to them. Better to remain a celibate, they say, than to make so tremendous a commitment. Had Christ taught no more than Shammai had taught before him there would have been no such reaction. Jesus had obviously gone beyond this.

6) If there were no bond still persisting after the adulterous wife had been put away then the person who married her would be guilty of fornication not of "adultery" as the sentence states: "he who marries a woman who has been put away commits adultery."

The scientific conclusion must be that of the ages; the important text must signify what the overwhelming majority of the scholars down the centuries have held it to signify: "It is not lawful for any man to put away his wife except for impurity; and if a man putteth away his wife (for that or any other cause) and marrieth another woman, he committeth adultery." Taken out of the context of the sentence, the paragraph, the incident, the Gospel, the New Testament, the phrase "except for adultery" is ambiguous; within the total context there is only one meaning possible.

Legitimately Contracted Marriage Always Sacred

PIUS XII

Even where the parties are not baptized, marriage legitimately contracted is a sacred thing in the natural order. The civil courts have no power to dissolve it, and the Church has never recognized the validity of divorce decrees in such cases.

Modern Enemies of Christian Marriage

THE REV. LUCIUS F. CERVANTES, S.J.*

Sociologically the question of the family resolves itself to the question of the differences of the sexes. If the traditional characteristic behavior patterns of men and women are moored irresistibly to nature then marriage is moored unalterably to nature; but if the traditional masculine-feminine characteristic qualities are merely a product of our culture and an imposition of our environment, then sociologically monogamic marriage is likewise merely a product of our culture and might perfectly well be discarded.

The modern concern and confusion about questions of sex are not as superficial as they sometimes appear to be. . . . There is more at stake than the acceptance or rejection of the orthodox Communist doctrine that "sex is a drink of water" or the Kinsey evaluation of sex functions as "outlets" and sex cultural patterns as merely the result of taboos. . . . These statements are superficial social verbalized seismographic oscillations recording the deeper stress and incipient split in the philosophical underpinnings of the total marriage structure itself. It is the foundation of the institution of marriage itself which is at stake.

Academically it is extremely easy to swing from the basic stand that sexual differences are invalid to the terminal conclusion that monogamic marriage is invalid. . . . If one grants Plato's premise that "men and women differ only in this that one begets and the other bears children" one may likewise easily follow Plato's conclusion that men and women should do the same kind of work, that they should play the same roles, that marriage might as well be abolished and the children brought up in state institutions. . . .

* From *Marriage and the Family, A Text for Moderns*, Carl C. Zimmerman and Lucius F. Cervantes, S.J.; Copyright, 1956, Henry Regnery Co.

It is not the logic of such an anti-familial conclusion that should be questioned: it is the premise. For if men and women differ only in that one is the bearer of the sperm and the other the bearer of the ova, then there is no compelling sociological reason why the monogamic family should be firmly institutionalized. There would be no basic scientific reason for a child to be brought up rather by his monogamously mated parents than by two men or by two women or in a state institution by a group of men or women if beyond the function of procreation and gestation men and women are identical in function, outlook, and demeanor.

So it is entirely comprehensible that those who minimize the differences between the sexes should likewise minimize the need for the institution of marriage. . . .

Not many steps in logic nor many years in time intervened between the Communists' premise that the masculine and feminine characteristic qualities were a mere imposition of a capitalistic society and their conclusion that the family was no longer necessary. Marx, Engels, Bebel, Lenin—these men were most intelligent and clear-sighted and absolutely ready to accept the consequences of their own primary doctrines. They early proclaimed that the characteristic differences of the sexes had been imposed by the brutal capitalistic male to bring about the "world historical defeat of the female sex." . . . Marx concluded: "The modern family contains in germ not only slavery but . . . it contains in miniature all the contradictions which later extend throughout society and its state."

Lenin stated: "No nation can be free when half of the population is enslaved in the kitchen."

Within two years after their violent ascent to power and immediate imposition of their anti-familial laws in Russia, the Communist State could triumphantly announce: "The family has ceased to be a necessity, both for its members and for the State."

The same anti-familial attitude is evident not only in the early Communistic literature—whether of Plato or of Marx—but in the sociological writings of practically all those who minimize the differences of the sexes.

Margaret Mead is one of the most frequently quoted of contemporary anthropologists. Her basic postulate has been that "we no longer have any basis for regarding such aspects [i.e. the traditional masculine-feminine characteristics] of behavior as sex-linked." Knowing this to be her premise we are not surprised that she should likewise come to the conclusion that: "Were state responsibility for children to be substituted for the present family organization, we would again obtain a type of guarantee for children which the present bilateral family group fails to give." . . .

Bertrand Russell minimizes the disjunctive characterology of the sexes in such words as: "Maternal emotions altogether have been so long slobbered over by men who saw in them subconsciously the means to their domination that a considerable effort is required to arrive at what women sincerely feel in this respect. . . . As women become fully emancipated their emotions turn out to be, in general, quite different from what has hitherto been thought. . . . Assuming the break-up of the family and the establishment of rationally conducted State institutions for children, it will probably be found necessary to go a step further in the substitution of regulation for instinct. Women accustomed to birth control and not allowed to keep their own children would have little motive for enduring the discomfort of gestation and the pain of childbirth. Consequently in order to keep up the population it would be necessary to make child-bearing a well paid profession, not of course to be undertaken by all women or even by a majority, but only by a certain percentage who would have to pass tests as to their fitness from a stock-breeding point of view." . . .

This array of quotations may be concluded with appropriate quotations from *The Second Sex*, by Mlle. Simone de Beauvoir. This book has had a most remarkable reception from the reviewers. . . . One (Philip Wylie) has declared the book to be "one of the few great books of our era," another (Ashley Montagu) has called it "a great book, a book that will be read long after most works which have been written on the subject will have been forgotten." . . . She writes such passages as these: "It has been said that marriage diminishes man, which is often true; but almost always it annihilates women. . . . Both must be free. . . . Individuals are not to be blamed for the failure of marriage: it is—counter to the claims of such advocates as Comte and Tolstoy—the institution itself, perverted as it has been from the start. To hold and proclaim that a man and a woman, who may not even have chosen each other, are in duty bound to satisfy each other in every way throughout their lives is a monstrosity that necessarily gives rise to hypocrisy, lying, hostility, and unhappiness. . . . Adultery is indeed the form that love will assume as long as the institution of marriage lasts." . . .

Mlle. Beauvoir follows these statements with this concluding statement: "But is it enough to change laws, institutions, customs, public opinion, and the whole social context, for men and women to become truly equal? 'Women will always be women,' say the skeptics. Other seers prophesy that in casting off their femininity they will not succeed in changing themselves into men and they will become monsters. This would be to admit that the woman of today is a creation of nature; it must be repeated once more that in human society nothing is natural and that woman, like much else, is a product elaborated by civilization. . . . Woman is determined not by her hormones or by mysterious instincts, but by the manner in which her body and her relation to the world are modified through the action of others than herself. The abyss that separates the adolescent boy and girl has been deliberately opened out between them since earliest childhood; that past was bound to shadow her for life. If we appreciate its influence, we see clearly that her destiny is not predetermined for all eternity." . . .

Charlotte Perkins Gilman put it: "Mere promiscuity, indulged from mutual desire, is not in itself a vice." . . . W. L. George was more forthright in his *Atlantic Monthly* article when he stated the feminists' anti-institutional aims:

"In the main we are opposed to the indissoluble Christian Marriage. The present increase in the divorce rate is of course gratifying; but it is not enough. Personally I believe that the ultimate aim of Feminism is the suppression of marriage and the institution of Free Alliance. It may be that only thus can woman develop her personality."

George Bernard Shaw's recurrently resurrected play, *Man and Superman,* along with many other of his feminist works have identical overtones. As he stated in his *Sociological Papers:* "What we need is freedom for the people who have never seen each other before and never intend to see one another again, to produce children under certain public conditions, without loss of honor." . . .

According to the Communist theory the abolishing of private property would mean that the family would lose its *raison d'être* and disappear with all the other evils of capitalism. Communist "free-love" propaganda differed little from that of the Feminists; they uniformly maintained that the progress of society would mean that the former functions and responsibilities of the family would be taken over by the state. Bebel maintained that "Marriage is sexual slavery" and that "free love must be absolute." Engel declared that "Marriage differs from prostitution in that one is purchase and the other hire." . . .

And the early Communist government had promoted their usual "free love" doctrine. Yet a mere twenty-five years later, the Soviets put out an official directive stating: "The State cannot exist without the family. Marriage is a positive value for the Socialist Soviet State only if the partners see it as a lifelong union." By 1943 it was evident that, in line with the other complete reversals and rejections of former orthodox Communistic dogmas, the Feminist and Evolutionist and Communist premise of the basic identity of the sexes was gone. Post-card divorces, free love, abortaria, identical education, "bachelor suburbs," community kitchens, display creches, idealized children's institutions —all were gone. The rising generation of Communists would not be reared according to original Communist doctrine.

"Free love is a bourgeois invention," "Marriage is the most serious affair of life," "The right to divorce is not the right to sexual laxity," "Illegitimate children and their mothers will receive no alimony" now became propaganda harbingers of the new way of life. Perhaps the most violent reversal of all, involving as it did a complete surrender of the Feminist and Evolutionist and Communist premise, was the declaration of August 4, 1943, that coeducation on the elementary and secondary level would be abolished. Not even the most conservative of the opposing biocultural school of thought demanded this. But the Communist now maintained: "A boy must be prepared for service in the Red Army while he is still at school. He receives physical and purely military training for a stern soldier's life. . . . What of the girl? She is essentially a mother. School must give the girl special knowledge of human anatomy, physiology, psychology, pedagogy and hygiene."

Curiously enough, this tremendous piece of experimental evidence is all but ignored by the advocates of the cultural theory in our English-speaking world. The total anti-familial program as implemented within Communist Russia was the great test-case of the practicability of the conclusions drawn by the proponents of the cultural school of sex differences. The experiment was a gigantic failure. The cultural hypothesis as envisioned by Feminism, Evolutionism and Communism could not stand the absolutely definitive test of practical application.

Fundamental Differences between Man and Woman

ALEXIS CARREL, M.D.

The differences existing between man and woman do not come from the particular form of the sexual organs, the presence of the uterus, from gestation, or from the mode of education. They are of a more fundamental nature. They are caused by the very structure of the tissues and by the impregnation of the entire organism with specific chemical substances secreted by the ovary. Ignorance of these fundamental facts has led promoters of feminism to believe that both sexes should have the same education, the same powers, and the same responsibilities. In reality, woman differs profoundly from man. Every one of the cells of her body bears the mark of her sex. The same is true of her organs, and, above all, of her nervous system. Physiological laws are as inexorable as those of the sidereal world. They cannot be replaced by human wishes. We are obliged to accept them just as they are. Women should develop their own nature, without trying to imitate the males. Their part in the progress of civilization is higher than that of men. They should not abandon their specific functions.

Marriage: A Part of the Divine Plan of Society

FATHER CUTHBERT, O.S.F.C.

It belongs to the genius of Christianity to discover in the temporal the germ of the eternal. The spirit of Christ entering into human life does not destroy but perfects; it takes our life as it is, and out of the merely natural or earthly raises up the supernatural and heavenly. . . . When rightly understood and dealt with, the visible world leads us to the knowledge and enjoyment of the invisible and eternal; draws us into communion with the spiritual. The Christian spirit thus beholds a sacramental value in all nature, but especially in human nature. For this reason any abuse of the gifts and joys of nature is so much more a sin, since it is a perversion to evil, brutish ends, of what in itself is destined to lead us on to the spiritual and usher us into the eternal. It is the consciousness of the eternal in the temporal which more than aught else differentiates man from the brute; and it is the object of the Church to foster and develop this consciousness in all the relations of human life. When Pope Gregory the Great told St. Augustine not to destroy the pagan temples of the Anglo-Saxon nor to abolish pagan festivals, but to purify and consecrate the temples for Christian worship, and transform the festivals into Christian festivals, he did but apply in this particular instance the universal principle of Catholic Christianity.

It is not nature which is evil, but our abuse of nature, and our blindness to the sacramental character of nature.

This truth is nowhere more intimately revealed than in the Catholic conception of marriage. Here we have one of the primary institutions of the civilized state taken over into the Christian life, consecrated by a sacramental blessing and regarded as one of the seven sacramental foundations of the Church. Marriage is not regarded by Christianity as a mere accident of life, it is not tolerated as a necessary evil; but it is taken as a recognized vocation essential to the building up of the Church on earth, and thereby entering into the scheme of the world's salvation. Husband and wife have their part to do in the life of the Church and in the work of transforming the world into God's kingdom, just as the priest and the consecrated virgin have their part; and it is from its relation to the divine economy of the Church that Christian marriage derives its sanction and peculiar sanctity. Christians, according to the mind of the Gospel, marry in order to give effect to the divine plan of human society; and this they do not merely by carrying on the human race, but by the creation of a domestic society, which shall be in itself a microcosm, containing the germ of a larger society of the Christian world; and it is upon the foundation of this smaller society of the Christian home that the larger society of the Church is built. The home is, as it were, the domestic chapel from which is fed the more extended life of the basilica; and as the Christian character of that is, so will this be. Marriage, therefore, in the Christian dispensation cannot be separated from the idea of that home-life upon which the Christian society is built as upon a prototypal foundation. Marriage is for the home, and the home for the Church.

Such is the Catholic idea, and it at once gives the answer to the free-love theories so unhappily undermining the domestic morality of the modern nations. All these theories assume that marriage is a matter of merely personal convenience or pleasure. They ignore the truth, oftentimes so painfully borne in upon us, of the social responsibilities attaching to individual life; they seem unconscious of the fact that mere personal pleasure or inclination is no criterion of true self-development. The free-love theory in its furthest application is a denial of all social responsibility whatever; in its less extreme forms it is a denial of Christianity. Whether from a Christian or non-Christian point of view marriage is always the ordering and control of a natural instinct for the purpose of realizing social unity. In every case mere personal interest and gratification is subordinated to more unselfish ends. But from a non-Christian or secularist point of view the social purpose of marriage, while it imposes certain restraints, does not absorb the natural instinct into an abiding law and purpose, ever present in a man's life, and rendering mere self-indulgence always sinful; whereas in Christian society this is the case. Christianity places the sexual instinct under a spiritual law, and permits its gratification only for the definite purpose of creating a Christian home. Apart from this end any gratification of the sexual instinct is sinful, since it contravenes the divine purpose in human nature.

Marriage, therefore, according to Christian teaching, demands an entire surrender of mere natural impulse to one only purpose, the building up a Christian society through the home; and it is only when we recognize this that the laws of the Church regarding marriage are seen to be intelligible and consistent. . . .

We can see now what answer the Church must make to all arguments in favor of divorce. Marriage, it is urged by the advocates of divorce, is meant to enable the husband and wife to live more happily in this world; its primary object is to secure the happiness of the married parties. Consequently, when it proves to be conducive rather to their misery than their happiness, it is only just that they should be freed from each other. Further, it is urged, to force a man or woman to live together when they prove to be unfitted for each other is to tempt them to throw off all responsibility and seek pleasure unlawfully, thus putting the legal bond to scorn and robbing it of all respect. But to this argument the Church can only reply that though it is true that marriage is meant to conduce to the happiness of husband and wife, yet it is not true to say that this is its ultimate object, except in so far as the happiness of anyone is bound up with their true vocation in life. Husband and wife are supposed to find their happiness in their home and in each other's companionship; but the right object of their marriage is to create the home and make it a center of Christian life. To this purpose husband and wife are supposed to dedicate themselves when they take the marriage vow; and this purpose alone justifies them in taking their vow. Marriage, therefore, under the Christian law demands a sacrifice of that ultra-individualism which is taken to justify divorce, nor can the Church consistently consider such ultra-individualism afterwards as a plea for the dissolution of the marriage bond. Marriage, in fact, implies in the contracting parties a surrender of the individual to the Christian purpose, and in this surrender the individual who is properly called to the marriage state finds that higher development of his personal self, which is found in all self-sacrifice which proceeds from a sense of duty and religion.

What the Church then demands of husband and wife, from the moment that they are united in wedlock, is that they put aside all thought of self in so far as it tends to turn them aside from their proper purpose; for husband and wife no longer belong to themselves, they are consecrated to a purpose above and beyond themselves, and to turn their thoughts backwards upon their personal interests or pleasure to the detriment of the purpose to which they are dedicated, is a violation of their vow and a sacrilege. The Church, therefore, can never sanction any law or institution which tends to introduce personal pleasure or interest into the marriage relation to the detriment of that purpose for which alone under the Christian dispensation marriage is instituted, or which tends to foster an ideal at variance with that of the Gospel. To sanction divorce would be to recognize a purpose in marriage other than that which alone she does recognize.

This only can the Church grant in consideration of human weakness and fallibility, that in certain cases husband and wife may be permitted to live apart. Even in this matter the action of the Church is controlled by the idea of the stability of the home or the general welfare of society. Permission to live apart is granted only when it is evident that the continuing to live together will not conduce to the sanctity or integrity of home life. Such permission, too, is granted only by way of exceptional legislation designed to lighten the burden of useless suffering, but not to infringe in any way the essential stability of the marriage institution. It may happen even to the most thoughtful and conscientious man or woman to have chosen a partner in marriage with whom it is morally impossible to live with self-respect or whose entire want of sympathy or moral conduct renders the life of the other an excessive burden. To such the Church extends the indulgence of a legal separation; yet in bending so far to human weakness she preserves the radical bond; husband and wife still remain husband and wife. The ideal of the Church is thus vindicated in legal separation, and neither party, therefore, is at liberty to marry again. . . .

Christ came into the world to lift the world up; to free men from the tyranny of sense-pleasure by which they are ever drawn downwards towards the level of the brute creation, and so to constitute man once more in that spiritual perfection which is properly his. For this reason he appealed always to man's higher nature; to the spiritual in man, not to the brutish. The law of marriage which He promulgated is hard only in so far as men are guided in their desires by the lower instincts, whereas Christ will recognize as a legitimate rule of human life only the higher, more spiritual, instincts. Before the coming of Christ the recognized purpose of marriage was largely the gratification of passion, within certain limits made necessary by the well-being of the community. But Christian marriage was put at once upon a more spiritual foundation. Christ's union with humanity became the law of the union between husband and wife, and Christ's love of the Church became the law of conjugal affection. As Christ loves the Church with a pure, self-sacrificing love, and as His love finds its gratification in realizing God's kingdom amongst men by the union of Himself with humanity, so must husband and wife love each other and find their highest gratification in realizing through each other God's kingdom on earth. This true love—true at once to God and to man's own higher nature—was to supplant more sensual passion and be the basis upon which the sacramental structure of the marriage state was to be reared. And it is only where this love exists that the perfection of the Christian ideal can be realized. It is this love which the Church demands of husband and wife when they vow to love each other and take each other "for better, for worse," till death do them part. But this vow implies that there be already in their hearts that love for each other which they vow to give till death; and when this love is wanting marriage is a desecration and hardly less than perjury before God.

Marriage and Celibacy Compared

THE REV. FRANCIS DEVAS, S.J.

Sex and the power of love are united by God. In marriage and the consummation of marriage you get, where it is done perfectly by perfect lovers and perfect lovers of God, the very final culmination of love, a complete man and complete woman, body, soul, imagination, emotion—all united in subservience to God. . . .

That God should have given us this thing as a test is something for which we ought to try to be grateful. Thank God, He has given us something that we can do to prove our sincerity. You cannot succeed in a day; the struggle may go on to the end of your life, you have got something to achieve, a constant enemy to overcome. It is not something despicable, but something that can be made useful. The body, the imagination, the emotions—these are all absolutely good things, meant to be under your control (hence the necessity of mortification) in order that you may offer them to God.

To say that because the Church teaches the vow of celibacy is something better than marriage, does not mean that there is something in marriage . . . less than good. The true view can be seen from the nature of a vow, which is always to do something more perfect. You cannot take a vow to do something less perfect. The value of the vow varies with the value of the thing you vow to do or give up. If marriage were something low and common, there would not be much glory given to God in making the sacrifice of it for His sake. To give that up for God's sake would not be anything very wonderful. The Church puts such tremendous value on this vow of chastity precisely because the thing given up is one of the most precious things we have to give up. God intended men to be married; marriage is the normal state of mankind; it is essential to civilization that there should be married people in order that there should be families, and so, normally, it is God's intention and wish that men should be married. Our Lord blessed marriage and raised it to a sacrament. He used marriage as the sign and symbol of the union of the soul with Himself. The union of one man and one woman in marriage is the strongest bond of union that there is on earth, and it is the symbol of the eternal union between the soul and Christ. If we realize that the Church blesses marriage, recognizes that it is the natural fulfillment of our nature, we see that she certainly does not consider it as something lower than celibacy. Man alone is not complete human nature; the completion is man and woman, and when God has joined them together in marriage they become, as He said, one, and that union cannot be broken. There you get perfect and complete human nature. Our Lord has put that state as high as He can, and the Church has blessed and consecrated it, and so we see that to give that up is to give God something immensely worth having. It is not that priests and monks and nuns are better than other people because they have discarded something bad. They are better—in the sense in which I must use the word—because, for the sake of God, they have given up something so essentially good, because they have made the sacrifice which is the most perfect they can make.

Notice again with regard to the sacrifice of marriage for God's sake, how the Church in ages past has brought constant pressure on those who deliberately give up marriage, has hedged them round and protected them against themselves, because they are entering on a course of life which is not natural. But the Church knows that they are doing it for God, and appreciates immensely what they do. Why is this sacrifice of such value? Because their sacrifice of this good thing for God helps the laity to appreciate what a good thing it is. Marriage is not just self-indulgence; there would be no merit in making a sacrifice of what was merely self-indulgence. But not to practice something which is holy, which is meant by God to be the normal perfection of human nature, to give that up under the inspiration of the Holy Ghost—which is what we call vocation—is to be called, as a few are called in every generation, to make this great sacrifice for God and so it is very pleasing to God and useful to the rest of mankind, because it helps them to appreciate how holy the thing must be, since to renounce it for God's sake is almost the holiest thing one can do on earth.

Total Unity in Marriage

R. DE MONTJAMOT

It has been said that *unity* is a divine dream and *union* a human dream. In reality, all human dreams are the first faltering steps, humbly conscious of their limits, of a divine aspiration, a tentative beginning, a departure in the right direction.

When we consider our world, the unity Christ prayed for seems to be of the celestial order. But it implies immediate consequences that are of the earth. No state of life appears more marked with their imprint than marriage. For no state of life recalls so insistently to man closed in upon himself by sin that, saved by Christ, he must, day after day, break through the barrier of his ego by means of love of others to begin his pilgrimage towards the liberation that will one day mark his entry into the unity of life.

Called by God to eternal life, to the perfection of unity, we are therefore called as of now to the perfection of union which leads to it. There is no discontinuity between the two, and to realize union is already to answer, within our present limits, His call to unity.

It is in this perspective that conjugal union appears so magnificent, so pleasing to God, and truly, the seed of eternity. The first words of the Introit of the Nuptial Mass are: "May the God of Israel unite you." This union is perfectly and totally orientated towards God. . . .

Love is the one force in the world most capable of uniting two persons and added to it are the powerful forces of the sacrament which sustain and fortify it. Yet in every home contrary elements work against both love and grace. That is why everything in our personalities and in our lives must fall under the marriage contract. . . .

We are not forgetting that here it is a question of a union between two complementary persons, a union far richer than of two similar persons, since each must fill up what is lacking in the other and not merely duplicate. It is richer and also more difficult. Such a union demands more than an adaption; it demands a harmonization on all levels of masculine and feminine personalities so different and often, in many respects, so conflicting.

On all levels—The harmonious accord of two beings and two lives can neglect nothing. It supposes the union of activities, of bodies, of characters, of hearts, of sensibilities, of intelligences and of souls.

It is not enough to envisage such a union, to desire it, or to dream imaginatively of its beauty. We should will it and effect it. . . .

This union will only be fruitful if each personal life is rich and continually enriching itself; if the efforts of two personal lives fructify in a common work; and finally if this collaboration reflects back upon the personal life of each, conditioning it and enriching it. Thus the whole sweep of married life is magnificently unified.

Union of Activities—Evasions are most contrary to such unity. They can range from a personal activity that becomes a manifestation, more or less conscious, of independence, to the absence of any deep communal life. . . .

If a certain kind of independence is good, an absence of interest in our personal activities is not. Our activity is part of ourselves; it conditions very deeply what we are and what we are striving towards. To be disinterested in our activity is tantamount to being disinterested in ourselves.

For the same reason, an arbitrary elimination of the other party from our activity is also to refuse oneself. Disinterestedness that excludes a part of ourselves or our lives from the common goal of marriage is a refusal to work together and lays the foundation for serious divergences in our lives. . . .

Union of Bodies—This union reveals the essential characteristics of all unity. Because it rests upon an indisputable state of things, we can refer to it to understand the value, in any union, of complementary diversity, of the leadership of the man over the woman, of the joyful and living submission of the woman in whom passivity would be an absence of life. Passivity would be a submission deceptive to the husband and without any positive influence on the profound harmony of their personalities. The reality of the marriage act is concrete evidence of this. . . .

Marriage then appears to us as the most human union in the world; the only union that is fully so, because in it no element is foreign to the other. Here, moreover, are established the closest possible bonds between domains reputed to be foreign or even opposed to each other. Far from conflicting, they reinforce one another mutually. . . .

Union of Characters—Upon this depends the harmony, joy and peace of the home.

For characters are also complementary. There are evident psychological differences between man and woman; there are, in addition, differences that issue from diverse educations and backgrounds. It is important to be fully cognizant of these differences. For marital harmony is realized out of the raw materials of divergent notes of character. We should bear in mind that it is never a question of becoming identical; it is rather a question of accord.

Does this include defects of character as well? Certainly. In the work of harmonizing our mariage we cannot forget that our characters are sinful and the common accord of our lives must take into account our contrarieties and imperfections.

To love someone is to love that person as he is and not as we would like him to be. We are under no obligation to love his faults, but we must love him enough that his faults will not set up enmity between us. . . .

But these mutual faults, even though they diminish, will not always be overcome immediately. Due to the psychological differences between man and woman, even defects of character can frequently become the basis of harmony. One efficacious means of keeping peace in the home is to cultivate the antidote of the other's faults: calmness and patience, for example, if the other conspicuously lacks these virtues. This practice will help the other partner acquire what he does not have (the educative influence of daily examples needs no demonstration) and contribute to the maintenance of the equilibrium of the home.

Union of Hearts—Numerous nuances differentiate the love of a man from that of a woman. Neither can expect to be loved as he or she loves.

Man wants to protect, to lead the woman he loves. He reveals himself more the conqueror in love than the receiver; yet he has an immense need of woman. Woman offers herself to the man she loves. She needs, above all, to be necessary and submissive to him. To be no longer necessary, is a kind of death. Her love restores and appeases man. She wants to give him and to give herself; she wants to be received by man that her love might be a food to him. These are perhaps the general and habitual differences, visibly complementary, between their two manners of loving. There are certain other differences which lead to the false belief that one loves less than the other. It is a belief that leads one to suffer from what appears a lack of love, while the other suspects a kind of deception, a reproach which he cannot understand and which appears to him unjust.

We must at all costs abstain from this secret censure which separates hearts. . . .

Perfection here consists in refraining from all reproaches; if this proves impossible, if every effort to reason away a suspected deception fails, then the only solution is total frankness with each other. It is always better to express our thoughts in these matters as soon as possible. . . .

Happiness contributes greatly to the unity of marriage. So, too, in a still deeper sense, does suffering. A few years of marriage is sufficient to teach us to what point the suffering lived by two people cements their union and how, by a return to grace, this union helps them bear their suffering and offer it to God. Two weaknesses then become an astonishing strength. . . .

Union of Tastes and Sensibilities—This union invites us to exchanges which are, in the home, sources of multiple joys. The tastes of one are added to those of another to complete them. There are so many new ways of seeing, feeling, and understanding persons and things that married couples can communicate to each other.

They can do this easily for nothing is more communicable or even more communicative than tastes (or differences of taste), than impressions and sentiments—understood in the sense that we say certain people, more than others, have a taste for beauty. . . .

Our guiding principle should be not to insist upon sharing our personal sentiments with the other, but rather to seek out what we enjoy together. The young Beethoven used to say, when he began to compose: "I'm looking for notes that like each other." We must always try to pick out these notes with a light finger and, when they are struck, they frequently call forth others. . . .

The choice of friends and their welcome in the home seems to be of this order—a common joy in meeting enriching personalities, in kind attention to others, in a constant concern to make them feel welcome, in the desire to understand them, to help them and to open oneself to whatever they can bring to our home. . . .

To share our past also responds to an ardent desire of love. It is to relive for the other the atmosphere of our childhood, the people we loved then and draw forth a new evocation of the other's past. Actually, the past then becomes the present. . . .

Union of Wills—Marriage is two strengths, two wills joined in the service of each other, the service of the community, the service of their neighbor and the service of God.

This ideal can be achieved much better if husband and wife are united and not isolated; if they are in agreement on the essential points and then, in the measure of the grace that is given to them and depending upon circumstances, on the secondary ends; and if they are capable of harmonizing their means to this common end.

The essential accord here resides in a common objective. The end we pursue makes us what we are. We become the person of our objective. . . .

Harmony, if it were always thus, would be simple to realize. Practically speaking, however, one of the couple is almost always more energetic than the other. Whence the danger of one absorbing the other! If one partner has a dominating will, he should guard crushing the other's personality, an unfortunate phenomenon in many a home.

On the other hand, the more energetic of the two should sometimes come to the aid of the other's will, making up for what it lacks by adroitly and educatively playing the role of a lever. . . .

Union of Intelligences—Here again it is not a question of imitation but of completing each other. Masculine and feminine intelligences differ by their structures as they do by their methods of thought.

They are nevertheless called to enrich each other that their vision and comprehension of the world be more adequate.

Neither man nor woman has the right to become isolated in his or her "speciality" of thought; but, having thought first of all alone, they must share their intellectual discoveries. A warm life of the spirit is born of such exchanges. That is why, on this plane more than on others, it is important that each cultivate his personal life—developing it with the view of a fertile common life; enriching it that each might bring to his partner something of the treasure he has found. . . .

The intelligence must be nourished on everything. A varied intellectual life through the communion of two minds is certainly essential if the home is to be alive and if the children are to be nourished on the same spiritual plane. . . .

Union of Souls—Let us first of all insist upon the importance of *a personal life* in this respect. The primordial duty of a creature can be summed up by this threefold rule: God must be known, loved and served first!

Our union with God cannot therefore be subordinated to our conjugal love. This love is dependent upon the life of the soul and its union with God.

Each partner ought therefore to reserve certain moments of quiet with God—moments of heart to heart prayer in which the other partner is not the first pre-occupation. At this point one partner has no need of the other to benefit by his prayer, for here the union of souls takes the full meaning of "communion of saints."

Our imperious vocation is above all that sanctity which bears the beautiful name of union with God: the sanctity of our souls first, then the sanctity of our marriage. We must desire not only union of God with our souls, but also union of God with our union itself, with the "we" consecrated on our wedding day and the family that is born of this love.

Thus an indispensable personal life of the soul with God far from excluding, fosters that common pooling which realizes the integral union of husband and wife and the union of their family with God. Their communion of soul is precisely what interiorly animates their life on all levels; it is the soul of their union.

(*Translated by Bernard G. Murchland, C.S.C.*)

The Pledge to Christian Marriage

In gratitude to Almighty God for all the blessings that family life has brought me, I pledge myself always to uphold the great dignity of Christian marriage.

Therefore, in the presence of the Blessed Sacrament, I profess my belief in the sanctity of marriage. I acknowledge it as a sacrament and a symbol of the union of Christ and His Church.

I believe: "What God hath joined together, let no man put asunder."

I renew my deep reverence for fatherhood and motherhood.

I believe that in family life parents co-operate with God.

I believe that in family life the child is paramount.

I abhor and condemn every sinful interference with the role of parenthood.

With the help of our Immaculate Mother I pledge myself anew to wholesome family life.

I resolve to do all in my power to foster the virtue of purity, the bulwark of the family.

May the Holy Family—Jesus, Mary and Joseph—bless our families and our homes.

(First recited by fourteen hundred couples at the closing session of the Catholic Family Life Conference, 1947, in Chicago)

Two

HUSBAND AND WIFE

Put me as a seal upon thy heart, as a seal upon thy arm, for love is strong as death, jealousy hard as hell, the lamps thereof are fire and flames.

Many waters cannot quench charity, neither can floods drown it: if a man should give all the substance of his house for love, he shall despise it as nothing.

CANTICLE OF CANTICLES 8:6-7

The Triumph of Subjection

WINGFIELD HOPE

Unity is the pervading idea in the Marriage Service and in the Proper of the Nuptial Mass, and it is the first essential for the future happiness of both bride and bridegroom and of the children who will be born of their unity.

To understand, in some measure, this vital principle of unity, and to express it in our married lives in the fullest measure possible, is, therefore, necessary if we are to follow the pattern [given by God].

The husband and wife who hope for an ideal unity will do well to study the Epistle of the Nuptial Mass, although this Epistle has caused many a woman keen vexation by its opening words: "Brethren, let women be subject to their husbands, as to the Lord." The chivalrous husband, too, may feel apologetic that such words should be considered appropriate to his bride.

There is real danger that we may be blinded to the extraordinary beauty of this reading from St. Paul if we register a first impression that he is preaching something derogatory to women and that he spoils the whole concept of the unity of marriage by assigning to the wife a position of the doormat order; that he assigns to her a position in which her personal development will be stunted, and in which she must put herself out for her husband without expecting any unselfishness from him.

Actually the exact opposite is the case. To read these first few words of the Epistle for the Nuptial Mass and mentally run away from them recalls the old rhyme about the nettle. If we do this we shall certainly be stung and the irritation of our sting will remain with us.

But to grasp the whole of the Epistle prevents the sting or heals it. For it is a wonderful relationship that is here suggested to us, a relationship strengthening the whole essence of unity in the life of the couple and in the family pattern. It is also a relationship which gives the wife a personal development far fuller and richer than anything she could achieve by herself, provided that she fulfills this part of the pattern with intelligence and good will.

Let us then get beyond the first words of the Epistle and admit to our minds the full beauty of the whole idea: "Brethren, let women be subject to their husbands as to the Lord; for *the* husband is the head of the wife, as Christ is the head of the Church." This comparison should impress us profoundly with the excellence of what God ordains for us in married life. That these words should be selected for our Marriage Service shows, too, the dignity which the Church, in making use of this comparison, allots to every Christian wife.

Is the Church humiliated in her subjection to Christ, her Head? Or is she not on the contrary ennobled by her subjection, and able by it to achieve perfect unity with Him, which would otherwise be quite impossible?

It seems incredible that the plan of unity between husband and wife should be compared to this great unity. Yet this comparison does actually come to us through Scripture and through God's infallible Church.

As, then, with the union between Christ and the Church, so must it be with the union of husband and wife in the family pattern. In giving, the wife receives; in receiving, the husband gives. This is the first principle of their united lives.

Will the wife's subjection involve sacrifice? Most certainly, in the sense that sacrifice is something offered to be made holy; and something which is offered—sometimes at her own immediate cost—for the infinite gain of her husband and herself united.

The hasty critic has quite often implied that the wife's sacrifice is a one-sided one, except for the matter of worldly goods. To explode any such idea we must turn again to our Epistle of the Nuptial Mass to see whether sacrifice is demanded only of the wife in the Christian union of Marriage. And actually, St. Paul demands of the husband the most complete and sublime sacrifice conceivable: "Husbands, love your wives, as Christ also loved the Church *and delivered Himself up for it.*" The Church was founded for our redemption, and its Founder prayed and worked and suffered and died for it, and for all its members.

The husband then, to fulfill the pattern, must have such love for his wife that he will pray and work for her; that he will be ready to suffer for her and to die for her. Here is the perfection of sacrifice and of Christian chivalry. The husband must "deliver himself up to his wife." And, in the same Epistle, we read that "he that loveth his wife loveth himself." Thus, in delivering himself up for her he identifies himself with her, and this is the foundation of their unity.

But, in their close unity, the husband remains the head, the person of first responsibility to God for his wife and for their children.

The Priest's Customary Address to the Bride and Groom

Dear friends in Christ: As you know, you are about to enter into a union which is most sacred and most serious, a union which was established by God Himself. By it, He gave to man a share in the greatest work of creation, the work of the continuation of the human race. And in this way He sanctified human love and enabled man and woman to help each other live as children of God, by sharing a common life under His fatherly care.

Because God Himself is its author, marriage is of its very nature a holy institution, requiring of those who enter into it a complete and unreserved giving of self. But Christ our Lord added to the holiness of marriage an even deeper meaning and a higher beauty. He referred to the love of marriage to describe His own love for His Church, that is, for the people of God whom He redeemed by His own Blood. And so He gave to Christians a new vision of what married life ought to be, a life of self-sacrificing love like His own. It is for this reason that His Apostle, St. Paul, clearly states that marriage is now and for all time to be considered a great mystery, intimately bound up with the supernatural union of Christ and the Church, which union is also to be its pattern.

This union then is most serious, because it will bind you together for life in a relationship so close and so intimate, that it will profoundly influence your whole future. That future, with its hopes and disappointments, its successes and its failures, its pleasures and its pains, its joys and its sorrows, is hidden from your eyes. You know that these elements are mingled in every life, and are to be expected in your own. And so, not knowing what is before you, you take each other for better or for worse, for richer or for poorer, in sickness and in health, until death.

Truly, then, these words are most serious. It is a beautiful tribute to your undoubted faith in each other, that, recognizing their full import, you are nevertheless so willing and ready to pronounce them. And because these words involve such solemn obligations, it is most fitting that you rest the security of your wedded life upon the great principle of self-sacrifice. And so you begin your married life by the voluntary and complete surrender of your individual lives in the interest of that deeper and wider life which you are to have in common. Henceforth you belong entirely to each other; you will be one in mind, one in heart, and one in affections. And whatever sacrifices you may hereafter be required to make to preserve this common life, always make them generously. Sacrifice is usually difficult and irksome. Only love can make it easy; and perfect love can make it a joy. We are willing to give in proportion as we love. And when love is perfect, the sacrifice is complete. God so loved the world that He gave His Only-begotten Son; and the Son so loved us that He gave Himself for our salvation. "Greater love than this no man hath, that a man lay down his life for his friends."

No greater blessing can come to your married life than pure conjugal love, loyal and true to the end. May, then, this love with which you join your hands and hearts today, never fail, but grow deeper and stronger as the years go on. And if true love and the unselfish spirit of perfect sacrifice guide your every action, you can expect the greatest measure of earthly happiness that may be allotted to man in this vale of tears. The rest is in the hands of God. Nor will God be wanting to your needs; He will pledge you the life-long support of His graces in the holy Sacrament which you are now going to receive.

Counsel for Newlyweds

PIUS XII

You also, my dear newlyweds, should give yourselves unreservedly to God in the new state of life to which you have been called. Beginning with this day, take upon yourselves seriously the grave obligations it imposes upon you. Guard yourselves against continuing a life which was perhaps thoughtless and frivolous: lazy and dissolute for the young men, frivolous and self-indulgent for the young women. Expend all your energies upon the duties of your new state. The time has passed when little girls were married without understanding the meaning of marriage; but unfortunately the time is still with us when many young married people believe they can in the beginning, permit themselves a period of moral liberty and enjoy their rights without a thought for their duties. This is a serious mistake which brings down upon it the wrath of God. It is the source of even temporal unhappiness, whose consequences should cause everyone to be afraid. A duty that one will not recognize or that he despises, is always put off so long that one ends by almost forgetting it, and with it goes the happiness that its courageous performance would have brought. And when one does remember and is sorry, he sometimes arrives at the sad truth that it is too late. A couple who has been unfaithful to its mission, can only shrivel up, without hope, in the desert of its sterile selfishness.

Then Tobias exhorted the virgin, and said to her: Sara, arise, and let us pray to God today, and tomorrow, and the next day: because for these three nights we are joined to God: and when the third night is over, we will be in our own wedlock.
For we are the children of saints, and we must not be joined together like heathens that know not God.
So they both arose, and prayed earnestly both together that health might be given them.   (Tobias 8:4-6)

Reverence Between Husband and Wife

F. J. SHEED

In marriage the view of the essential magnificence of man is at once most urgently needed and most sharply tested. It is harder for the married to go on holding it and grimmer to go on, not holding it. No man is a hero to his valet, says the proverb; and no valet is bound as tight to his master's unposed self as wife and husband to each other. Distant hills are greenest: in marriage there is no distance at all to create the illusion of any verdure that is not there, or deepen the greenness of any that is. Every man's private face is different from his public face: but the face that the married see is something more private than private—private is too public a word for it. No one sees the husband as the wife sees him—not the husband, certainly; and he has his own unshared view of her for compensation. For being thus unique, the view each has of the other is not necessarily accurate or profound. Each will note the elements in the other that he or she personally responds to most—the response being either of attraction or repulsion: but whereas one may get used to the qualities that attract and take them for granted and cease to respond to them, the irritating more often continues to irritate.

The average issue of all this is hard to set down: indeed it is hard to say if there *is* an average, or if the word average has any meaning, where there is so wide an arc—with something that verges on bliss at one end, and something that skirts the upper edges of the intolerable at the other. But those marriages surely rank high where husband and wife love each other, would feel all lost without each other, are amiably tolerant of each other's faults (and aware of their own); and even in this smaller group the phrase "essential magnificence" applied to either might cause the other to smile. In less happy marriages—which would yet count as successful, which neither party regrets having entered upon—the rejection would be more violent.

Only in the rarest cases will a husband and wife discover each other's magnificence by looking at each other: the way to learn is the way Christian civilization learnt it, by listening to God, who says that it is so. Learn it they must, for it is the truth about themselves, and it is the one sure ground of reverence. Reverence is everywhere essential. In marriage reverence is more important even than love: love will not find its own self without it. Reverence does not mean remoteness or exclude lightheartedness; two who reverence each other can play together. But it does mean a steady awareness in each that the other has a kinship with the eternal.

It is essential that husband and wife reverence each other: it is essential that they reverence the marriage relation. And as the one reverence comes from knowledge of what man is, the other comes from knowledge of what marriage is. In one as in the other, as we have seen, the essential magnificence is as real as any existential degradation there may be. In normal Christian marriage, of course, there is no question of degradation. Yet there may be a failure to realize what marriage essentially is which prevents the marriage reaching its full stature. It may be a failure either to see marriage as a union of personalities, based upon self-giving, or to achieve a bodily union worthy of the total personal relation it is meant to express.

The bodily union may lack perfection either from coldness, where one party goes through the motions mechanically or with positive distaste; or from excess, with one or both concentrated wholly and gluttonously upon the pleasure the body can get out of it and so, with whatever protestation of love, each using the other as a means, a convenience, a thing and not a person. . . .

Marriage seems to work magic. But it is not all magic. Husband and wife must work hard at it. If one is making no effort, the other must work twice as hard. Love helps, though it is precisely love that is in danger of losing its élan with so much to depress it; prayer helps tremendously. But in the purely psychological order, nothing helps so much as the reverence that flows from a right vision of what man is—that this loutish man, this empty-headed woman, is God's image, an immortal spirit, loved by Christ even to the death of the Cross: whatever the surface looks like, this is in the depth of every human being, this in him is what God joined together with this in her. The realization that there is this welding of two into one in the depths of their being, below the level that the eye of the mind can see, is the most powerful incentive to make that union in depth effective through every layer of personality.

This reverence is a safeguard against one of the great dangers of family life—the tendency of one partner to form, or re-form, the other (or for a parent to form the children) in his own image. There is a sort of imperialism to which the self is liable, the desire to impose its own likeness. . . . One should not lightly try to remake another: but, if remaking there *must* be, assuredly the only image in which anyone should be remade is the image of God in which he was made. . . . Any imposing of oneself on another is a sin against reverence. Reverence is due to all men.

The Payment of the Marriage Debt

THE REV. CHARLES HUGO DOYLE

Marriage is a contract. The formal object of this contract is the mutual *right* of the contracting parties, to the exclusion of all others, that each party has over the body of the other for those acts which normally result in the generation of offspring. This includes the *obligation* of allowing that right to be exercised.

The giving and accepting of the exclusive and perpetual right to those mutual bodily functions is based on the Word of God as found in St. Paul's Epistle to the Corinthians: "Let the husband render the debt to his wife: and the wife also in like manner to the husband. The wife hath not power of her own body; but the husband. And in like manner the husband also hath not power of his own body; but the wife" (I Cor. 7:1-4).

Since the obligation of giving and accepting marital rights is seriously binding on both husband and wife, any violation of this right is a sin directly against justice. At the same time it endangers the purity of the other partner since it denies him/her the formal satisfaction of physical desire. In view of this, any refusal on the part of the husband or wife to the other party *without just cause* is a violation of the marriage contract. Just causes for refusal of the marital rights would be drunkenness, even partial intoxication, refusal to support the family, sickness, extreme fatigue, the period prior to final stages of pregnancy (at least five weeks) or immediately after delivery (say, three or four weeks), proven adultery, grave inconvenience, or danger of scandal.

When there is no *just* reason, simple excuses such as a slight headache, the weather, anger at something the other has said or done, do not constitute just reason for refusal. Most of the trumped up reasons are a cover-up in these modern days for plain old fear of pregnancy.

There are those authorities who say that if husbands were a little more subtle and stopped demanding the act as their right and sought it as if it were a privilege, the response might be more warm-hearted. . . . As noted by Pope Pius XI in his great Encyclical, *Casti Connubii*. "This subjection," writes the Pontiff, "does not deny or take away the liberty which fully belongs to the woman both in view of her dignity as a human person, and in view of her noble office as wife, mother and companion; nor does it bid her obey her husband's every request if not in harmony with right reason or with the dignity due a wife."

The marriage act ought not to be something roughly demanded or taken but something tenderly sought and mutually given, with each party realizing his or her obligation in justice to cooperate. Each maritial act between husband and wife ought to be a renewal of love, for love, as St. Thomas defines it "is to wish another well," or as Webster puts it: "a desire for and earnest effort to promote the welfare of another."

Nothing is so calculated to inspire loathing for the act than anything which tends to make of it something lustful, something detached from its sublime end. Archangel Raphael put it plainly to Tobias: "Hear me, and I will show thee who they are, over whom the devil can prevail. For they who in such manner receive matrimony as to shut out God from themselves, and from their mind, and to give themselves to their lust, as the horse and mule, which have not understanding; over them the devil hath power" (Tob. 6:16-17).

Married persons must never forget that all love comes from God and that it is through love of one another, as St. John points out, that we rise to love of God. Whenever married people let the maritial act become isolated from the general consecration of their union to God, the love which at first prompts it sours, and becomes the prey of selfishness and caprice.

The Splendor of Sex

F. J. SHEED

If we consider sex in itself and ask what Nature had in mind in giving sex to human beings, there can be only one answer: Sex is meant for the production of children, as lungs for breathing or the digestive organs for nourishment. The physical and psychological mechanism is so complex in the man and in the woman, so delicately ordered for the generating of new life, that it would be monstrous to deny (nor, one imagines, has anyone ever denied) that that is what sex is meant for, that is why we have sexual powers. The fact that man can use sex for other, sterile purposes of his own choosing does not alter the certainty that child-bearing is sex's own purpose. . . .

But to say that Nature had children in mind when she gave human beings sex does not mean that when two people decide to marry their motive is to have children. If a man draws a girl's attention to the falling birthrate and asks her to marry him in order to improve it, she would be well advised to refuse him: his wooing is a good deal too sociological. People marry, usually anyhow, because they want each other: they may want children, too, or they may merely see their advent as probable but regrettable: either way, their purpose in marrying is not to have children but to have each other: and Nature does not mind a bit. She is all for people having their own purposes, provided they do not frustrate hers.

Because custom dulls wonders, dulls advertence even, we hardly realize how extraordinary it is that sex should be for child-bearing. It is extraordinary in two ways. For in the first place it gives a grandeur to sex—a remote and even unwanted grandeur you may feel it, but a grandeur that is incomparable. . . . Creation is the work of omnipotence. But procreation is pro-creation, a kind of deputy creation. So that sex in its essential nature is man's greatest glory in the physical order.

Sex as men have it, sex existential as we may call it, is not always, or perhaps even commonly, glorious. Which brings us to the second way in which it is extraordinary that sex should be for child-bearing. It is extraordinary because the bearing and rearing of children requires a maximum of order, stability, tranquillity; and sex is the most turbulent of man's powers.

What clouds almost all present discussion of sex is that its demonic energy is not adverted to: the sex reformers write of it as though it were a sort of amiable pet, to be played with and put back in its little basket.

But sex is not like that: in its beauty and ferocity it can be more like a tiger, and even in the mildest it is no domestic pet. Man does not play with sex: it is nearer the truth to say that sex plays with him, and it can be a destructive game. For sex begins powerful and can become uncontrollable. Short of that extreme, it can become a vast tyranny, harrying the individual man, poisoning every sort of human relationship. . . .

So we return to our anomaly: the continuation of the race, which requires above all things an ordered framework of life, is entrusted to sex, which of itself makes for chaos. It is in marriage that these two irreconcilables are reconciled. The critics of marriage have simply not realized how incredibly difficult, and how totally necessary, is the reconciliation it effects. In marriage sex loses none of its strength, but it serves life.

But if marriage is to serve life fully—bring the child not only to birth but to maturity—it must be permanent. The new-born child has to be shaped into a fully developed member of the human race; and for this he needs both parents. Humanity is not man or woman, but both in union. A child brought up by a father only or a mother only is only half-educated. He needs what the male can give him and what the female can give him. And he needs these not as two separate influences, each pushing him its own way, so that he moves on some compromise line that is neither, but as one fused influence, wholly human, male and female affecting him as conjoined not as competing influences. For that the parents must be united—and indissolubly united. It is not enough that they should agree to live together only while the children need them—because then they would already be separated in spirit, and their two influences would bear upon the child as two not as one. So that if nature is to solve its problem and reconcile its irreconcilables, to make sex serve life, it needs unbreakable marriage.

Are we, then, to see the love of the man and woman for each other as a trap set by nature to lure them into prison, with every sentence a life-sentence? Are human beings no more than pawns in nature's game of preserving the race?

Nothing could be further from the reality. Men, in nature's plan, are never pawns. They cannot serve nature's purpose without serving their own. In marriage the power of sex is not weakened. Marriage provides strong banks within which sex can course at the utmost of its power, but for the service of life and not for destruction.

There is a common error here—that the great lover is the multiple lover, that sex is made perfect in promiscuity. But it is in the love of one for one that men have always seen sex supremely manifested. . . .

Marriage, as the union of one man and one woman, gives opportunity for a splendor of sex impossible outside it, and this both at the level of technique, which does not concern us here, and at the deeper level of personality, which does. The sexual act, merely as a union of bodies, can give exquisite physical pleasure (though it is surprising how often it does not). But it has a double effect.

First, it cannot continue to satisfy even its own unambitious level: it follows the law of diminishing returns that governs the merely physical pleasures—the dose must be increased to give the same effect. The body craves for the sensation. But after a time grows used to it, is unstimulated by it and craves for more intense sensation. . . . It is the universal human experience that a point comes when the craving for the act is overmastering and the pleasure from the act all but nil, so that the act can be neither refused nor enjoyed: that being the way of the body's cravings.

Second, a union of bodies is not the fulness of sexual union. It is valid only as an expression of the union of two personalities. Apart from that, it is a meaningless acrobatic. In other words, the sex act is not the marriage union, but is a marvellous way of expressing the marriage union. When, into the union of two bodies, all the shared life and shared love of a man and a woman are poured, then you have the sexual union in its fulness. And in this sense it is no paradox to say that the promiscuous, however many experiences they may have had, remain inexperienced. The giving of the bodies at once symbolizes, expresses, and helps to effect, the giving of the selves. The completer the self-giving, the richer the bodily union. The giving of one's self to another is the decisive act, the act that transforms. . . .

But the giving of a self and the receiving of a self, the union of personalities—all these can only in their completeness be of one to one—they belong in marriage, and precisely in marriage that is indissoluble. They are not always found in marriage but they are not easily to be had outside it. Where they are found, there is sexual union in its perfection; so that, in falling in with the plan nature has for the carrying on of the race, sex is enriched. The bodily union merely as such—and indeed the whole sexual experience of which it is the normal culmination—can bring a new value into ordinary life, a heightened awareness, an intensification of all vital processes. The thing called glamor is real and valuable. But in marriage as nature would have it all this is increased and given a new hope of permanence. The sexual union has more to utter; and there is not the certainty of ultimate boredom which goes with all purely bodily pleasures. For while one soon comes to an end of what the body has to give, there is no end to the exploration of a personality. So that an act which becomes stale when repeated for its own sake, need never become stale when it is regarded as the expression of a profounder reality that is always growing. . . .

Humanity is composed of man and woman: but putting a man and woman together does not of itself constitute the true human compound: something else must happen, something electric perhaps. There must be that real giving and receiving we have already spoken of, a free-will offering of the self by each to the other. Obviously you can have marriage where this mutual giving is at the barest minimum: but it is not marriage at its best, and it does not bring the enrichment of personality that each needs.

The Marriage Act

ST. THOMAS AQUINAS

Since no act proceeding deliberately from the will is indifferent, the matrimonial act is always either sinful or meritorious in one possessing grace. For, if one is led to perform the marriage act, either by virtue of justice, in order to render the debt, or by virtue of religion, that children may be procreated for the worship of God, the act is meritorious.

(*Translated by E. C. Messenger*)

Restraint

PIUS XI

Even the very best instruction given by the Church, however, will not alone suffice to bring about once more conformity of marriage to the law of God; something more is needed in addition to the education of the mind, namely a steadfast determination of the will, on the part of husband and wife, to observe the sacred laws of God and of nature in regard to marriage. In fine, in spite of what others may wish to assert and spread abroad by word of mouth or in writing, let husband and wife resolve: to stand fast to the commandments of God in all things that matrimony demands; always to render to each other the assistance of mutual love; to preserve the honour of chastity; not to lay profane hands on the stable nature of the bond; to use the rights given them by marriage in a way that will be always Christian and sacred, more especially in the first years of wedlock, so that should there be need of continency afterwards, custom will have made it easier for each to preserve it. . . . Let them constantly keep in mind, that they have been sanctified and strengthened for the duties and for the dignity of their state by a special sacrament, the efficacious power of which, although it does not impress a character, is undying. To this purpose we may ponder over the words full of real comfort of holy Cardinal Robert Bellarmine, who with other well-known theologians with devout conviction thus expresses himself: "The sacrament of matrimony can be regarded in two ways: first, in the making, and then in its permanent state. For it is a sacrament like to that of the Eucharist, which not only when it is being conferred, but also whilst it remains, is a sacrament;

for as long as the married parties are alive, so long is their union a sacrament of Christ and the Church."

Chastity

ST. THOMAS AQUINAS

Chastity takes its name from the fact that reason *chastises* concupiscence, which, like a child, needs curbing. . . .

Chastity does indeed reside in the soul as its subject, though its matter is in the body. For it belongs to chastity that a man makes moderate use of bodily members in accordance with the judgment of his reason and the choice of his will.

(*Translator Anonymous*)

Gentleness in Love

THE REV. GERALD VANN, O.P.

"With my body I thee *worship*," we say in the liturgy [used by the Catholic Church in England] of marriage; without worship there is disaster as well as sin. At the height of passion especially it is easy to forget the person, to forget the breadth and depth of love, to let the hard-won unity of the self be split up again into fragments, and passion in autonomy becomes a preying brute. It is only by a habitual reverence and humility and worship that the danger can be forestalled. And always love-making demands patience and gentleness and sometimes heroic generosity if there is not to be the proud snatching of a selfish pleasure where there should be the deep oneness of a shared joy. Sexual pleasure is not a king in its own right; it is one element in a whole, and being one element only, it may not rule. It is one element in the totality of the oneness of two *persons*; if it is not that, it is a dictator, it ceases to be human at all. . . .

Think of the immensity of the total love of two human beings. At the height of the passion, love produces ecstasy. The word means being outside the self: it means "I live, now not I," it means "It is thyself." A man and a woman are each unique and infinite: "I have said, Ye are gods." Here you have two infinites that are one: not a drab assuagement of tumescence, not a slick exercise of a biological function, not the feckless gathering of rosebuds, but the marriage of gods. Ecstasy means living in another. Here, you are living in the being you love; you are living in the race whose history you summarize, whose function you fulfill, whose life you gather in your hands and pass on to the future ages; you are living (if you have eyes to see) in God, to whose life and love you thus do homage, whose infinite mighty art waits upon you to work with you—you making the body, He the spirit—to fashion another infinity. This is the immensity that sex can open out to you; and will you isolate it and turn it into a toy? For here if anywhere it must be clear that you are not the master of heaven and earth, and that you must go down on your knees to receive a gift greater than yourself. It is the snatcher and the mauler who destroy; the temperate man adores. . . .

Humility . . . is the root of the whole matter. The other virtues, too, are grounded in humility and destroyed by pride; but the death of the false self day by day, the challenging of the false self where its brutality and the effects of its arrogance can be most marked, is especially the task of temperateness. . . . The chaste man is free, not because he is passionless, but because his passion does not destroy but expresses and enlarges the spirit; and chastity brings not death but life because, just as in the aesthetic vision it is in and through the senses that the whole being is enlarged, so here, too, and to an infinitely deeper and wider extent, it is in and through the senses that the two infinities meet and are made one.

You have to be so careful when you hold in your hands a

thing of great loveliness and value. Think how tenderly we treat a glass of wine of rare vintage, and rightly; yet that is not infinite, that is not a person, that cannot be hurt as a man or a woman can be hurt. You can hurt love and yourself and the other, if you wrench the physical from its human totality; or if you are selfish and use the other as a means; or if you are proud in the primal sense of denying the mystery and excluding God. Christian temperateness is not the tempered possessive enjoyment of things, but rather a worshipping union *with* things *in* God; it is saying to another human being, "It is thyself," so that both together in their oneness may make the final affirmation to the Infinite Love, "It is Thyself."

This gentleness is not just an external thing. It is not primarily an external thing. It is primarily gentleness of mind. How terrible when people are led to believe, or left to believe, that once they are in love they have nothing to do but live happy ever after, they have nothing further to learn. Love is an endless creative process; the oneness of the two is not born but made. Do you think that two people, however much in love, will love each other in exactly the same way? Do you think they will never differ in the way they want to express their love? Do you think that because they are living in love they cease to be individuals, or that the false self is wholly dead? There is always the tension; there is always the temptation to sink back into the separate selfhood, there is always the danger that passion may destroy the unity of the person; it is only by long, patient labor that you can hope to forge the unity of the deep personal will which can govern separate superficial desire.

So when you make love you must be gentle and humble, because it is to the mystery of a human being that you are making love. Love is an endless creative process; it is also an endless voyage of discovery. Because you are in love with each other do you think you know each other? Perhaps when you are both old you will have learnt a little—but only if all the time you have loved deeply and been deeply aware of your ignorance. . . .

If you degrade love by brutality or selfishness or pride, you destroy it; and you will find its wholeness broken up into two fragments, each of them ugly; you will find passion twisted into lust, and emotion twisted into sentimentality. Both of them are superficial, both of them are unreal, both of them are disruptive; and their fruit is loneliness. . . .

We live a many-levelled life, and real love is a sharing of life on all these levels, but a sharing of them in their integrity, a sharing of the whole being; and that is why the fullness of love is not likely to be given us this side of the grave for we are not likely this side of the grave to be completely whole. But though the fullness of love is something that must wait upon our wholeness, love itself is precisely what makes us whole; when we have the fullness we say, "It is thyself," but it is love that makes us begin to say it. . . .

If you skim along the surface of life, you will never know the need of a Saviour except by hearsay, for you will never know the depths of the human heart. If love were an endless idyll unflecked by sorrow you would be endlessly happy, but you would still not know the depths of the human heart. But if you know the love that can lead you near to heartbreak, if you know not only the heights of ecstasy but the depths of pain, then you will know you stand before a mystery and you will be silenced, and you will have seen the abyss of the human heart which only infinity can fill, and perhaps you will find yourself forced to look beyond the barriers of the finite for the Love in which all other loves are fulfilled. . . .

Love, like prayer, has its moments of ecstasy; but it is made up not of these but of the simplicities, the common joys and burdens, of every day. It is a long and arduous process, though its drudgeries are suffused with joy. We are led to it because of our incompleteness, because the heart is a hunger, because we are always seeking for fulfillment of the body, mind and will. Man and woman complete one another, but the demands of passion will not always coincide: there is the labor and sometimes the agony of approaching, touching, entering, another mind, there is the long labor of forging the unity of the deep personal will. . . .

This is the greatest tragedy: when two who are one, who have been reborn in one another, who have, therefore, gone infinitely beyond the empty unreality of the man who remains alone, and stand as it were at the gates of paradise, nevertheless turn away—because they, too, have great possessions. This is the greatest tragedy: that you can repeat in company with another the lonely disintegration of the primal sin; that even though you are living in love you can turn away from Love. And then the original disruption is repeated: just as pride tears man from God and robs his nature of its wholeness, so this pride, too, tears love from its eternity and robs it even of its temporary wholeness.

"Collaborators of God"

PIUS XII

The eternal love of God called the world and humanity into being from nothing; the love of Jesus for His Church generates souls to supernatural life; the love of a Christian husband for his wife participates in these two divine acts because, in accordance with the will of the Creator, man and wife prepare the dwelling of the soul in which the Holy Spirit shall live with His grace. In this manner, through the mission providentially assigned to them, husband and wife are really the collaborators of God and His Christ; their very actions have something of the divine in them, and here too they may be called *divinae consortes naturae*.

Sexual Moderation

PIUS XII

The truth is that matrimony as a natural institution, by virtue of the will of the Creator, does not have as its primary, intimate end the personal improvement of the couples concerned but the procreation and the education of new life. The other ends though also connected with nature are not in the same rank as the first, still less are they superior to it. They are subordinated to it. This holds true for every marriage, even if it bear no fruit, just as it can be said that every eye is made for seeing although in certain abnormal cases, because of special internal and external conditions, it will never be able to see. . . .

Does this mean that we deny or diminish what there is of good and right in the personal values arising from marriage and its carrying out? Certainly not. In matrimony, for the procreation of life, the Creator has destined human beings made of flesh and blood, endowed with minds and hearts: they are called as men, not animals without reason, to be the makers of their descendants. For this end God wishes that couples be united. . . .

Not only the common work of external life but also intellectual and spiritual endowment, even the depths of spirituality in conjugal love as such, have been put by the will of nature and the Creator at the service of our descendants. By its nature, perfect married life means also the complete dedication of the parents for the benefit of their children, and in its strength and tenderness, conjugal love is itself a postulate of the most sincere care for the offspring and the guarantee of its being carried out.

To reduce cohabitation and the conjugal act to a simple organic function for the transmission of seed would be converting the home, the sanctuary of the family, into a mere biological laboratory. . . . In its natural structure, the conjugal act is a personal action, a simultaneous and immediate cooperation on the part of the husband and wife which by the very nature of the agents and the propriety of the act is the expression of the mutual gift which according to Holy Scripture brings about union "in one flesh only."

This is something much more than the union of two seeds which may be brought about even artificially, without the natural action of husband and wife. The conjugal act, ordained and willed by nature is a personal act of cooperation, the right to which husband and wife give each other when they marry. . . .

The Creator Who in His goodness and wisdom has willed to

conserve and propagate the human race through the instrumentality of man and woman by uniting them in marriage has ordained also that in performing this function, husband and wife should experience pleasure and happiness both in body and soul. In seeking and enjoying this pleasure, therefore, couples do nothing wrong. They accept that which the Creator has given them.

Nevertheless, even here couples must know how to restrict themselves within the limits of moderation. As in eating and drinking, so in the sexual act, they must not abandon themselves without restraint to the impulse of the senses. The right norm therefore is this:—The use of the natural inclination to generate is lawful only in matrimony, in the service of and according to the order of the ends of marriage. From this it follows that only in marriage, and by observing this rule, the desire for and the fruit of this pleasure and satisfaction are lawful. Hence, enjoyment is subordinated to the law of action from which it derives and not the other way about, the action to the law of enjoyment. And this law, so reasonable, concerns not only the substance but also the circumstances of the act, with the result that although the substance of the act be unimpaired, one may sin in the manner of performing it. . . .

If nature had aimed exclusively or even primarily at a mutual gift and mutual possession of couples for pleasure, if it had ordained that act solely to make their personal experience happy in the highest degree and not to stimulate them in the service of life, then the Creator would have adopted another plan in the formation and constitution of the natural act. But this act is completely subordinated to and ordered in accordance with the sole great law of *"generatio et educatio prolis,"* the fulfilling of the primary end of matrimony as the origin and source of life. . . .

The seriousness and sanctity of the Christian moral law do not admit unbridled satisfaction of the sexual instinct tending merely to pleasure and enjoyment. The moral law does not allow man with his reason to let himself be dominated to that point, be it a question of the substance or the circumstances of the act.

Some people are of the opinion that happiness in marriage is in direct proportion to mutual enjoyment in conjugal relations. This is not so. Happiness in marriage is in direct proportion to the respect the couple have for each other even in their intimate relations: not that they should deem immoral and refuse that which nature offers and the Creator has given, but because the respect and the mutual esteem it generates is one of the strongest elements of a pure, hence, more tender love.

Married People Need Chastity

ST. FRANCIS DE SALES

For those who are married, it is most true, though the vulgar cannot conceive it, that chastity is very necessary, also, for them; because, in respect of them, it consists not in abstaining absolutely from carnal pleasures, but in containing themselves in the midst of pleasures. Now as this commandment, *Be angry and sin not*, is, in my opinion, more difficult to be observed than this, *Be not angry*; and as one may more easily abstain from anger than regulate it; so it is easier to keep ourselves altogether from carnal pleasures than to preserve a moderation in them. It is true, that the holy liberty of marriage has a particular force to extinguish the fire of concupiscence; but the frailty of them that enjoy this liberty passes easily from permission to dissolution, and from use to abuse; and as we see many rich men steal, not through want but avarice, so also may we observe many married people fall into excesses by mere intemperance and incontinency, notwithstanding the lawful object to which they ought and might confine themselves; their concupiscence being like wildfire, which runs burning here and there, without resting in any one place. It is always dangerous to take violent medicines, for if we take more than we should, or if they be not well prepared, they may be attended with fatal consequences. Marriage was blessed and ordained in part as a remedy for concupiscence, and, doubtless, it is a very good remedy, but yet violent, and consequently very dangerous, if it be not used with discretion.

I add, that the variety of human affairs, besides long diseases, oftentimes separates husbands from their wives; and therefore married people have need of two kinds of chastity: this one for absolute abstinence, when they are separated upon the occasions of which I have been speaking; the other for moderation, when they are together in the ordinary course.

(Translator Anonymous)

Unnatural Birth Control

PIUS XI

But no reason, however grave, may be put forward by which anything intrinsically against nature may become conformable to nature and morally good. Since, therefore, the conjugal act is destined primarily by nature for the begetting of children, those who in exercising it deliberately frustrate its natural power and purpose sin against nature and commit a deed which is shameful and intrinsically vicious. . . . Any use whatsoever of matrimony exercised in such a way that the act is deliberately frustrated in its natural power to generate life is an offence against the law of God and of nature, and those who indulge in such are branded with the guilt of a grave sin. . . . Holy Mother Church very well understands and clearly appreciates all that is said regarding the health of the mother and the danger to her life. And who would not grieve to think of these things? Who is not filled with the greatest admiration when he sees a mother risking her life with heroic fortitude, that she may preserve the life of the offspring which she has conceived? God alone, all bountiful and all merciful as He is, can reward her for the fulfilment of the office allotted to her by nature, and will assuredly repay her in a measure full to overflowing.

Holy Church knows well that not infrequently one of the parties is sinned against rather than sinning, when for a grave cause he or she reluctantly allows the perversion of the right order. In such a case, there is no sin, provided that, mindful of the law of charity, he or she does not neglect to seek to dissuade and to deter the partner from sin. Nor are those considered as acting against nature who in the married state use their right in the proper manner although on account of natural reasons either of time or of certain defects, new life cannot be brought forth. For in matrimony as well as in the use of the matrimonial rights there are also secondary ends, such as mutual aid, the cultivating of mutual love, and the quieting of concupiscence which husband and wife are not forbidden to consider so long as they are subordinated to the primary end and so long as the intrinsic nature of the act is preserved. . . .

There is no possible circumstance in which husband and wife cannot, strengthened by the grace of God, fulfil faithfully their duties and preserve in wedlock their chastity unspotted.

The Natural Law

ST. THOMAS AQUINAS

The light of natural reason whereby we discern what is good and what is evil, which is the function of the natural law, is nothing else than an imprint on us of the Divine Light. It is therefore evident that the natural law is nothing else than the rational creature's participation of the eternal law.

(Translated by the Most Rev. Fulton Sheen)

When the Natural Law Is "Blotted Out"

ST. THOMAS AQUINAS

There belongs to the natural law, first, certain most common precepts that are known to all; and secondly, certain secondary and more particular precepts, which are, as it were, conclusions following closely from first principles. As to the common principles, the natural law, in its universal meaning, cannot in any way be blotted out from men's hearts. But it is blotted out in the case of a particular action, in so far as reason is hindered from applying the common principle to the particular action because of concupiscence or some other passion. But as to the other, *i.e.*, the secondary precepts, the natural law can be blotted out from the human heart, either by evil persuasions, just as in speculative matters errors occur in respect of necessary conclusions; or by vicious customs and corrupt habits, as, among some men, theft, and even unnatural vices, as the Apostle states (*Rom.* 1:24), were not esteemed sinful.

(*Translated by Anton C. Pegis*)

Families Are Not Required to Have as Many Children as Biologically Possible

THE REV. THURSTON DAVIS, S.J.

You will not find any reputable and responsible theologian who holds or teaches that *any* limitation of the family by self-restraint is a lack of trust in God. In fact the statement is false.

Similarly you will not find any theologian who holds that all families should have as many children as God sends. Of course this statement should be "as many as God might send if parents cooperated with Him." If this were true, most Catholic married people have been wanting in their duties since the beginning of Christianity. All along, the Church has known of small families. Yet she did not reproach them.

Married people are not obliged to have as large families as possible biologically, and regardless of the effects on the wife's health and the maintenance of living children. The husband is seriously bound not to jeopardize the health of the wife or the decent economic condition of the family.

A husband's duty to wife and existing children is more pressing than his obligation—if there is one—to procreate more children.

Those people who maintain that the family should be the largest biologically possible, *coûte que coûte*, are thinking irrationally. Surely God does not wish Heaven to be peopled with citizens of Heaven, at the cost of duties unfulfilled by man and woman.

The Use of Rhythm

PIUS XII

Then, there is the serious question today as to whether and how far the obligation of ready disposition to serve motherhood can be reconciled with the ever more widely diffused recourse to the periods of natural sterility (the so-called agenetic periods of the woman) which seems to be a clear expression of the will contrary to that disposition. . . .

There are two hypotheses to be considered. If the carrying out of this theory means nothing more than that the couple can make use of their matrimonial rights on the days of natural sterility too, there is nothing against it, for by so doing they neither hinder nor injure in any way the consummation of the natural act and its further natural consequences. It is in this respect that the application of the theory of which we have spoken differs from the abuse already mentioned which is a perversion of the act itself. If, however, it is a further question—that is, of permitting the conjugal act on those days exclusively—then the conduct of the married couple must be examined more closely.

Here two other hypotheses present themselves to us. If at the time of marriage at least one of the couple intended to restrict the marriage right, not merely its use, to the sterile periods, in such a way that at other times the second party would not even have the right to demand the act, this would imply an essential defect in the consent to marriage, which would carry with it invalidity of the marriage itself, because the right deriving from the contract of marriage is a permanent, uninterrupted and not intermittent right of each of the parties, one to the other.

On the other hand, if the act be limited to the sterile periods insofar as the mere use and not the right is concerned, there is no question about the validity of the marriage. Nevertheless, the moral licitness of such conduct on the part of the couple would have to be approved or denied according as to whether or not the intention of observing those periods constantly was based on sufficient and secure moral grounds. The mere fact that the couple do not offend the nature of the act and are prepared to accept and bring up the child which in spite of their precautions came into the world would not be sufficient in itself to guarantee the rectitude of intention and the unobjectionable morality of the motives themselves.

The reason for this is that marriage obliges to a state of life which, while conferring certain rights also imposes the fulfillment of a positive work in regard to the married state itself. In such a case, one can apply the general principle that a positive fulfillment may be omitted when serious reasons, independent from the good will of those obliged by it, show that this action is not opportune or prove that a similar demand cannot reasonably be made of human nature. . . .

The individual and society, the people and the state, the Church itself depend for their existence in the order established by God on fruitful marriage. Therefore, to embrace the married state, continuously to make use of the faculty proper to it and lawful in it alone, and, on the other hand, to withdraw always and deliberately with no serious reason from its primary obligation, would be a sin against the very meaning of conjugal life.

There are serious motives, such as those often mentioned in the so-called medical, eugenic, economic, and social "indications," that can exempt for a long time, perhaps even the whole duration of the marriage, from the positive and obligatory carrying out of the act. From this it follows that observing the non-fertile periods alone can be lawful only under a moral aspect. Under the conditions mentioned it really is so. But if, according to a rational and just judgment, there are no similar grave reasons of a personal nature or deriving from external circumstances, then the determination to avoid habitually the fecundity of the union while at the same time to continue fully satisfying their sensuality, can be derived only from a false appreciation of life and from reasons having nothing to do with any proper ethical laws.

The Morality of Rhythm

THE REV. DONALD F. MILLER, C.SS.R.

One simple statement can be made about the use of rhythm in marriage and it is this: Every case in which it is considered is an *individual* case, and should be presented, with all the attendant circumstances, to the judgment of the confessor. The confusion arises from the fact that a decision given for one case is so often passed around as a norm for other cases, and these other cases may not be similar to it at all. Another difficulty is that advertisers of rhythm charts and booklets have so often made general statements affirming the universal acceptability of the practice, for the sake of making sales. Of course they do not take into account any of the many circumstances that can make the practice evil.

According to the natural law, it is not sinful for husband and wife voluntarily and mutually to limit the use of their marriage privileges to certain times for a variety of reasons, some of which may have nothing to do with the possibility or expectation of conception. The natural law demands only that there be no interference with the proper method and end of the marriage privilege whenever it is used.

Circumstances that can, and frequently do, make limitation of the use of marriage to certain times wrong are the following: 1) If this is dictated by one partner alone, so that the other is unwillingly made to follow it. This forcing of one's will on the other is contrary to the very essence of the marriage contract. The unwillingness of one partner may be expressed or merely implied, and may be temporary or permanent; but wherever such unwillingness is present, the partner may not insist on rhythm without a grave and objective reason. 2) If the limitations demanded by rhythm lead to frequent sins at times when it has been decided not to use the marriage privilege. The adoption of the rhythm system becomes a serious and unnecessary occasion of sin when it leads to sins of adultery, self-abuse, and other forms of impurity during the fertile periods, and as such is wrong itself. 3) If it leads to quarrelling, bickering, unhappiness in the home, and even the possibility of divorce. Rightly to take into account all these circumstances demands of married people that they have the right attitude toward children. While it is true that there is much selfish avoidance of the responsibilities of children in modern families, it is also true that if all husbands and wives would take a serious view of the responsibility and mutuality of their duties to each other, they would at the same time be cultivating the right attitude toward the size of their families. . . .

There are few subjects on which there is more confusion of thought than on this topic of limiting offspring. The reason for the confusion is that the publicists for birth control have abandoned all the logic and reason that support the natural law, and have made up a morality of expediency on the question of contraception. Therefore the best way to arrive at an understanding of [this] question is by starting out with simple, universal principles and then applying them to the morality of rhythm and contraception.

First of all, the Catholic Church, in promulgating the natural law, does not blindly object to limitation of offspring on the part of parents. Sometimes she even advises and urges such limitation, as for example, in cases of severe or contagious disease on the part of parents, extreme poverty, etc. She does maintain, according to the natural law, that such limitation may be effected only by limitation of intercourse, because it is contrary to the natural law ever to use the marriage right while frustrating its primary purpose.

Secondly, the Catholic Church does not maintain that the sole purpose of intercourse is the begetting of children. She maintains that that is the first and primary purpose—the one that may never be deliberately avoided through the manner of exercising the marriage right. But the Church states the natural law that there are secondary purposes of intercourse, which are the showing of mutual love between husband and wife and the avoidance of the wrong use of sex. These purposes may still be sought and fulfilled in the use of the marriage right, even when the primary purpose cannot be achieved because of age, sterility, etc., so long as the marriage act is properly performed. In other words, a husband and wife are bound always to act in their relations with each other in cooperation with the primary purpose of sex, even though they know it cannot be attained.

Contraception, therefore, is wrong because it means attacking the primary purpose of the marriage act in the very manner of performing it. The use of rhythm may be justified in certain circumstances because in this no attack is made on the primary purpose of the marriage act in the way it is performed. It should be remarked that rhythm is not universally permissible to married persons; they must have a reason for using it, and should ordinarily subject that reason to a confessor's decision.

The Mother or the Child?

PIUS XII

It is one of the finest and most noble aspirations of the medical profession to search for ever new ways of ensuring the life of both [mother and child in child-birth]. But if, notwithstanding all the progress of science, there still remain, and will remain in the future, cases in which one must reckon with the death of the mother, when it is the mother's wish to bring to birth the life that is within her, and not to destroy it in violation of the command of God: Thou shalt not kill!—nothing else remains for the man, who will make every effort up to the last moment to help and save, but to bow respectfully before the laws of nature and the dispositions of Divine Providence.

But—it is objected—the life of the mother, especially the mother of a large family, is of incomparably greater value than that of a child yet to be born. The application of the theory of the equivalation of values to the case which occupies Us has already been accepted in juridical discussions. The reply to this harrowing objection is not difficult. The inviolability of the life of an innocent human being does not depend on its greater or lesser value. It is already more than ten years since the Church formally condemned the killing of life considered to be "without value"; and whosoever knows the sad events that preceded and provoked that condemnation, whosoever is able to weigh up the direful consequences that would result, if one were to try to measure the inviolability of innocent life according to its value, knows well how to appreciate the motives that determined that disposition.

Besides, who can judge with certainty which of the two lives is in fact the more precious? Who can know what path that child will follow and to what heights of achievement and perfection he may reach? Two greatnesses are being compared here, one of them being an unknown quantity. . . .

On purpose We have always used the expression "direct attempt on the life of an innocent person," "direct killing." Because if, for example, the saving of the life of the future mother, independently of her pregnant state, should urgently require a surgical act or other therapeutic treatment which would have as an accessory consequence, in no way desired nor intended but inevitable, the death of the fetus, such act could no longer be called a direct attempt on an innocent life. Under these conditions the operation can be licit, like other similar medical interventions, granted always that a good of high worth is concerned, such as life, and that it is not possible to postpone the operation until after the birth of the child, nor to have recourse to other efficacious remedies. . . .

Innocent human life, in whatsoever condition it is found, is withdrawn, from the very first moment of its existence, from any direct deliberate attack. This is a fundamental right of the human person, which is of general value in the Christian conception of life; hence as valid for the life still hidden within the womb of the mother, as for the life already born and developing outside of her; as much opposed to direct abortion as to the direct killing of the child before, during or after its birth. . . .

Never and in no case has the Church taught that the life of the child must be preferred to that of the mother. It is erroneous to put the question with this alternative: either the life of the child or that of the mother. No, neither the life of the mother nor that of the child can be subjected to an act of direct suppression. In the one case as in the other, there can be but one obligation: to make every effort to save the lives of both, of the mother and of the child.

Must the Sterile Seek Medical Attention?
THE REV. DONALD F. MILLER, C.SS.R.

Problem: My husband and I have been married for seven years and have no children, through no fault of our own. Friends have told me that we are supposed to see a doctor and find out whether through some treatment or operation it may not be possible for us to have children. Personally, I am content to leave everything in God's hands and I do not care to undergo tests and examinations. My question is: Am I obliged to see a doctor with the idea that he may be able to correct whatever it is that keeps us from having children?

Solution: On the general principle that childless marriages are subject to difficulties and dangers that grow with the passage of the years, and on the ground that you and your husband would be on the way to becoming victims of selfishness if you suppressed all interest in parenthood, I would say that you would be very foolish not to submit at least to a general examination into the causes of your failure to become a mother. It might turn out that some very slight and easy corrective treatment would make all the difference in the world. The blessing of children, from many angles, is so great, that anyone who advises married couples would strongly urge that those who find themselves childless over a period of years should at least try to find out if there is any specific cause of sterility.

If you ask what your exact obligations are, I shall tell you: 1) You have no strict obligation of consulting a physician if both you and your husband are equally content to permit things to go on as they are now. 2) If your husband, however, is eager to have children, and is deeply disappointed and grieved because of your failure to become a mother, then you would have a strict obligation of taking at least the ordinary steps to find out whether anything can be done to correct the present cause of sterility. (It may be added that this works both ways: if a wife strongly desires children and does not become pregnant over a period of years, the husband would have the obligation of seeking professional advice as to whether he might not be the cause of childlessness.) 3) If medical examination brings out the fact that only through a serious operation can the sterility be corrected, there is no obligation of undergoing such an operation, though the wife may undergo it and may be advised to do so. 4) If the examination reveals that a very minor operation or very simple treatment would correct the situation, there would be some obligation of undergoing it, depending on the nature of the operation or treatment and on the urgency of the husband's desire for a family. It may be remarked, for the sake of those who may be ignorant of the fact, that great advances have been made by the medical profession, both in ascertaining the causes of sterility and in removing them. Wise and normal married couples will ordinarily not hesitate to utilize these advances of science.

Artificial Insemination

PIUS XII

The practice of artificial insemination, when it is applied to man, cannot be considered exclusively, nor even principally, from the biological and medical viewpoint while leaving aside the viewpoint of morality and law.

Artificial insemination outside marriage is to be condemned purely and simply as immoral.

In fact, the natural law and the positive Divine Law are such that the procreation of new life may only be the fruit of marriage . . . marriage alone provides for the good and education of the offspring. Consequently, there is no possibility of any divergence of opinion among Catholics regarding the condemnation of artificial insemination outside marriage. A child conceived in such condition is, by that fact alone, illegitimate.

Artificial insemination in marriage with the use of an active element from a third person is equally immoral and as such is to be rejected summarily. Only the marriage partners have mutual rights over their bodies for the procreation of a new life and these are exclusive, non-transferable and inalienable rights. So it must be, out of consideration for the child. . . .

With regard to the lawfulness of artificial insemination in marriage, it is sufficient for us at present to recall the principles of the natural law: the simple fact that the desired result is obtained by this means does not justify the employment of the method itself; nor does the desire of the marriage partners—most legitimate in itself—to have a child, suffice to prove the lawfullness of a recourse to artificial insemination for the fulfillment of that desire.

It would be false to believe that the possibility of a recourse to that method would render a marriage valid between two persons who are unfitted to contract a marriage because of the impediment of impotency.

Moreover, it is superfluous to indicate that the active element can never be lawfully attained by acts that are contrary to nature. . . .

Artificial insemination is something which must not just be regarded with extreme reserve, but must be utterly rejected.

When Love Falters, Transfigure It

THE MOST REV. FULTON J. SHEEN

Aridity in love is not the defeat of love, but rather its challenge. If there were no love above the human, or if life were only sex, there is no reason to suppose that love would ever become dull. The major tragedies of life come from believing that love is like a child in a progressive school, and that if left to itself without any discipline, it will grow to perfection. Dryness, mediocrity, and tedium are danger signals! Love, too, has its price, and no one ever became a saint, or made a marriage a joy, without a fresh struggle against the ego.

The modern solution in marriage is to find a new love; the Christian solution is to recapture an old love. Divorce with remarriage is a sign that one never loved a person in the first place, but only the pleasure which the person gave. The Christian attitude is that one must now love the same person, but on a higher level. To seek to overcome the depression by finding a new love is to intensify egotism, and make the other the victim of that egotism under the appearance of devotion and love. The Christian solution is to conquer egotism. Instead of discovering a new love, it discovers the same love. The modern solution is to chase new prey; the Christian solution is to bind up the wounds of the Divinely-sanctioned marriage.

Those who leave one thrill for another never really love, for no one loves who cannot love through disenchantment, disillusion, and deception. It is sex which seeks a *new* stimulus; but Christian love seeks a *higher* stimulus. Sex ignores eternity for the sake of passing experience; love tries to bring eternity more into love, and thus make it more lovable. Love, at the beginning, speaks the language of eternity. It says, "I will love you always." In the Crisis of Nothingness the idea of eternity cries to be reintroduced. There is this difference, however. In the days of romance, the eternal emphasis was on the ego's durability in love; in the Crisis of Nothingness, the eternal element is God, not the ego. Love now says, "I will love you always, for you are lovable through eternity for God's sake." He who courts and promises eternal love is actually appropriating to himself an attribute of God. During the Dark Night of the Body, he puts eternity where it rightly belongs, namely, in God.

Once purified, love returns. The partner is loved beyond all sensation, all desire, all concupiscence. The husband who began by loving the other for his own sake, and then for her sake, now begins to love for God's sake. He has touched the depths of a body, but now he discovers the soul of the other person. This is the new infinite taking the place of the body; this is the new "always," and it is closer to the true infinite because the soul is infinite and spiritual, whereas the body is not. The other partner ceases to be opaque and begins to be transparent, the glass through which God and His purposes are revealed. Less conscious of his own power to beget love in others, he sees his poverty and begins to depend on God to complement that poverty. Good Friday now passes into Easter Sunday with the Resurrection of Love.

Love, which once meant pleasure and self-satisfaction, changes into love for God's sake. The other person becomes less the necessary condition of passion and more the partner of the soul. Our Blessed Lord said that unless the seed fall to the ground and die, it will not spring forth into life. Nothing is reborn to a higher life without a death in the lower. The heart has its cycles as well as the planets, but the movement of the heart is an upward spiral, and not a circle which turns upon itself. The planetary circles are repetitious, the eternal return to a beginning.

There are some who say that their love lives on memories, but they know in their hearts that the memories are unsatisfying. The body that has lost an arm or a leg is not consoled by recalling the departed member. Life is progressive rather than reminiscent. If love does not grow, it becomes sterile and flat. The living on memories assumes that the heart, like the planets, travels in a circle and not in a spiral. He who loses his arm, and then utilizes the loss to incorporate himself more closely to the Will of God, has spiraled upwards in his love. He who takes the aridities and the ordinariness of love, and utilizes them to lift self and partner to new horizons, has proven that he belongs to the realm of life rather than to that of planets.

Progress begins with a dream, and progresses through the death of that dream. Marriage would never begin, if there were no dream of happiness. When finally the dream comes true, there will be no progress in joy unless one is prepared to die to that old dream and begin to dream new dreams. To live on the memory of a love is as unsatisfying as to live on the memory of food. The Crisis of Nothingness, which follows a dream come true, needs its purification and its Cross. The Cross is not a roadblock on the way to happiness; it is a ladder up which one climbs to a heaven of love.

Another name for the purification of love is transfiguration, which means the use of a loss, or a pain, or a mediocrity, or a disillusionment, as a steppingstone to a new anointing of joy. When Peter saw the face of Our Lord, as bright as the sun and with His robes white as snow, he wanted to capture that ephemeral glory in a permanent form. But all the while, Our Lord was talking to Moses and Elias of His death. He was reminding Peter that there is no true glory without a Cross. This momentary glory is only an anticipation and a preshadowing of a glory that comes after a crucifixion. Transfiguration in marriage comes through an intensive retraining of the ego. The more one gives up the self, the more one possesses self. It is the ego that stands in the way of all fine social relationships. The egotist has no friends in the social order, and the egotistic spouse precludes the possession in joy of the other.

Transfiguration is based on the idea that love resides in the will, and not in the emotions. The emotions lose their thrill, but the will can become stronger with the years. Those who identify love and the glands feel their love decreasing as time goes on, despite the injection of hormones. Those who identify love and the will admit the third which makes love, find that age never affects love. The will can really grow stronger as the body becomes weaker. One therefore always has it in his or her power to lift himself to new heights through a willed and deliberate sacrifice of the ego, even when the body-love has begun its decline.

Counsel for Husbands

ST. JOHN CHRYSOSTOM

Wouldst thou have thy wife obedient to thee as the Church is to Christ? Take thou thyself the same provident care of her as Christ takes for the Church. Yes, even if it shall be needful for thee to give thy life for her, yea, and to be cut to pieces ten thousand times, and to endure and to undergo any suffering whatsoever, refuse it not. . . .

A servant, indeed, one will be able, perhaps, to bind down by fear, nay not even him for he will soon start away and be gone. But the partner of one's life, the mother of one's children, the foundation of all one's joy, one ought never to chain down by fear and menaces but by love and good temper. For what sort of a union is that, where the wife trembles at her husband? And what sort of pleasure will the husband enjoy, if he dwells with his wife as with a slave and not as with a free woman? You should suffer anything on her account, do not upbraid her; for neither did Christ do this.

Thus, then, by your own language, teach her never to speak of "mine and thine" and again, never call her simply by her name, but with terms of endearment with honor, with exceeding affection. Honor her, and she will not need honor from others.

(Oxford translation revised by J. A. Broadus)

True Married Love

PIUS XI

Matrimonial faith demands that husband and wife be joined in an especially holy and pure love, not as adulterers love each other, but as Christ loved the Church. . . . The love, then, of which We are speaking is not that based on the passing lust of the moment nor does it consist in pleasing words only, but in the deep attachment of the heart which is expressed in action, since love is proved by deeds. This outward expression of love in the home demands not only mutual help but must go further; must have as its primary purpose that man and wife help each other day by day in forming and perfecting themselves in the interior life, so that through their partnership in life they may advance ever more and more in virtue, and above all that they may grow in true love towards God and their neighbour. . . .

Domestic society being confirmed, therefore, by this bond of love, there should flourish in it that "order of love," as St. Augustine calls it. This order includes both the primacy of the husband with regard to the wife and children, the ready subjection of the wife and her willing obedience. . . .

This subjection, however, does not deny or take away the liberty which fully belongs to the woman both in view of her dignity as a human person, and in view of her most noble office as wife and mother and companion; nor does it bid her obey her husband's every request if not in harmony with right reason or with the dignity due to wife; nor, in fine, does it imply that the wife should be put on a level with those persons who in law are called minors, to whom it is not customary to allow free exercise of their rights on account of their lack of mature judgment, or of their ignorance of human affairs. But it forbids that exaggerated liberty which cares not for the good of the family; it forbids that in this body which is the family, the heart be separated from the head to the great detriment of the whole body and the proximate danger of ruin. For if the man is the head, the woman is the heart, and as he occupies the chief place in ruling, so she may and ought to claim for herself the chief place in love.

Again, this subjection of wife to husband in its degree and manner may vary according to the different conditions of persons, place and time. In fact, if the husband neglect his duty, it falls to the wife to take his place in directing the family. But the structure of the family and its fundamental law, established and confirmed by God, must always and everywhere be maintained intact.

"The Obedience Woman Owes to Man"

PIUS XI

The same false teachers who try to dim the lustre of conjugal faith and purity do not scruple to do away with the honorable and trusting obedience which the woman owes to the man. Many of them even go further and assert that such a subjection of one party to the other is unworthy of human dignity, that the rights of husband and wife are equal; wherefore, they boldly proclaim, the emancipation of women has been or ought to be effected. This emancipation in their ideas must be threefold, in the ruling of the domestic society, in the administration of family affairs and in the rearing of the children. . . .

This, however, is not the true emancipation of woman, nor that rational and exalted liberty which belongs to the noble office of a Christian woman and wife; it is rather the debasing of the womanly character and the dignity of motherhood, and indeed of the whole family, as a result of which the husband suffers the loss of his wife, the children of their mother, and the home and the whole family of an ever watchful guardian. More than this, this false liberty and unnatural equality with the husband is to the detriment of the woman herself, for if the woman descends from her truly regal throne to which she has been raised within the walls of the home by means of the Gospel, she will soon be reduced to the old state of slavery (if not in appearance, certainly in reality) and become as amongst the pagans the mere instrument of man.

This equality of rights which is so much exaggerated and distorted, must indeed be recognised in those rights which belong to the dignity of the human soul and which are proper to the marriage contract and inseparably bound up with wedlock. In such things undoubtedly both parties enjoy the same rights and are bound by the same obligations; in other things there must be a certain inequality and due accommodation, which is demanded by the good of the family and the right ordering and unity and stability of home life.

As, however, the social and economic conditions of the married woman must in some way be altered on account of the changes in social intercourse, it is part of the office of the public authority to adapt the civil rights of the wife to modern needs and requirements, keeping in view what the natural disposition and temperament of the female sex, good morality, and the welfare of the family demands, and provided always that the essential order of the domestic society remain intact, founded as it is on something higher than human authority and wisdom, namely on the authority and wisdom of God, and so not changeable by public laws or at the pleasure of private individuals.

Must A Wife Obey Her Husband?

THE REV. FORREST MACKEN, C.P.

"Does a wife really have to obey her husband?"

A question like that does more than put a lecturer, panel member, or marriage counselor on the spot. It often gives voice to an exaggeration about the head of the home. It may echo the attitude of the husbands who overreach the limited authority they have over their wives. Or it may express the feeling of those wives who *"let him think* he is head of the home." . . .

Is the husband's authority in operation 24 hours a day—well, at least all the waking hours? Some husbands believe it is. Their misunderstanding of the nature of marriage as blueprinted by God results in two kinds of exaggerations.

The first one concerns the limits of a husband's authority. At first glance it could seem that the inspired words of God declare that there are no limits. "Just as the Church is subject to Christ, so also let wives be to their husbands in all things" (Eph. 5:24). However, as the Scripture scholars authorized by the Bishops explain in their footnote of the Confraternity of Christian Doctrine's American translation, that phrase "in all things" means in all things pertaining to the right relationship of husband and wife. . . .

A husband goes against right reason . . . when he requires something that is not related to husband-wife action toward the common goal of their married society. Such things are: ordering his wife to use a certain color of lipstick, forbidding her to visit a particular neighbor, and like things.

Again, a husband acts against right reason if he demands that the family dwell in a place where the wife will surely lose her health.

Likewise does a husband overreach the limits of domestic authority, says Pius XI, if he requires what is not "in harmony with the dignity due to a wife." . . . To treat a wife as an eldest daughter is not in harmony with her dignity. Her position requires that she be treated as an adult companion. Harry, it would seem, does not treat Helen in harmony with her dignity in this case: Helen talks of taking an evening course at the college one night a week to improve herself. Harry replies, "You'd better skip it. I can see you won't be neglecting me or the kids—but, I think you better skip it."

Furthermore, the demands of prudence require that husbands discuss their decisions with their wives. Such a statement will probably draw wry smiles. But by prudence, here, is meant the virtue, not merely a caution, that a consulted woman becomes a cooperative woman, whereas an ignored woman can become an obstructionist. The virtue of prudence often requires one to take counsel with others. A wife frequently has access to facts and knowledge although a husband does not. Therefore, if a husband is to avoid failing against the virtue of prudence, he will often consult his wife before making his decisions.

The second exaggeration of husbands regarding authority over their wives flows from overlooking the *community* aspect of their marriage. Pope Pius XI reminds us that married life has two different aspects when he develops in his encyclical letter *On Christian Marriage* the context of the husband's primacy and the wife's subjection. Marriage can "be looked at [either] in the restricted sense as instituted for the proper conception and education of the child, [or] more widely as the blending of life as a whole and the mutual interchange and sharing thereof." Here the Pope indicates the distinction of marriage as a *society* from marriage as a *community*. Viewed from one aspect marriage is a society; from a different aspect it is a community.

Married life implies a *society*, that is two persons combining their activities in view of a common goal. The common goal in marriage is chiefly "the proper conception and education of new life." Their intentions, of course, do not establish that common goal in the way that business partners, for example, trace the outline of their commercial objective. The common goals of marriage are instituted by God. By choosing to marry, couples implicitly desire these common goals.

But such a common objective does not assure the united action necessary to arrive at it. As couples approach forks in the road of their married life, both husband and wife may agree in determining which way they will take toward their common goal. But at times, as the saying goes, they will agree to disagree. To provide for united action at these junctions, God has built into each married society an arbiter with authority.

In marriage as a *community*, on the contrary, authority and obedience have no place. For one thing, the unifying bond in a community is friendship. Friendship harmonizes two (or more) persons in oneness of affection. The deep friendship involved in a married community links husband and wife as equals. (Of course, the children, too, share in family community.)

The reason a community exists lies in the fact that persons regularly share things in common. Such an exchange of goods and of acts of service cannot be traced to commands of authority. Wishes are indeed fulfilled and service given—but because of love. One submits to the other but simply out of a desire to please a loved one.

When husbands overlook the community aspect of marriage and think of it as a society alone, they tend to do more than "pull their rank" on their wives. They easily exaggerate their authority.

Husbands, however, do not stand alone in exaggerating their authority. Wives can do the same, although from different misunderstandings.

One of them makes the husband's authority a matter of make-believe. Such a wife goes through all the motions merely to let her husband think he is really head. Deep down she harbors the conviction he is not. Such a wife was Mrs. Hamilton. In chatting with her about domestic matters Mrs. Gary remarks, "You know, I just can't get my husband to buy a home on Smartset Lane." "Well, my dear," Mrs. Hamilton advises her, "you just keep after him. I always get what I want. I simply keep on talking and talking until my husband finally gives in." . . .

Divine wisdom could not allow the basic unit of human living to begin with anarchy and drift haphazardly . . . True, it is normal for newlyweds to yearn so to please each other that authority and obedience are hardly necessary during the honeymoon. When this wears thin, husband and wife would have to jockey for first position or else wait for indefinite months to find out who will prove to be head.

But why is the wife not head? The fundamental reason lies in the husband's God-given roles to provide and to protect. During the later stages of pregnancy and for some time after childbirth, wives are not in condition to protect and provide for themselves and their babies. Nor do they find themselves equipped at such times to face the requirements and the responsibilities of making decisions of concern to the common goal. Moreover, this reference to childbirth and child care amounts to much more than an example. It refers to the chief meaning of the husband-wife society. For, says Pius XII, "The primary function of marriage is service to new life."

These truths are not outmoded. They are called to the attention of present day couples by our present Holy Father: "To the man belongs the headship of the family unity." A wife who merely "lets her husband think he is head," does not merely indulge in make-believe. She walks through married life out of step with the reality of things—to her misfortune and frustration.

The second exaggeration of some wives amounts to a feeling that a submissive wife must acknowledge herself inferior (as though Mary, full of grace, pretended she was inferior to St. Joseph).

On looking more closely, we find here a confusion of personal dignity with obedience. As a matter of fact, obedience does not demand that one subordinate himself to someone who stands on his own level. To do such a thing is unworthy of a human person. Accordingly, it is truly contrary to the dignity of a wife. Genuine obedience can be rendered only to an agent of God. . . . Wives who, in practice, deny some of God's active influence in human affairs can be expected to rebel at what they consider the arbitrary imposition of "authority." Janet, for example, goes to Mass every Sunday. But she feels that away from church property and out of prayer time everyone is pretty much on his own as far as God is concerned, for all practical purposes. . . .

These truths recall a paradox of Christianity. Always have Christian wives been reminded that they are subject to their husbands. Yet, the same Christian teaching gradually lifted the condition of wives from the generally complete subjection to their husbands in the Roman Empire at the birth of Christianity, up to ever higher dignity. Wholesome feminist aims of today have blossomed from the stem of this Christian teaching. To the contrary, where this Christian doctrine has not penetrated, wives may be "treated well" but they remain even today at the lowly level of a plaything in a harem or a human chattel or something of the kind.

Christian husbands have always been taught that the authority they bear means a responsibility to serve the family's welfare. That responsibility answers to God and to Christ the King from Whom comes all authority on earth, whether in the family, in the state, or in the Church. . . .

The direct result of authority and obedience in Christian marriage is to foster united action toward the common goal of that married society. Grace and holiness grow in the exercise of obedience and authority according to the common norms of merit, in the ways all good actions are made meritorious.

Christian doctrine assures us that authority will be present in married society always. Nevertheless, says Pius XI, "subjection of the wife to the husband in its *degree* and *manner* may vary according to the different conditions of persons, place and time."

Why, then, are some people alarmed at the growing need for the head of the home to win loyal love in place of relying on his dominance? Some Catholics feel bound to insist not only on the fact of authority but also on some so-called "traditional" manner of exercising family authority.

Catholic scholars have expanded on this notion of a diminishing degree of a husband's authority in contemporary living. One striking example is the Benedictine, Reverend Edgar Schmiedeler, for some 25 years Director of the Family Life Bureau of the National Catholic Welfare Conference. He forecast favorable developments in a scholarly study, *Introductory Study of the Family*, written almost 30 years ago. He predicted that authority will remain less influential in family life than was the case previously, for example, under the semi-patriarchal systems of the past. "The ultimate result . . . may be a much more ideal family life . . . in which authority will be more closely allied with the elements of loyalty and love than with coercion and insistence upon rights. . . ."

It might be thought that a decrease in the degree and manner of family authority must mean a dangerous decline. On the contrary, it can signify that certain couples have attained a higher plateau. "The two wills in the home will involve possibility of conflict and clash," wrote Father Schmiedeler, "but will not necessarily imply actual disharmony. Indeed, the noblest harmonies of life arise when two disciplined and independent wills combine, and the truest comradeship is found when man and woman meet on the common ground of mutual interest and respect."

The Vocation of Women in the World
THE REV. GERALD VANN, O.P.

Underneath all the varieties of individual qualities and characteristics there lies the greatest of all natural differentiations: which is that between man and woman. It is true that we are none of us wholly male or female in our make-up; but it remains permissible to speak of the male mind or the female mind, and therefore of the vocation of a man and the vocation of woman, inasmuch as there are some qualities of mind and soul which ought to be predominant in man and others which ought to be predominant in woman. . . .

If you look at primitive societies, where human nature is at its simplest, you find a clear-cut division: the man is the breadwinner, the active one, the builder; the woman is the housewife, the receptive one, the conserver. It is the man who goes out to hunt; the woman who stays behind to preserve the home and the family. And as the intellectual life of a community evolves, the same fundamental distinction persists: it is the man, the builder and legislator, who represents reason; the woman, the conserver and consoler, who represents intuition. The man adventures in ideas, in science and philosophy, and builds up what is new; the woman conserves the deep lasting unchanging wisdom in her heart.

You hear a great deal nowadays about the equality of the sexes: there is a great danger here. If you are trying to defend woman from the degradation of being treated as a chattel, from the horrors of child-marriage and so on, then of course you are wholly right: these things are a crime against human nature and against the laws of God. But be careful: if by equality you mean an obliteration of the difference between the sexes you will end by destroying the integrity of both. For the whole idea and purpose of the difference is that the two together are complementary: they complete one another precisely because they differ from one another. Man and woman are meant to have the equality of true companionship; but true companionship does not exclude a subordination on one plane. If we had begun this meditation with some of the sayings of St. Paul about woman, would you have been irritated or depressed? If so, you would have been wrong. You will not achieve the freedom and dignity of woman by trying to turn her into a man; you will only destroy her, and man as well.

On one level there is a subordination, there is obedience. But be comforted: on another level it is woman who indisputably reigns. Her special role, spiritually, intellectually, as well as biologically and economically, is just as necessary to man as his is to her. They are partners, fellow-workers—you ruin everything if you try to give them both the same work. . . .

Man, the rational, active builder, tends to be concerned with the immediate and apparent needs of life, with the surface, and in consequence to take the short view; woman is meant by nature to be slower to leap to conclusions: it is for her to keep in her heart the words, the experiences, which life brings to them both; and having kept them in her heart to come to understand them in a different way. She must know the length; she must be able to take, not so much rationally as intuitively, a long view; she must see beyond the immediate necessities and advantages, and sense ultimate effects. She must know the breadth: it is easy for the man, all too easy, in the struggle for life, to find himself involved in facile enmities; it is for her to preserve in herself and in him the sense of the unity of the human family and indeed of all the creatures of God. She must know the height: it is easy for the man to become so wrapped up in his human work and human striving for progress that he comes to measure all things by purely human standards, or at least forgets that there are things that matter even more than daily bread; she must preserve his human labors along the horizontal line of human progress from the dangers of shallowness and perhaps idolatry by her upward, vertical striving of spirit towards divinity—she must be always bringing back the humanist world to the sense of God. She must know the depth. It is her heaviest cross and her greatest glory. The humanist world is a shallow world, a world of false and facile optimism, inasmuch as it forgets the fact of sin, or tries to ignore it. But you cannot ignore the underworld of life with impunity. Either you must go down into it, suffer it, understand it, and overcome it; or you can try to forget it for a time, and then, sooner or later, it will rise up against you and destroy you. And when a whole civilization tries thus to forget the sense of depth it may live very placidly on the surface for a while; it may make immense progress, but still on the surface; and then its nemesis too will come upon it, and it will find itself driven back to the darkness of the caves. That is why, even on a purely natural reckoning, we so desperately need the vocation of woman in the world of today; and why we need so desperately this aspect of the fullness of life of the saints. . . .

The rational mind of the male tends to take the short view, to become involved in rivalries and enmities, to ignore the heights of the eternal hills and the depths of evil and misery; and for any or all of these reasons the rational schemes of the male and all his work of building and all his ambitions tend to come tumbling down, sooner or later, in ruins about him; and it is then that woman is meant to find her true vocation as mother of man, and her share in the universal motherhood of Mary. Sometimes indeed it is only this catastrophe which can enable her to recall man to the sense of length and breadth and height and depth: when all goes well he refuses to listen, he meets her wisdom with a parade of logic and beats it down; and it is not till he has seen his own world crashing about him, seen the chaos to which he has brought himself, that he comes back to be re-born in the womb of her pity and realize belatedly that she was right, realizes perhaps that all the time he knew unconsciously that she was right and that his parade of reason was only an escapist mechanism of rationalization. But she for her part will throw away her destiny if in the moments of failure and abjection she despises him; if she does that she fails herself. She has to preserve her faith in him; and she has to preserve his own faith in himself, in his ability to start again, to re-build in a new spirit what is broken or to build something new and more worth while.

Here she may have to meet her greatest temptation, in this moment when her essential vocation is fulfilled. It is the temptation to make herself the triumphant rival of the work the man is meant to do. Not that the temptation is confined to these moments; on the contrary; but it is here that it can be most acute. . . .

The man has his home and his career; he may neglect one of them for the sake of the other; she for her part may be tempted to view the career either as a rival, withdrawing him from her, or at least as a part of his life in which she has no share. In either case she fails to fulfill her destiny. For it is no longer his career, his work. It is their career, their work. She is dependent on him, on the results of the work, that the home may be preserved; but he for his part is dependent on her, on the wisdom she can bring him if she has learnt her destiny aright, on her faith in him, on her love and the strength it gives her to support them and give them hope in times of crisis and distress. She has to learn her particular wisdom, she has to learn her particular work—the domestic arts—she has to learn the particular qualities she needs as a wife, precisely in order to help him achieve his vocation and to share in his work. . . . But it may happen that he for his part becomes so absorbed in his career that he loses interest in her; and it may be only failure that will bring him back; and it is then, when that happens, that she has to meet the keenest temptation, the temptation to spend all her energies simply on retaining this love permanently instead of giving him new heart for the work. She must, of course, want to retain his love; but she must try to re-integrate his life, not destroy a part of it: her vocation is still to minister to the work—and if she does that, it is surely probable that her faith and love and strength will themselves win back for her the fullness of his love, whereas if she sets herself up as a rival she will at best only triumph for a time, for you cannot frustrate half of a man's nature indefinitely.

That is her first temptation. The second comes of the duality of her life as wife and mother. When she is first married, perhaps the man's predominant attitude will be one of adoration; she will be in a position to command. The power that sex gives you over another's will is a terrible thing: it can be used to teach and to save, but it can also be used to destroy and ruin. Her temptation will be to preserve that relationship unchanged; to preserve at all costs the power, and therefore the endowments which give the power. And again if she does that she will be throwing away not only his destiny but her own. Her part, in the last resort, is not to command and make decisions but to cause him to command and make decisions; otherwise he will never reach his full stature as a man. But she herself will never reach her full stature as a woman unless she goes on to fulfill her destiny as a mother. Her life of labor in kitchen and nursery, with all the demands it puts upon her of courage and patience and dogged endurance: it is that that can teach her, more than anything, her own deep wisdom. But only if she does it wholeheartedly. You cannot create a family, a home, unless you love your children completely; but you cannot love them completely unless, feeling their dependence upon you, you give yourself entirely to them. That is why a woman has to stop being a goddess on a pedestal and become a worker in a kitchen and a nursery. And a year or two goes by, and one day the man realizes that his companion is not a goddess but a hard-worked woman, beginning to show signs of the work and worry that she has had to contend with; and then—and it is part of *his* growth to fullness—he should be moved with compassion to think that it is her devotion to him and to his children that has brought about this change; and he should be filled with a sense of the family's dependence on him, and a determination to take care of it and provide for it and cherish it, cost what it may. And if they both accept their vocation in this way, in the fullness of the demands it makes on them, then they learn a deeper love and unity than ever they could achieve in the more lyrical and idyllic stage of their career: they fulfill in their lives the image of the Holy Family. . . .

Keep the words of God, the things that God does and the events and experiences that he sends you, in your heart; use them in prayer and sacrifice to increase your vision of the length and breadth and height and depth; then, no doubt, you will share with Mary in the sorrows of the seven swords, but you will share with her also in the motherhood of man. And in the degree to which you can copy her humility, the humility of her *ecce ancilla Domini*, to that degree you will share in her glory: you of your own smaller life and smaller world will be able to say something approaching the words with which she described her future glory in the world as a whole: Behold from henceforth all generations shall call me blessed, for he that is mighty hath done great things in me, and holy is his name.

Love Creates Domestic Harmony

ST. JOHN CHRYSOSTOM

"To love their husbands." This is the chief point of all that is good in a household. "Man and wife that agree well together."

(Ecclas 25:2). For where this exists, there will be nothing that is unpleasant. For where the head is in harmony with the body, and there is no disagreement between them, how shall not all the other members be at peace? For when the rulers are at peace, who is there to divide and break up concord, as on the other hand, there will be no good order in the house. This then is a point of the highest importance, and of more consequence than wealth, or rank, or power, or aught else. Nor has he said merely to be at peace, but "to love their husbands." For where love is, no discord will find admittance, for from it, other disadvantages too spring up. . . .

She who despises her husband, neglects also her house; but from love springs great soberness, and all contention is done away. And if he be a Heathen, he will soon be persuaded; and if he be a Christian, he will become a better man. . . . For if it should happen that a believing woman, married to an unbeliever, should not be virtuous, the blasphemy is usually carried on to God; but if she be of good character, the Gospel obtains glory from her, and from her virtuous actions. Let those women hearken who are united to wicked men or unbelievers; let them hear, and learn to lead them to godliness by their own example.

(Translator Anonymous)

Pope Saint Gregory the Great Instructs the Clergy How to Counsel Husbands and Wives

For those who are bound in wedlock are to be admonished that, while they take thought for each other's good, they study, both of them, so to please their consorts as not to displease their Maker; that they so conduct the things that are of this world as still not to omit desiring the things that are of God; that they so rejoice in present good as still, with earnest solicitude, to fear eternal evil; that they so sorrow for temporal evils as still to fix their hope with entire comfort on everlasting good; to the end that, while they know what they are engaged in to be transitory, but what they desire to be permanent, neither the evils of the world may break their heart while it is strengthened by the hope of heavenly good, nor the good things of the present life deceive them, while they are saddened by the apprehended evils of the judgment to come. Wherefore the mind of married Christians is both weak and steadfast, in that it cannot fully despise all temporal things, and yet can join itself in desire to eternal things. Although it lies low meanwhile in the delights of the flesh, let it grow strong in the refreshment of supernal hope: and, if it has the things that are of the world for the service of its journey, let it hope for the things that are of God for the fruit of its journey's end; nor let it devote itself entirely to what it is engaged in now, lest it fall utterly from what it ought steadfastly to hope for. For he has a wife as though he had none who enjoys carnal consolation through her as still never to be turned by love of her to evil deeds from the rectitude of a better aim. He has a wife as though he had none who, seeing all things to be transitory, endures of necessity the care of the flesh, but looks forward with longing to the eternal joys of the spirit. . . . Love not the world abidingly, since the world ye love cannot itself abide. In vain ye fix your affections on it as though it were continuing, while that which ye love itself is also fleeting. Husbands and wives are to be admonished, that those things wherein they sometimes displease one another they bear with mutual patience, and by mutual exhortations remedy. For the law of Christ's Charity; since it has from Him bountifully bestowed on us its good things, and patiently borne our evil things. We, therefore, then fulfill by imitation the law of Christ, when we both kindly bestow our good things, and piously endure the evil things of our friends. They are also to be admonished to give heed, each of them, not so much to what they have to bear from the other as what the other has to bear from them. For, if one considers what is borne from one's self, one bears more lightly what one endures from another.

(Translated by James Barmby)

The Husband's Contribution to Happiness

PIUS XII

A husband's contribution to the happiness of the home must not stop at kindness and consideration toward his partner in life. It must advance to understand, appreciate, and recognize the work and effort of her who silently and diligently dedicates herself to making the common home more comfortable, more pleasant, more gay. With what loving care, for example, a young woman has arranged everything to celebrate, as joyously as the circumstances permit, the anniversary of the day in which she was united before the altar with him who was to become the companion of her life and happiness, and who is now about to return from his office or workshop!

But the man arrives, weary from the long hours of work, perhaps more exhausted than usual, nervous because of unforeseen vexations. He returns later than usual, somber and worried about other thoughts; the happy affectionate words that greet him go unheeded and he remains silent; he appears unaware of the meal prepared with so much love. He only looks and notes that the dish which was selected especially to make him happy has been cooking too long, and he grumbles, without thinking that the reason was his own delay and the long wait. He eats hurriedly, since, he says, he must go out immediately after dinner.

When the meal is over, the poor young woman, who had dreamed of the joy of a pleasant evening together with him, finds herself alone in the deserted room; she needs all her faith and courage to keep back her tears. . . .

When therefore you find yourselves at home . . . do not be quick to search for little defects inevitable in every human endeavor; be mindful, rather, of all that is good, be it much or little, which is offered to you as the fruit of toil, vigilant attention, affectionate feminine intuition, to make your home . . . a little paradise of happiness and joy.

Do not be content to contemplate and love such goodness only in the recesses of your thoughts and heart. Let your wife know it and feel it, since she has not spared herself in procuring it for you. For her the best and sweetest recompense is a loving smile, a gentle word, an appreciative glance, which makes her aware of your gratitude.

A Wife's Prayer

ANONYMOUS

Lord, bless my cherished husband, whom You have given to me; let his life be long and blessed, comfortable and holy; let me ever be a blessing and a comfort to him, a sharer in all his sorrows, a consolation in all the accidents and trials of life; make me forever lovable in his eyes and forever dear to him; unite his heart to mine in fondest love and holiness, and mine to him in all sweetness, charity, and submission. Keep me from all ungentleness; make me humble and obedient, that we may delight in each other according to Your blessed word. May both of us rejoice in You, having our portion in the love and service of God forever. Amen.

Should a Wife Ever Permit a Divorce?

THE REV. DONALD F. MILLER, C.SS.R.

Should a Catholic wife permit her husband to divorce her because he has lost his faith and become infatuated with another woman? . . .

This is one of those involved issues that require a great deal of investigation before a definite answer can be given. A few principles can be put down that cover some of the circumstances.

It must be remembered that for actual cooperation in divorce proceedings the permission of the bishop, obtained through the pastor, must be had. This law is a safeguard in this in that it involves consultation with the pastor, which is bound to bring out all the circumstances and to open the way for alternative suggestions. It is all but impossible for outsiders, even close friends, to know all the facts in a given problem between a husband and wife as they would be known to the priest consulted.

A second principle would be that so long as even a slight hope of the ultimate repentance and correction of the erring husband can be entertained, there should be no cooperation with his desire for a divorce. Especially if there are children, this hope of conversion from evil should be a deciding factor. If the desire for a divorce is based upon an infatuation, which is often a brief and, no matter how offensive to the wife, rather quickly passing thing, a prudent and good wife will balk a divorce with every means in her power.

On the other hand, if the husband seems to be incorrigible because all semblance of his faith is gone, and if he is making life miserable for his wife and children through public scandal and private mistreatment, then a Catholic wife should apply to her pastor for the permission to place counter charges against him, so that she may obtain the protection of the law from his abuse, and an economic settlement that will provide for herself and the children. She should not be deterred from this either by the thought that she does not want to give him what he calls "his freedom" (a man of this kind will never be happy anyway) or by a fear that in such a case there would be a stigma in divorce.

Avoiding Family Fights

THE REV. LEO J. KINSELLA

Some years ago I was faced with the necessity of working up a talk on the ideal wife. Naturally, I was open for suggestions, particularly from a few ideal wives whose friendship I highly prize. One evening, as I visited the home of one of these friends, I mentioned the task with which I was confronted.

"Mary, if you had to give an hour talk on the ideal wife to high school seniors or to a woman's club, what would you discuss?" . . .

Although she did not indicate that she considered patience the most important quality of the desired wife she unhesitatingly suggested it first. Not only did she mention patience first, but she also explained what she meant by patience in the wife. Notice that the discussion deals with the patience required of the wife, not of the mother in her relations with her children. A woman is first the wife of her husband before she is the mother of his children. . . .

The understanding, the sympathy, and the patience required for happy living cannot be measured out. The stupid expression "marriage is a fifty-fifty deal" implies yardsticks, tape measures, half cups, full table spoons, and the like. Love has nothing to do with these things—will not be fenced in by them, for love partakes of the very limitlessness of God. A wife's parsimonious measuring out of her imagined fifty per cent produces many serious fights. She wins these fights too and loses her husband.

Let us illustrate the above by concrete examples. The wife was getting supper ready. John was fighting the traffic on his way home from work. She was humming softly as she busied herself contentedly about the kitchen. He was muttering loudly the red light blues. She felt fine. He was half sick and out of sorts. Things had not been going well at work. He was upset and unwittingly looking for a fight.

As he entered the house and gave Mary a little hug and kiss, she noticed that he looked tense and jumpy. A few minutes later she could hear him scolding one of the children. The storm warnings should have been flying by now. They had better steer clear of him tonight.

Before the family was called to the supper table, Mary had been fully on guard. Unless she was very mistaken, her husband was going to demand much more than fifty per cent somewhere along the evening. So the measuring devices, the half cups and full table spoons were behind her for this evening. The meal was already prepared. She would not use them on her husband. She would not measure out her patience and understanding. Her husband was definitely off color this evening. She would give him her all. No matter what he said, she would pass it off.

The supper got off to as good a start as could have been expected with the cloud hanging over the table. Soon one of the children massacred table etiquette in such manner as to cause Emily Post to wince. Before her husband could draw in sufficient breath to let out a blast at the culprit, she quickly took the wind out of his sail by firmly correcting the child. Before the dessert appeared, she took in her stride a caustic remark about the quality of the pot roast and a criticism leveled at her through one of the children.

Mary was nobody's dish rag. She had a lot of fire and spirit. She could have stood up to him that night, "let him have it," and have had a fight which she might have won, or, at least in which she would have held her own. But, did anyone ever win a fight of this kind?

This ideal wife had made up her mind to carry her husband through the evening, come what might. He was not himself. Tomorrow would be another day. If he had been physically sick in bed and needed her care, would she have given only fifty per cent? Of course not. She would have nursed and lavished upon him all the warmth of her nature. Well, he was sick that night—sick in mind and spirit. He needed her intelligent, loving and patient consideration. She would have considered herself a very shallow person to have reacted otherwise. She was in love with her husband that night, too, unreasonable though he was.

A few weeks later the tables were turned. She was the one who was at wits end with herself. She started the day with a headache and things went from bad to worse. It was a rainy day, and for some unfathomable reason the school shut its doors on the children. They were under her feet all day. Often she had to act as referee in their squabbles. As the afternoon wore on toward supper time, she was becoming conditioned for more adult opposition.

An unsuspecting husband made his entry. He was back to his little castle in the suburb with roses round the door (metaphorically speaking) and babies on the floor (literally speaking).

During the meal Mary "blew her top" about something. Oh yes, the car did not start that afternoon. The battery or something must have been dead. Some junk! It was time they had a new car.

So it was junk, was it? John could think of the days of work it took to buy that old bus a few years previous. It was still a good car. What did women know about cars anyway? There ought to have been a law against women ever— There is no future in this kind of thought, so John quickly banished the hideous little devil from his mind. Mary was worked up tonight. He would have to be cautious. Did he defend the car against his wife? John was a little too sharp for that. He jumped on the band wagon and lambasted the car too. Yes, we would have to do something about that nuisance. He felt like going out then and burning it up. He knew by the time they got to the dishes, Mary would have forgotten all about the car.

Mary purred through the rest of the meal contentedly with that wonderful feeling that her husband was all for her. Together they stood against the whole world.

Suppose that John had been a little thick between the ears and that he took exception to her remarks about the car and defended the car against his wife. A fight would have ensued. Feelings would have been hurt. And there was danger that their tempers would have swept them on to the name calling stage. Once this has been reached, real harm frequently has been done to a marriage.

Mary finished her explanation of what she meant by patience by saying that she and her husband had never had a fight in the twelve years of married life. Then she added what I thought was the epitome of her whole conversation by saying that she and her husband did not intend to have any fights. This determination not to fight was indicative of their intelligence and maturity. Surely it was one of the factors contributing to the happy stability of their marriage.

If Love Dies

THE REV. ALBERT H. DOLAN, O.CARM.

It is sad but true that love sometimes not only cools but actually dies. I fear that *after* that happens, the married couple concerned are in no mood to listen to the only possible advice that can cover their case, which is: "Since your marriage vows still bind you in God's sight, since you may not remarry, then is it not God's will that you do your best to revive your love?" Impossible? Nothing is impossible with God's help. Moreover, in all but the most extreme and rare cases (when husband and wife are Catholics), their former love does not change to hatred; there remains a spark of friendship, and where there is goodwill and prayer for God's help, that friendship may be used as a basis on which to build, not an ardent love, but an endurable and even at times pleasant companionship. In no case need the marriage become a "mockery." . . . We admit of course that the degree of success attained will depend upon how much "God's will" and "God's plan," and "heaven" mean to both husband and wife. But surely no reasonable person will deny that a Catholic couple can, if they wish, live together until death as God planned and because God planned and wills it. That it will take a lot of doing is obvious; that it will take a lot of prayer is clear; but it is by no means impossible with God's help.

And to the couples whose love is young and fresh, we say: "Don't let your love die! Then you will never be confronted with this situation we have been discussing." Don't let your love die! There is much trash written about love as if it were utterly beyond our control. We will not go into that question here but this much is certain: the wife can so foster her own love for her husband and his for her that it need never entirely die even where it fails to become the deep, strong friendship that is the ideal. A very wise woman who has made a splendid success of her marriage writes: "It is important to keep married love alive and healthy. It must not be permitted to languish and die. A woman's love does not seem to need the careful attention which is necessary to keep a man's love flourishing. A man's love will languish if his wife doesn't keep the spark alive by constant little manifestations of affection."

Let husbands not rest however upon the assumption that it is not their business also to keep their wife's love alive by these "constant little manifestations of affection." If both practise this rule throughout their marriage, their love will remain very much alive indeed.

"The Child Is a Sort of Bridge"

ST. JOHN CHRYSOSTOM

How do they become one flesh? It is as if you were to take the purest part of gold, and mingle it with other gold. In the same way, indeed, the woman receiving the richest part of man, fused as it were, by pleasure, nourishes it and cherishes it, and at the same time contributes her own share, and then restores it back as a human being. Thus, the child is a sort of bridge, so that three become one flesh. . . . Hence it says, with an accuracy of expression, not "they shall be one flesh," but "into one flesh," namely the flesh of the child, which connects them together. But does this imply, that, when there is no child, they will still be two and not one? No . . . for their coming together has this effect: it diffuses and commingles the bodies of both. And as one who, by putting ointment into oil, makes the whole mass one, so in truth we have here.

I know that many are ashamed at what I am saying. The cause of this is their lasciviousness and unchasteness. The fact that marriages are made and depraved in that manner has given them an evil repute. Yet "marriage is honorable, and the bed undefiled." Why are you ashamed of what is honorable? Why do you blush at what is undefiled?

(Translator Anonymous)

Three

PARENTS AND CHILDREN

A woman about to give birth has sorrow, because her hour has come. But when she has brought forth the child, she no longer remembers the anguish for her joy that a man is born into the world.

ST. JOHN 16:21

The Parents' Obligations as Educators, as Stated in the Code of Canon Law

Canon 1113: Parents are bound by a most grave obligation to provide to the best of their ability for the religious and moral as well as for the physical and civil education of their children, and for their temporal well-being.

Canon 1372: From childhood all the faithful must be so educated that not only are they taught nothing contrary to faith and morals, but that religious and moral training takes the chief place.

Love for Children

ST. JOHN CHRYSOSTOM

Then were brought to him little children that he might lay his hands on them and pray; but the disciples rebuked them. But Jesus said to them, "Let the little children be, and do not hinder them from coming to me, for of such is the kingdom of heaven." And when he had laid his hands on them, he departed from that place. St. Matthew 19:13-15.

And wherefore did the disciples repel the little children? For dignity. What then doth He? Teaching them to be lowly, and to trample under foot worldly pride, He doth receive them, and takes them in His arms, and to such as them promises the Kingdom: which kind of thing He said also before.

Let us also then, if we would be inheritors of the Heavens, possess ourselves of this virtue with much diligence. For this is the limit of true wisdom; to be simple with understanding; this is angelic life; yes, for the soul of a little child is pure from all passions. Towards them who have vexed him he bears no resentment, but goes to them as friends, as if nothing had been done; and how much soever he be beaten by his mother, after her he seeks, and her doth he prefer to all. Though thou show him the queen with the diadem, he prefers her not to his mother clad in rags, but would choose rather to see her in these, than the queen in splendor. For he useth to distinguish what pertains to him and what is strange to him, not by its poverty or wealth, but by friendship. And nothing more than necessary things doth he seek, but just to be satisfied from the breast, and then he leaves sucking. The young child is not grieved at what we are grieved, as at loss of money and such things as that, and he doth not rejoice again at what we rejoice, namely, at these temporal things, he is not eager about the beauty of persons. Therefore He saith, "Of such is the kingdom of Heaven," and that by choice we should practice these things, which young children have by nature.

(Translator Anonymous)

An Ancient Legend

Amel, a Breton fisherman, and Penhov, his wife, accompanied by their child, were tending their nets when overtaken by the tide. As the water rose higher and higher and cut off their escape, Amel called to his wife: "Penhov, this is our final hour; stand on my shoulders that you may live longer than me." As Amel sank rooted into the sand his wife followed his instructions, and in addition instructed the child to stand on her shoulders. The mother, too, disappeared beneath the sea and presently only the child's golden hair showed above the water. Suddenly an angel appeared, seized the child's hair and pulled. "Goodness, how heavy you are" said the angel as he began to draw the child from the water. Then another head appeared out of the water; it was Penhov, still clutching the child's feet. Then Amel came to the surface, clinging to Penhov's feet.

Thus by the child are father and mother saved.

"A Paternity Like to That of God"

THE REV. JEAN BAPTISTE LACORDAIRE

It is not in the substances capable of disturbing the reason or in the tragedies of chance that is found the most seductive sensation of man, his primary joy and his most poignant ecstasy, not beyond him or around him, but in himself, in the living circle of his personality, he finds a palpable flesh, a living and sensible flesh, which cleaves to his soul, which receives orders from it, but which acts upon it in its turn and offers to it a theatre where it can summon life from the very bosom of God. For God has not given us life for ourselves alone, as a miser's treasure, incapable of being communicated. Life is, by its nature, fruitful; it comes of an inexhaustible source, and springs up of itself in generations without end. He, then, who has given it to us, the God Who has said to all that is: *Live and multiply*, has, with still more reason, given to His chosen creature the command to live outside himself by transmitting himself to posterity.

But this commandment, divine for all, was so, in a very different manner, for us. For, as to others, He addressed Himself only to the body, to an organization composed of parts which might divide and discover in their division a seed of themselves. In man, the foundation of life was the soul; the soul, one, indivisible, incapable of dividing for the purpose of imparting itself, and being, like its Author, under the necessity of existing in its entirety or of ceasing to exist. There must needs be for man, then, at this supreme degree of existence, a paternity like to that of God, and as God [the Father] in the inaccessible light of His essence, said to Himself, speaking to another than Himself [the Son]: *Thou art my Son, this day have I begotten Thee,* so man, who is primarily soul and secondarily body, must evoke, at one and the same time and in the same act, a living soul and body of his image, and be also able to say to them like God: *Thou art my son, this day have I begotten thee.* . . .

What has God not done to elevate this mystery to the height of its nature and its end! Sacred union of souls beneath the immortal yoke of love freely promised, pleasures and duties for ever in common, misfortunes borne together, joys of paternity tempered by the anxieties of the future, indescribable mingling of good and evil, virtue ever present to sustain the feebleness of the heart against the chafings and trial of life.

(Translator Anonymous)

To Fathers

For it is a most sacred law of nature that a father must provide food and all necessaries for those whom he has begotten. And, similarly, nature dictates that a man's children, who carry on, as it were, and continue his own personality, should be provided by him with all that is needful to enable them honorably to keep themselves from want and misery in the uncertainties of this mortal life.

Leo XIII

You are rightly solicitous for your daily bread and a suitable home, which are indispensable for your maintenance and that of your families: see that this solicitude is not in conflict with your heavenly destiny. Let it not make you forgetful or neglectful of your soul and of the imperishable treasures which God has entrusted to you in the souls of your children.

Pius XII

The Romance of Fatherhood

JOSEPH A. BREIG

Much is written in poetic praise of motherhood. Little is written in that vein of fatherhood. The father is generally regarded as a kind of noble but weary beast of burden, silently enduring the tedium of providing for his family. Of the rewards of fatherhood almost nothing is said. Yet I suspect that the most gigantic of all human joys are experienced by fathers.

My own father used to embarrass me by the way in which he looked at me. It was as if I were something too wonderful to be true, merely because I was there. I felt that if he were to utter what was in his heart, I would be covered with confusion at the vision of the marvel of my own existence. But of course he could not utter it. He simply looked at me, and at the other children, as if he were asking how he—inconsequential he—could be the father of beings so mysterious and marvelous.

That was humility; but it was realism too. Humility may be defined as right realism. And humility is necessary for joy. A man will hardly appreciate a sunset if he imagines, in his pride, that he can paint something better. A woman will not rejoice in a rose if she thinks she can make a more beautiful rose of crepe paper. And a father will not be happy in his children unless he realizes that they came from God, that they are held in existence from moment to moment by the power of God, and that but for God they would vanish in an instant into nothingness.

I wonder whether there can be a father so unappreciative as not to have felt, from time to time, a pang of unutterable happiness in his children, like a wound in the heart. These moments come and go. But I have felt tears of joy in my eyes at the sight of the sturdy straight back of one of my boys, or in the presence of a small daughter's smile.

There is a scene that I have seen several times; and to have seen it once would have repaid me immeasurably for every effort I have invested in fatherhood. It was the sight of a small boy, my son, and a small girl, my daughter, walking hand in hand into the twilight. Symphonies could be written about that. The greatest poets and dramatists could exhaust themselves attempting to express it in words. But it is unutterable.

I remember that Betty and Joe walked with me one evening to the church which was halfway to the point where I was to take a bus. After they had said their little prayers, I started them up the hill toward home. It was that moment in the day when the sun is setting and the moon rising, and the first stars beginning to glow blue-green in the sky. Upon the trees and houses there lay a glow of pale rose light. The birds had ceased their sweet clamor, and the air was motionless, as if expectant.

I watched our daughter and our son as they trudged toward our house. In a moment Betty, who was the elder, took Joe's hand. Then they advanced together into that magic twilight, slowly receding from me; and I knew that if I had lived and worked for a century, I could never have earned that scene. Above all, I could never have earned the tremendous joy which came to me, which made me want to shout cheers to God who had made this moment. For an instant I wished that I might shake God's hand, and thank Him. . . .

I don't know what other fathers may feel, but I know what I feel at such moments. I feel that I am shouting together with all the sons of God. I know that there has been given to me a happiness which in an instant repays me a thousand times for all the weary waiting, for all the anxiety, for all the sitting in hospital corridors, for all the endless hours of working, which I have invested in my children.

This vision of the privilege of existence, and of the pricelessness of fatherhood, may come upon a man at any moment. I have seen it in a youngster's overshoes tossed carelessly in the vestibule of the house. I have seen it in a doll dropped in the middle of the living room floor. I have seen it when I entered a bedroom and found my son sleeping with his new hat on the side of his head. It can arise from anything at all—from the jaunty shape of a boy's shoulders, from the way a little girl wrinkles her nose, from a child's first awkward attempt at coloring in a coloring book. . . .

If I stepped out of this room, or went upstairs, I could at this moment multiply examples of the things that should make a father rejoice and praise God. I could—and later will—go from room to room looking down at the sleeping little ones with their tousled hair and their happy innocence and carefreeness. I will go from bed to bed calling down a blessing on each one. And I will feel myself in partnership with God. I shall see myself for what I am—an Associate Father, a God-father, another Joseph. And I will be more than content. I will be happy with the happiness that the world cannot give.

Provider for the Family

EUGENE GEISSLER

We commonly speak of a new baby as "another mouth to feed." And so it is. By the time of adolescence it is no small mouth either. There is something basic and elementary about this classic expression. We can imagine the possibility of getting along, at least in some climates, without clothing and shelter, but no one can do without food.

In our land of plenty and vitamins the threat of scarcity seems so remote that a father may, momentarily, show a lack of anxiety about this first duty of his to provide food for his family. Yet, the loss of his job, the threat of sickness, or merely missing a day's work leaves him disturbed. Just the thought of not having enough to go around can make him toss in his sleep. The mere idea that somewhere some other father's children do not have enough to eat can fill him with concern. Even the far-off cry of hunger is fearful to a father.

Fathers have been known, at least in the truth of fiction, to kill their children because, being unable to provide for them, they could no longer stand their cries of hunger. Fathers have been known to "steal" in order to keep their children alive. It is so fundamental a duty to provide food that "stealing" can cease to be a sin when a father appropriates someone else's bread for his own children's dire need.

But normally it is by the "work of his hands" and the "sweat of his brow" that a father provides this first and elementary necessity. Since the greatest gift a man can give another person is life, it follows that the work and sweat expended to support life also has great dignity. Often, very often, a father is himself kept going at a hard job and at monotonous work, not by the satisfaction he gets from doing what he is doing, but by the sheer truth that what he does sustains the lives of those he is dutybound to feed. In doing his duty he is giving himself and dying to himself, the greatest thing a man can do for another. If indeed it took all a father's energies and waking hours to keep his children alive, his life's work would be complete.

In a way, these extreme cases are an academic consideration, but it seems useful sometimes to return to bare essentials in order to rediscover the basic values that are the dignity of fatherhood.

A father works for his family, first of all, in and around the home, but mainly in modern times at his place of employment. It is never far from a father's consciousness that indirectly this "employment" is the work that feeds his family. What may happen, unfortunately, is that he may forget the exalted dignity that the fundamental duty of providing livelihood gives to the lowliest of jobs.

There are types of work that in themselves are more dignified than others because they are more spiritual, more intellectual, or more human in the sense that they use more of the person in their planning and execution. But a father must know that the dignity of whatever honest work he does to provide for his family is unassailable. For, by it he fulfills his primary duty of cooperating with God in completing the work of creation. The father's job is related to the Creator's own work of keeping alive the children who were brought into the world by God and by himself and his wife. . . .

It becomes apparent that the father gives not so much himself as things. His reputation as provider rests, a little like fame, on things exterior to himself. The woman lives at the heart of the family, giving herself. Not so the man. That is why, from one point of view, a father must continually "reason" his way to the true dignity of his contribution; why, from another point of view, he so needs the understanding and encouragement of his wife, who knows better than he himself the value of his contributions.

Obviously this time-hallowed word, "provider," is no idle or ill-chosen word; it truly represents the basic role of the father, who is doomed in a way, but not without dignity, to bring in from the outside what the family needs. This is not all there is to it, but it is basic.

The Father—An Important Factor in the Development of the Child

ROBERT P. ODENWALD, M.D.

The recognized presence of the father in the home is necessary for the healthy development of any child. The father must not be regarded only as the one who makes money, as much money as possible, even to the point of having a second job directly after supper. A father devoting all his time to the support of his family neglects the most important duty of fatherhood, and he becomes a stranger to his children. A mother one day complained to her husband that their little girl put up a fight every night when it was time to go to bed. He replied that he would see about that, he would put her to bed that night. It was a threat but the little one regarded it as a promise. That night the child refused to stay in bed unless her father put her there. He was astonished when he heard of it and went up the steps two at a time with a shout, "Get into that bed quick." With a happy laugh the child fled to her bed and cuddled down, smiling happily at her father. She insisted upon saying her prayers again and added a word of thanks for her "dear daddy." That father was wise enough to realize the love he had denied his child and that he had denied himself. . . .

The boy submits to the dominating person and should this be his mother, he falls in too readily with her wishes and takes on feminine attitudes. He tends to become a mother's boy, a "sissy." He may draw away from competitive sports and prefer quiet, domestic activities to the more active and boisterous ones of the typical child. Such submissive children are too often regarded as "ideal" children, for they cause no disturbance in the house. Very often they are made to act as servants rather than as children of the house. In extreme cases these children are unable to marry, or if they marry, prove unsatisfactory mates. "Momism" is recognized as one of the causes of insecurity in men of today.

The girl reared by the dominating type of mother is apt to show unfeminine trends; she may assert herself by engaging in boys' sports and games. After adolescence these activities tend to cease but she may develop a coarseness and aggressiveness out of line with an attractive feminine manner. To excuse her unbecoming masculinity she blames her father, since he is unresponsive and denies her all affection.

Down through the ages the father was recognized as the head of the family; it was the father who made decisions and saw that they were carried out. The children gave the father utmost confidence, believed in his unlimited strength and felt that their destiny was safe in his hands. In those times the father had a true sense of values, and by all means a sense of humour; he was lively, high in his aims; he had a lot of time for his family and was every ready to play a game. He tossed a ball or played horseshoes with his son, took him for hikes in the woods or went fishing with him. He took the boy or girl on his knee and told tall tales from his life which the child loved for their exaggeration. For the proper development of the child a father must keep himself and his soul young enough to maintain direct contact and understanding with these youngsters. . . . The father spends most of his day in the world outside, a great "unknown" which he must interpret to the child, a place where the child will assume a role some day. "What do you want to become when you grow up?" is a favorite question on radio and television today and the answers are funny rather than intelligent. A recent study made at the Catholic University revealed that only 41 per cent of the freshmen boys understood the type of work their fathers were doing. This failure on the part of the modern fathers explains why children entering adolescence have little idea of what the world has to offer them. If the mother has had a too-protective influence, the youth enters a competitive outside world with no preparation for finding his way.

The father should serve as intermediary between the world and the home. He should discuss with the young minds the happenings in the world and should answer patiently and understandingly the many questions his children ask him. . . .

The infant's rearing, his whole emotional upbringing is achieved through complete identification. Children sense the presence of the father and the positive tender feelings aroused in the play period is an essential role in their ego development. The father who romps with the little child, sits on the floor and plays with its mechanical toys, mends a broken doll or shoots at a target, develops a rapport with the youngster that brings them together as part of a family unit. And both the father and the child profit from this feeling of oneness.

Very quickly the little child reciprocates the father's love with an inspiring devotion. The son admires his strength and masculine prerogatives and the little girl coquettishly woos the father's affection; both children feel safe and secure. . . .

The presence of a wise and affectionate father gives to the child a sense of security, a control which directs him safely and within which protection he can adventure; an ideal to which he can strive. Close relationship with the father is naturally of first importance to the boy in his adaptation to his social role in life and as a member of his sex. The girl finds ease and tranquil enjoyment in the presence of her father, the same ease and comfort which it is necessary for her to develop later in the company of the male sex, an important factor for the choice of the right mate.

The child assumes the patterns of behavior of those whom he loves; usually of those whose strength and security he envies. . . .

There is a group in which any demonstration of affection is considered in poor taste and plebeian, while lack of emotion is regarded as aristocratic and noble. . . .

Children do not understand this unnatural repression of affection, being candid and open in all their thinking. They desire and need physical contact with persons they love. When children shy away from parents, there has been something wrong with the previous contact of the parents with the children. The child who is denied the opportunity to romp with his father and the baby who is denied his need for cuddling will come to think of affection in an unhealthy light. He may develop a personality that puts the wrong emphasis on affection and seek it unwisely, or he may assume his parents' attitude of rigidity which unfits him for normal romance and proper intersocial relationship. . . .

The importance of the father in the formation of a strong ego development in the child cannot be denied; it must be remembered that in the harmonious home the child's relationship is not to mother or father as separate entities; it is the totality of their relationship as parents. It is a shared relationship, a feeling of oneness, father, mother, child. A child should have the feeling that he can turn to the parents if the problem of living is too difficult. If the unity of the parents is torn in pieces by jealousy, envy, or any other unhappy human emotions, the child has lost an anchorage which for him was the foundation of living. . . .

Parenthood must be a shared relationship to the child, a shared responsibility. The child should be brought up to a feeling of being an individual part of a unity which is his strength and guide. The love and care of the mother alone is not enough. The wisdom and affection of the father are equally necessary for the development of the child into a noble adulthood. It is a wise father who will direct his footsteps right. You probably all know the story of the man who went out of the house one winter's day through the deep unbroken snow. He walked a block, crossed over and went another block and entered a building. His little son, coming out to play, saw the tracks of his father and stretching his little legs, put one foot after another into the footprints of his father and followed along. It was a frightened father sitting at a bar who saw the door open and his little son walk in.

The Mother's Sacred Ministry

THE REV. JEAN BAPTISTE LACORDAIRE

To whom should man, on rising into life, be confided? To whose charge should he be given, that he may be inspired with sentiments of good? What hand is sufficiently delicate, sufficiently ingenious, sufficiently tender, to make that wild animal tractable which is just born between good and evil, who might be a wicked sinner or a saint? Let us not seek so far. Already his education has commenced, even in the womb which bore him. Each thought, each prayer, each sigh of his mother, was a divine nourishment for him, which flowed even to his soul, and baptized it in honor and holiness. The father is powerless directly to influence him in this stage of his being. To the mother alone it has been given, that her soul during the nine months should touch the soul of the child, and impose upon it predispositions to truth, gentleness, goodness, the culture of which precious germs she should complete in the light of day, after having sown them in the mysterious mysteries of her maternity. The infant appears; he escapes from that first education of the Gospel by the bowels of his mother; but he is received into the hands which the Gospel has blessed; . . . he sleeps tranquilly under the guardianship of his mother, armed by Jesus Christ. And as soon as his eyes open, what is the first look which meets them? The pure and pious regard of a Christian woman. And as soon as a word, gliding through the tortuous channels of the hearing, can be introduced to his intelligence, who will be the first to pronounce it? Who will convey to him the first word, the first revelation, the first cry of one intelligent being to another? Who! It was once God, it is God still, by our purified and sanctified mother. The Christian woman has succeeded to God in the sacred ministry of the first word. When Adam heard it, and when the flame of his mind was kindled by that action, beneath the splendid horizon of Heaven, it was God Who had spoken to him. And when our hearts awaken to affection, and our minds to truth, it is under the hand, under the language, under the influences of maternal love that the prodigy is accomplished.

(Translated by Henry Langdon)

A Mother's Prayer

ANONYMOUS

Mary, my Mother, grant that my little child may instruct me in the ways of God. Let its innocent eyes speak to me of the spotless holiness of Jesus. Let its open smile remind me of the great love God has for His creatures. Let its helplessness teach me the unbounded power of God. May its first feeble effort to speak call to my mind the wisdom of the Almighty. May my love for God be stimulated by the deep-rooted affection my child has for me. May I, in all these things, grow in greater appreciation of my holy motherhood. Mary, I trust in you to obtain this favor for me.

I put my little baby under your protection, Mary, my mother. Make its tiny mind grow up to love the truths of faith; consecrate its will to the service of God; fill its heart with love for its Creator. Fashion its little body in all perfection; let its organs be sound, its senses acute, all its members strong and healthy. You can obtain this favor for me and my child, most powerful Mother. I put my trust in you. Amen.

Duties and Responsibilities of Mothers

PIUS XII

Mothers, your sensibility is greater and your love more tender, and therefore you will keep a vigilant eye upon your babies throughout their infancy, watching over their growth and over the health of their little bodies, for this is flesh of your flesh and the fruit of your womb. Remember that your children are the adopted sons of God and specially beloved of Christ; remember that their angels look forever on the face of the heavenly Father; and so you too as you rear them must be angels in like manner, in all your care and vigilance keeping your eyes fixed upon heaven. It is your task from the cradle to begin their education in soul as well as in body; for if you do not educate them they will begin, for good or ill, to educate themselves. . . .

Notwithstanding what certain thinkers have maintained, we are not born endowed with knowledge or with the memories and dreams of a life already lived. The mind of the child as it comes forth from its mother's womb is a page upon which nothing is written; from hour to hour as it passes on its way from the cradle to the tomb its eyes and other senses, internal and external, transmit the life of the world through their own vital activity, and will write upon that page the images and ideas of the things among which it lives. Hence an irresistible instinct for truth and goodness turns "the simple soul that nothing knows" upon the things of sense; and all these powers of feeling, all these childish sensations, by way of which mind and will come gradually to their awakening, need to be educated, trained, and carefully guided, otherwise the normal awakening and proper direction of these noble faculties of the spirit will be compromised and distorted. . . .

Study the child in his tender age. If you know him well you will educate him well; you will not misconceive his character; you will come to understand him, knowing when to give way and when to be firm; a naturally good disposition does not fall to the lot of all the sons of men.

Training the Mind

Train the mind of your children. Do not give them wrong ideas or wrong reasons for things; whatever their questions may be, do not answer them with evasions or untrue statements which their minds rarely accept; but take occasion from them lovingly and patiently to train their minds, which want only to open to the truth and to grasp it with the first ingenuous gropings of their reasoning and reflective powers. Who can say what many a genius may not owe to the prolonged and trustful questionings of childhood at the home fireside!

Training the Character

Train the character of your children. Correct their faults, encourage and cultivate their good qualities and co-ordinate them with that stability which will make for resolution in after life. Your children, conscious as they grow up and as they begin to think and will, that they are guided by a good parental will, constant and strong, free from violence and anger, not subject to weakness or inconsistency, will learn in time to see therein the interpreter of another and higher will, the will of God, and so they will plant in their souls the seeds of those early moral habits which fashion and sustain a character, train it to self-control in moments of crisis and to courage in the face of conflict or sacrifice, and imbue it with a deep sense of Christian duty.

Training the Heart

Train their hearts. Frequently the decision of a man's destiny, the ruin of his character, or a grave danger threatening him, may be traced to his childish years when his heart was spoiled by the fond flattery, silly fussing and foolish indulgence of misguided parents. The impressionable little heart became accustomed to see all things revolve and gravitate around it, to find all things yielding to its will and caprice, and so there took root in it that boundless egoism of which the parents themselves were later to become the first victims! . . .

Adolescence

But the day will come when the childish heart will feel new impulses stirring within it; new desires will disturb the serenity of those early years. In that time of trial, Christian mothers, remember that to train the heart means to train the will to resist the attacks of evil and the insidious temptations of passion; during that period of transition from the unconscious purity of infancy to the triumphant purity of adolescence you have a task of the highest importance to fulfill. You have to prepare your sons and daughters so that they pass with unfaltering step, like those who will pick their way among serpents, through that time of crisis and physical change; and pass through it without losing anything of the joy of innocence, preserving intact that natural instinct of modesty with which Providence has girt them as a check upon wayward passion. . . . You will keep a watchful eye on their steps; you will not suffer the whiteness of their souls to be stained and contaminated by corrupt and corrupting company; you will inspire them with a high esteem and jealous love for purity, advising them to commend themselves to the sure and motherly protection of the Immaculate Virgin. Finally, with the discretion of a mother and a teacher, and thanks to the open-hearted confidence with which you have been able to inspire your children, you will not fail to watch for and to discern the moment in which certain unspoken questions have occurred to their minds and are troubling their senses. It will then be your duty to your daughters, the father's duty to your sons, carefully and delicately to unveil the truth as far as it appears necessary, to give a prudent, true and Christian answer to those questions, and set their minds at rest. If imparted by the lips of Christian parents, at the proper time, in the proper measure and with the proper precautions, the revelation of the mysterious and marvellous laws of life will be received by them with reverence and gratitude, and will enlighten their minds with far less danger than if they learned them haphazard, from some unpleasant shock, from secret conversations, through information received from oversophisticated companions, or from clandestine reading, the more dangerous and pernicious as secrecy inflames the imagination and troubles the senses. Your words, if they are wise and discreet, will prove a safeguard and a warning in the midst of their temptations and the corruption which surround them, "because foreseen an arrow comes more slowly." . . .

The Aid of Religion

But in this great work of the Christian education of your sons and daughters you well understand that training in the home, however wise, however thorough, is not enough. It needs to be supplemented and perfected by the powerful aid of religion. From the moment of baptism the priest possesses the authority of a spiritual father and a pastor over your children, and you must co-operate with him in teaching them those first rudiments of catechism and piety which are the only basis of a solid education, and of which you, the earliest teachers of your children, ought to have a sufficient and sure knowledge. You cannot teach what you do not know yourselves. . . .

However eminent school-teachers may be in their professions they will have little success in the formation of your children without your collaboration—still less if instead of helping and lending support to their efforts you were to counteract and oppose them. What a misfortune it would be if at home your indulgence and fond weakness were to undo all that has been done at school, at catechism or in Catholic associations, to form the character and foster the piety of your children!

But—some mother may say—children are so difficult to manage nowadays! I can do nothing with that son of mine; that daughter of mine is impossible! Admittedly many boys and girls at the age of twelve or fifteen show themselves intractable. But why? Because when they were two or three years old they were allowed to do as they pleased. True, some temperaments are ungrateful and rebellious; but however unresponsive, however obstinate, he is still your child. Would you love him any the less than his brothers and sisters if he were sickly or deformed? God has given him to you; see that you do not treat him as the outcast of the family. No child is so unruly that he cannot be trained with care, patience and love; and it will rarely happen that even the stoniest and most unpromising soil will not bear some flower of submission and virtue, if only an unreasonable severity does not run the risk of exterminating the seed of good will which even the proudest soul has hidden within it. The whole education of your children would be ruined were they to discover in their parents—and their eyes are sharp enough to see—any signs of favoritism, undue preferences or antipathies in regard to any of them. For your own good and for the good of the family it must be clear that, whether you use measured severity or give encouragement and caresses, you have an equal love for all, a love which makes no distinction save for the correction of evil or for the encouragement of good. Have you not received them all equally from God? . . .

Conclusion

What a majestic figure is that of the mother in the home as she fulfills her destiny at the cradle side, the nurse and teacher of her little ones! Hers is truly a task full of labour, and We should be tempted to deem her unequal to it were it not for the grace of God which is ever at hand to enlighten, direct and sustain her in her daily anxieties and toil; were it not, too, for those other educators, mother-like in spirit and energy, whom she calls to aid her in the formation of these youthful souls.

Parents' Duty to Children

ST. AUGUSTINE

The blessing of children involves the duty of the married couple to receive them with love, to look after their temporal wants with solicitude, and to educate them with religious care. . . . Such is the law of marriage, which sets off the glory of fecundity while it puts a brake to the shameful disorder of incontinence.

(Translated by J. A. O'Brien)

Papal Pronouncements on the Education and Training of Children

In the first place the Church's mission of education is in wonderful agreement with that of the family, for both proceed from God, and in a remarkably similar manner. God directly communicates to the family, in the natural order, fecundity, which is the principle of life, and hence also the principle of education to life, together with authority, the principle of order.

The Angelic Doctor [St. Thomas Aquinas] with his wonted clearness of thought and precision of style says: "The father according to the flesh has in a particular way a share in that principle which in a manner universal is found in God. . . . The father is the principle of generation, of education and discipline and of everything that bears upon the perfecting of human life."

The family therefore holds directly from the Creator the mission and hence the right to educate the offspring, a right inalienable because inseparably joined to a strict obligation, a right anterior to any right whatever of civil society and of the state, and therefore inviolable on the part of any power on earth.

That this right is inviolable St. Thomas proves as follows: "The child is naturally something of the father . . . so by natural right the child, before reaching the use of reason, is under the father's care. Hence it would be contrary to natural justice if the child, before the use of reason, were removed from the care of its parents, or if any disposition were made concerning him against the will of the parents." And as this duty on the part of the parents continues up to the time when the child is in a position to provide for himself, this same inviolable parental right of education also endures. "Nature intends not merely the generation of the offspring, but also its development and progress to the perfection of man considered as man, that is, to the state of virtue," says the same St. Thomas.

The wisdom of the Church in this matter is expressed with precision and clearness in the Codex of Canon Law: "Parents are under a grave obligation to see to the religious and moral education of their children, as well as to their physical and civic training, as far as they can, and moreover to provide for their temporal well-being."

On this point the common sense of mankind is in such complete accord, that they would be in open contradiction with it who dared maintain that the children belong to the State before they belong to the family, and that the state has an absolute right over their education. Untenable is the reason they deduce, namely that man is born a citizen and hence belongs primarily to the State, not bearing in mind that before being a citizen man must exist; and existence does not come from the state, but from the parents, as Leo XIII wisely declared: "The children are something of the father, and as it were an extension of the person of the father. To be perfectly accurate, they enter into and become part of civil society, not directly by themselves, but through the family in which they were born. . . . And therefore the father's power is of such a nature that it cannot be destroyed or absorbed by the state; for it has the same origin as human life itself."

Pius XI

It . . . belongs to the State to protect the rights of the child itself when the parents are found wanting either physically or morally in this respect, whether by default, incapacity, or misconduct, since, as has been shown, their right to educate is not an absolute and despotic one, but is dependent on the natural and divine law, and therefore subject alike to the authority and jurisdiction of the Church, and to the vigilance and administrative care of the state in view of the common good. Besides, the family is not a perfect society, that is, it has not in itself all the means necessary for its full development. In such cases, exceptional no doubt, the state does not put itself in the place of the family, but merely supplies deficiencies, and provides suitable means, always in conformity with the natural rights of the child and the supernatural rights of the Church.

Pius XI

According to the divine plan parents are the first educators of their own children. It is well nevertheless to recognize the fact that under actual conditions of life the necessary preoccupation of making a living makes the fulfillment of this essential duty difficult.

Pius XII

Families have certain rights and liberties which the State must always protect; which it must never violate or sacrifice to a pretended common good. We have in mind, to cite a few examples, the right to honor and to a good reputation, the right and the freedom to worship the true God, the inherently primary right of parents over their children and their children's education.

Pius XII

Instinct endows even irrational animals with affection for their young. Hence it should not be necessary to teach affection to newlyweds and future Christian parents. It could, none the less, come about that excessive severity or a lack of understanding would raise a sort of barrier between the hearts of the children and those of their parents. St. Paul said: "To the weak I became weak. . . . I became all things to all men, that I might save all." It is a great good quality to know how to become little with the little, children with the children, without compromising paternal or maternal authority in so doing.

Pius XII

As regards family life, it is of the highest importance that the offspring of Christian marriages should be thoroughly instructed in the precepts of religion; and that the various studies by which youth is fitted for the world should be joined with that of religion. To divorce these is to wish that youth should be neutral as regards its duties to God; a system of education in itself fallacious, and particularly fatal in tender years, for it opens the door to atheism, and closes it on religion. Christian parents must therefore be careful that their children receive religious instruction as soon as they are capable of understanding it; and that nothing may, in the schools they attend, blemish their faith or their morals. Both the natural and the divine law impose this duty on them, nor can parents on any ground whatever be freed from this obligation.

Leo XIII

The souls of children given to their parents by God and consecrated in Baptism with the royal character of Christ, are a sacred charge over which watches the jealous love of God. The same Christ Who pronounced the words "Suffer little children to come to me" has threatened, for all His mercy and goodness, with fearful evils, those who give scandal to those so dear to His Heart.

Pius XII

By educating your children to a life that is deeply and courageously Christian, you will give them and yourself the best guarantee of a happy life in this world and of a happy reunion in the next.

Pius XII

Keep before the eyes of the child, from its early years, the commandments of God and accustom it to observe them. The youth of today no less than of former days is prepared and is ready to do good and to serve God, but it must be educated to do so.

Pius XII

Immoderate pursuit of pleasure and lack of moral discipline likewise seek to invade even the ranks of Catholic youth. . . . Counteract this with the education of self-control, of sacrifice and renunciation, beginning with smaller things and gradually going on to greater ones; promote education of fidelity in fulfillment of one's duties, of sincerity, serenity and purity, especially in the years of development into maturity. . . . Try to arouse and mold a sense of responsibility and to remind them that liberty is not the only one among all the human values, although it is numbered among the foremost, but that it has its limits, intrinsic in the unescapable norms of decency and extrinsic in the correlative rights of others, both as regards the rights of each one in particular as well as the rights of society in general.

Pius XII

Counteract the desire for luxury and pleasure with an education in frankness and simplicity! Youth must learn again to control itself and face privations. It must not happen that youth should burden parents with requests that parents cannot satisfy.

Pius XII

In an ideal home the parents, like Tobias and Sara, beg of God a numerous posterity "in which Thy name may be blessed forever" and receive it as a gift from heaven and a precious trust. They strive to instill into their children from their early years a holy fear of God, and true Christian piety; they foster a tender devotion to Jesus, the Blessed Sacrament, and the Immaculate Virgin; they teach respect and veneration for holy places and persons. In such a home the children see in their parents a model of an upright, industrious, and pious life; they see their parents holily loving each other in our Lord, see them approach the holy sacraments frequently and not only obey the laws of the Church concerning abstinence and fasting, but observe the spirit of voluntary Christian mortification; they see them pray at home, gathering round them all the family, that common prayer may rise more acceptably to heaven; they find them compassionate toward the distress of others and see them divide with the poor the much or the little they possess.

Pius XI

Religious Instructions for Children

ST. JOHN CHRYSOSTOM

Let no one tell me that our children ought not to be occupied with these [religious] things; they ought not only to be occupied with them, but to be zealous about them only. And although on account of your infirmity I do not assert this, nor take them away from their worldly learning, just as I do not draw you either from your civil business; yet of these seven days I claim that you dedicate one to the common Lord of us all. For is it not strange that we should bid our domestics slave for us all their time, and ourselves apportion not even a little of our leisure to God; and this too when all our service adds nothing to Him (for the Godhead is incapable of want) but turns out to our own advantage? And yet when you take your children into the theatres, you allege neither their mathematical lessons, nor anything of the kind; but if it be required to gain or collect anything spiritual, you call the matter a waste of time. And how shall you not anger God, if you find leisure and assign a season for everything else, and yet think it a troublesome and unseasonable thing for your children to take in hand what relates to Him?

Do not so, brethren, do not so. It is this very age that most of all needs the hearing these things; for from its tenderness it readily stores up what is said; and what children hear is impressed as a seal on the wax of their minds.

(Translator Anonymous)

The Child: Citizen of Two Worlds

CATHOLIC BISHOPS OF THE UNITED STATES
(1950)

The child must be seen whole and entire. He must be seen as a citizen of two worlds. He belongs to this world surely, but his first and highest allegiance is to the kingdom of God. From his earliest years he must be taught that his chief significance comes from the fact that he is created by God and is destined for life with God in Eternity.

The child's prospects for fulfilling this great hope which God has reposed in him must be viewed realistically. He will come to maturity in a society where social, moral, intellectual and spiritual values are everywhere disintegrating. In such a society, he will urgently need the integrating force of religion as taught by Christ. Such a force will give him a complete and rational meaning for his existence.

First of all, it will arouse in him a consciousness of God and of eternity. His vision will be opened out upon a supernatural world revealed by faith which differs from the world of nature his senses reveal. Thus he will discover a higher life than this daily one and a brighter world than that he sees. Secondly, it will give him a continuing purpose in life, for it will teach him that he was made to know, love and serve God in this world as the condition for meriting eternal happiness. Thirdly, it will induce in him a deep sense of responsibility for those rights and obligations he possesses by reason of his citizenship in heaven as well as on earth. Finally, religion will challenge him to sanctify whatever walk of life he chooses and to seek and accept the Will of God in whatever way it may be manifested. Thus, as a principle of integration, religion will help the child to develop a *sense of God, a sense of direction, a sense of responsibility and a sense of mission* in this life.

The child is not complete in himself. He will find his completion only in his life with God; and that life must begin here on earth. Parents, therefore, should make early provision for their child's growth in God. This is not something to be postponed for nurture by school authorities. It must begin in the home through simple and prayerful practices. . . .

Only two courses are open to the child—either he will be God-centered or self-centered. He is made and destined for God, but he bears in his nature the lingering effects of original sin which incline him to seek the satisfaction of every selfish whim. To correct this bend in his will so that God, rather than self, will occupy the center of his life is one of the most challenging tasks facing parents.

In meeting this challenge, let parents make use of the strong, supernatural motivation which can be drawn from the life of Christ. Let them encourage the imitation of Him, particularly in His obedience, patience and thoughtfulness of others; and let them foster the emulation of that spirit of unselfish giving so characteristic of Christ. This can be done in many practical ways, particularly through providing the child with frequent opportunities for making acts of self-denial in the home. If he is taught to deny his selfish whims for the sake of Christ, he will not only discover a supernatural motive for his actions, but he will learn to give God that central place in his affections which God must occupy if the child is to come to his full spiritual stature.

Little point would be served in intensifying the child's awareness of God during his pre-school years, if later his schooling were to rob him of that. That child's education during school years should be of a piece with his education at home. . . .

When it is impossible for parents to take advantage of the God-centered education which Catholic schools offer, they have a grave obligation to provide for their child's religious instruction in some other way. At least they must see that their children attend Catechism classes and vacation schools and receive the benefit of other activities of the Confraternity of Christian Doctrine. . . .

When we speak of parents' responsibilities, it should be remembered that they do not devolve entirely upon the mother. The father has his responsibilities, too, and he must not shirk them. It is not enough for him to provide the material means of support for the family. He also has the obligation to identify himself with the interests and activities of his child. If the full benefits of parental direction are to be reaped by the child, such direction should include that steadying and stabilizing influence which it is the father's duty to exert.

Fathers and mothers have a natural competence to instruct their children with regard to sex. False modesty should not deter them from doing their duty in this regard. Sex is one of God's endowments. It should not be ignored or treated as something bad. If sex instruction is properly carried on in the home, a deep reverence will be developed in the child and he will be spared the shameful inferences which he often makes when he is left to himself to find out about sex. . . . Sex is more than a biological function. It is bound up with the sacredness and uniqueness of the human personality. It can be fully and properly appreciated only within a religious and moral context. If treated otherwise, the child will see it apart from the controlling purpose of his life, which is service to God. . . .

No point is urged with greater insistency by religion than the accountability of each individual before God. It is the duty of parents to see to it that their child develops a deep sense of personal responsibility; learning at the earliest possible period that he is accountable to God for his thoughts, his words and his actions. His home training must reinforce this teaching in every practical way. . . . He must be made to see that each member of the family has a part to play in the service of God by carrying out an assigned role.

St. Thomas More Instructs the Tutor of His Children

Let them put virtue in the first place, learning in the second, and esteem most in their studies whatever teaches them piety towards God, charity to all, and Christian humility in themselves. . . .

Warn my children to avoid the precipices of pride and to walk in the pleasant meadows of modesty; not to be dazzled by the sight of gold, not to sigh for those things which they mistakenly admire in others; not to think more of themselves for the possession of gaudy trappings, nor less for the want of them; not to spoil by neglect the beauty that nature has given them, nor to heighten it by artifice.

I do desire that you, and their mother and all their friends, would sing this song to them, and knock or repeat it into their heads, that vain glory is a despicable thing, and that there is nothing more sublime than the humble modesty so often praised by Christ. . . .

And in a letter to his daughter Margaret, St. Thomas More said:

"I assure you that, rather than allow my children to be idle, I would make a sacrifice of wealth and bid adieu to other cares and business, to attend to my family, amongst whom none is more dear to me than yourself, my beloved daughter."

Present-Day Errors in Child Training

ROBERT P. ODENWALD, M.D.

Training of a child has two objectives, namely, the development of his potential abilities and personality, and development of an awareness of his own place in the community and his responsibilities as a member of that community. . . . According as his training is good or bad, according as its prepares him to meet the problems of life, the child approaches or fails to attain an ideal of Christian adulthood. How successful his adulthood will be is dependent less upon his inherent tendencies than upon the mold into which his parents cast the tender, impressionable infant and child. . . .

Most of the errors in child training lie within two categories—those arising from faulty parent-child relationships and those coming from unhappy father-mother relationships. The autocratic parent, the laissez-faire or disinterested parent, the inconsistent parent, the over-protective parent—all fail to establish the feeling of being loved so necessary in developing the sense of security required in making a happy child.

The *easy-going or disinterested parents* permit the youngster to do as he pleases, when and where he pleases, believing or hoping that a proper self-development will result. These parents sometimes are so anxious to avoid arousing an antagonism on the part of the child that they anticipate every wish and satisfy every whim. This over-solicitude results in a child who considers his own welfare of paramount importance, and the parents become slaves to him.

The *inconsistent parents*, swayed by emotions, alternately pet and punish the child, condemning acts one day which they approved or applauded perhaps the day before. These children lose confidence, are puzzled and uncertain in actions. They lose their way.

The *over-protective parents* shield the child from every danger, solve every problem that presents itself. The child is provided with a constant crutch, so that he never stands alone. He develops no initiative; he never loses his dependence upon his parents or upon another's judgment.

The *repressed parents* because of their own frustrations and maladjustment fail to give the child the assurance and close contact of love which he so requires. He feels unwanted, unloved and insecure and, in turn, becomes secretive, unresponsive and depressed. . . .

Then there is the *autocratic parent*. His theory is that of the earlier centuries, that man is born into evil and only strict discipline can crush out the evil in the child. Neighbors and friends may give lavish praise to the parent of a docile child who gives robot-like unquestioning obedience to every command, but do not realize that back of this slavish docility may lie a rebellious hostility toward the parent and toward the whole world, a hostility that may develop into an offensive aggression. All initiative may be crushed in the child, but resentment may express itself at a later time in shocking antisocial acts. . . .

This brings up the old question of how much *authority* shall be exercised in rearing a child. Truly, the child is receptive to suggestion, but often in his sturdy individualism he goes contrary to suggestion just to express that individualism, or "to show off." He must recognize authority, moral, social and legal, if he is to grow in appreciation of the rights of others, if he is to acquire the power of self-government, if he is to become a good citizen. . . . Parents are the first court of authority to the child. Through his obedience he is prepared to take his useful place in society or in his disobedience or in lack of authoritive direction, he becomes set in patterns of defiance and expresses his hostility in antisocial acts. Defiant of authority and social laws the delinquent may finally reach the juvenile court, to be judged and sentenced to corrective measures.

In addition to the question of authority comes the question of *discipline* required to maintain that authority. . . .

Discipline should be used by those who by virtue of their maturity and experience, are invested with authority; once proper authority has been set up and recognized by the child, he must be taught to respect it. Where there is no respect for authority, anarchy will inevitably exist. Actually, the child leans on adult authority, so that when it is exercised properly he does not resent its presence. As in all things, authority can be detrimental in unscrupulous hands. Discipline becomes easy when there is a mutual understanding between adults and children. Discipline is not fear which has an inhibiting effect upon the child. Always teach love before you give punishment. Put yourself in the place of the child and only then consider the value and limits of punishment.

How far punishment shall go, whether it is of a physical nature or consists of deprivation of desired privileges or awards, depends upon the nature of the child himself. Each child must be considered and treated as an individual in every step of his training. No rule can be established that is applicable to all children. . . . A normal development demands mutual love and understanding between parent and child, a growing respect and appreciation for each other's individuality and personality. From such a concept the child gains a respect for the rights of other individuals in the community and the world at large. . . .

We may pause for a moment to point out a very common error in the home created by the *over-fastidiousness* of the mother with a desire to have an *orderly house and cleanly children*. Children of these mothers prefer to play in the homes of other children because at home they must not have toys lying around, they must not disturb the furniture or climb on it, they must make no litter. These mothers spend so much time and effort keeping the house and children immaculate that they have none left for playing with the children, for taking them out, or for sitting down to listen to their questions and fanciful stories. Just as children are uncomfortable in overly neat homes, so are they distressed by having to be always neat in their appearance. Freedom to play in dirt, to get thoroughly dirty in face, hands and clothing is an important step and happy privilege in the development of an autonomous human being. . . .

The affectionate, trusting parent-child relationship can be no more important in the training of the child than is the *mother-*

father relationship. When there is bickering between parents or marital incompatibility in the home, the child is upset in his loyalty; he sides first with one and then with another. The youngster's emotions are strained in two directions at once and he is emotionally torn apart. Said a 10-year-old boy, "I'd rather be here in the Detention Home than live with my parents." His home was made so unhappy by the parental quarrels that he preferred to sleep out at night and beg his food. An emotion-provoking relationship with the parents can produce a lonely, frustrated child. He may become a truant and a delinquent.

There was a time when families knew the security founded on love—love of God, of one's self respect, of the family and of the neighbors in the Theocentric (God-centered) rural culture of that time. Families worked, played and prayed together. Most of the needs of the family were filled within the confines of the family, provided on the homestead or on the farm. Each family member contributed to the whole. Each child was an asset, welcomed on arrival and given his proper place in the family structure. The mother remained in the home as bearer, rearer and educator of the children. From their mothers girls acquired a spiritual security in their future role as potential mothers and learned the art of "mothering."

The onslaughts of secularism and individualism inevitably brought a change in that rural culture to one of urban individualism, with a rise of the evils of greed, indifference to one's neighbors and the concept of children as liabilities. Selfishness replaced selflessness, love depreciated in concept and value. With the basic need for love essentially unfulfilled, frustration followed. The denials suffered by the parents were visited upon the children. . . .

I need not raise the question, how important and necessary a role *love* plays in the training of the child. It needs *real loving.* If love is absent, we have all the crucial factors in development of maladjustment. These neurotic children need affection and appreciation to be able to survive. However, no one can give love who has not received love. The lack of love in a child becomes paramount in an adult.

The greatest preventative of poor training in children is the establishment of a love relationship of father-mother-child. What is the nature of love? It is practically impossible to give a good description of love—however, I venture to offer here a paraphrase of St. Paul in his first letter to the Corinthians, XIII chapter. "Love is patient, is kind. Love envieth not, dealeth not perversely, is not puffed up, is not ambitious, seeketh not its own, is not provoked to anger, thinketh no evil, rejoiceth not in iniquity, but rejoiceth with the truth; beareth all things, believeth all things, hopest all things, endureth all things." (Corinthians I:XIII)

Finally, the greatest error in the rearing of children today is the neglect of proper religious training by the parent. If religion is left out of the early training of the child, the one compelling motive for continuous good behavior is omitted. A child has a natural susceptibility to religious ideas when they are presented against a background of affectionate care. Teaching a child to pray gives him his first realization of his dependence upon a will higher than his own. He learns very early that the true basis for doing or not doing certain acts is moral and religious. . . . Having an inherent tendency to revere a higher Being, children who have been instructed in the power and love of God will turn to that abiding Fatherhood in their times of doubt and need when the love of their own parents has failed them. . . .

The security of love—the shared parent-child love and particularly the love for the divine Father—this must be the basis of child training today and tomorrow.

A Lesson from the Eagle

SISTER M. TERESA GERTRUDE, O.S.B.

We can learn from the world of the eagle. Underneath the soft down which lines the eagle's nest there is a layer of brambles and thorns. If the eaglet refuses to learn to fly or refuses to go for its food when it is able to do so, the mother bird pulls out the soft down and lets the eaglet rest on the thorns. It immediately changes its attitude towards its part in the duties of life. Will anyone say that the mother eagle is harsh? Will the eaglet be happier in taking its place in the activities of its species or in remaining dependent?

Sometimes individualism, clinging to babyhood, is fostered by the mother who gets what she calls "maternal satisfaction" in waiting on this youth and spoiling him. She is merely dramatizing herself. She will not be proud of that dependent child when he is 17 or 18 years of age, and what is more, he will blame her for his own dissatisfaction with life.

There Is No Substitute for Parents

THE REV. JOHN L. THOMAS, S.J.

The personal obligation of parents to instruct and train their children in religious life remains as absolute as ever. This training, in the words of Pius XII, "must start with the cradle." Parents should see in the school an indispensable aid, but only an aid, in carrying out their primary obligation of developing the future "citizens of two worlds." However, several recent surveys . . . indicate that many children receive almost no religious instruction and training in the home. . . .

Various explanations of this parental neglect have been offered. Some point out that the Catholic parent is suffering from the same inferiority complex in regard to education as is the average American parent. No doubt, there are parents who are quite aware of their obligations but feel they are incapable of doing the job. Others may argue that the pre-school child is too young to understand. Some may contend that in spite of shorter hours of work and the addition of numerous labor-saving gadgets in the home, modern parents are too busy "about many things" to have time to instruct their children. All of these explanations may have some weight, but the obligation of parents to personally supervise the religious instruction and training of their children remains. Catholic parents may not sit back complacently merely because they support parochial schools and send their children to them.

The objection is sometimes raised that the Catholic school is eminently fitted to handle the entire religious training of children. The religious teacher is more skilled in teaching than is the average parent. Why not entrust the schools with the entire religious training of children? This objection utterly misconceives the meaning of religion in life. Religion is more than habit and practice. It is understanding life and living life in terms of Christ's teaching and the supernatural. This training cannot be confined to the classroom. It implies a basic ordering of life which cannot be postponed until the child reaches first grade. Further, to confine religion to the classroom is to cut it off from life, thus laying the foundation for the false view that "business is business" and moral precepts apply only in specific areas of living or on Sundays. . . .

If we wait until the child reaches school age in order to start religious training, the child is deprived of religious influences during his most formative years. The child starts learning as soon as it is born. Never is this learning process more active and more enduring than in the early formative years of life. . . .

The school should be a continuation of the training in the home. Successful teaching in the school must build on previous training in the family and on training going on in the home every day. . . .

Finally, to confine religious training primarily to the classroom leads to a dangerous confusion of religion and school in the child's mind. This confusion may have seriously harmful effects once the child leaves the environment of the school. The child comes to identify the precepts of religion with the rules and regulations of the school. He readily falls into the habit of attending Mass and fulfilling other religious obligations only because it is demanded by the school. Some children develop a positive distaste for this regimentation and refuse to practice their religion faithfully once they are away from school. More commonly, children acquire highly superficial views of religion and religious practices since the service of God is not stressed by their parents, whom they love and admire, but is imposed by "outsiders," whose motives they may misunderstand and sometimes distrust.

But there are even more cogent reasons why parents should personally initiate and continue the religious instruction and training of their children. The whole problem of parental control and guidance is involved here. . . .

Modern parents tell us that they no longer have control over their children. They say that their children refuse to obey them. We hear the complaint, "They simply won't listen to what we tell them! Every time we try to guide them or supervise their actions they call us 'old-fashioned' and point to the 'modern' parents of their companions who don't share our 'narrow ideas.' " . . .

Why have some parents lost control over their children? The answer is that they have failed to lay the foundations for that control from the child's earliest years. Parents cannot expect to step into the role of moral protector and guide for their child at puberty if they have not fulfilled that role in the child's life from the cradle. Parent-child relationships have to be worked at. They do not spring up spontaneously through the development of some mysterious kind of instinct. If the ten-year-old or fifteen-year-old child thinks of his parents as those who know best, or, at least, as those who should be obeyed, it will be because they have played this role in his life from infancy. In other words, parents will be accepted as the moral directors and guides of their children only if it is they who have introduced the child to God, have taught him his first prayers, have shown him what is right and wrong, have day by day, as the years go by, lovingly yet firmly, taught him to distinguish good from evil.

When the child starts school, parental roles change somewhat. They must encourage him by showing an active interest in his progress. At this time, both parents must realize that their child is constantly developing and meeting new experiences. He is seeking answers to himself and to the world around him. Their role is to act as interpreters for the child as his world grows more complex and extensive. They will explain his developing body to him, the meaning of the difference between boys and girls, where life comes from, how God runs His world. Their explanations will be graded according to the advance of the child, slowly, one step at a time, giving him at each stage the kind of answer he is capable of understanding.

By the time the child reaches puberty and the experience of new powers, he is ready for the advance. His parents have already taught him much of their meaning and he confidently turns to them for the rest. As his experience broadens and he encounters conflicting values and practices, he will not find it strange or unnatural if his parents step in and offer guidance, if they lay down seemingly restrictive rules which he must follow. Since they have been identified as his moral guides and teachers from the cradle, he does not find their care for his conduct unreasonable now. There will be youth's normal desire for independence and self-assertion, of course, but this will develop within the framework of parental respect rather than revolt.

The Role of the Father in the Christian Home

THE REV. GREGORY SMITH, O.CARM.

Christ was the Master. He was for His Father's great family a Teacher sent from God. He taught by what He said, by what He did, and by what He was. So in the Christian family the father speaks with authority given to him by God. . . .

As a teacher should, the father speaks with authority. "My father said—" is the last word that clinches any childhood argument. Because his children are his faithful flock, who will believe as gospel truth whatever he says, deceit is foreign to the lips of a father. This does not mean that dad has to be a walking encyclopedia or a university graduate. It does mean, however, that he should supplement the teaching grace that comes to him in the sacrament of matrimony by frequent recourse to the word of truth in Sacred Scripture. Dad, if he wants to faithfully fulfill his teaching office, should steep himself in the Gospel of Christ. Christ is pivotal in the Christian family. Mother and children will be brought to know Him better and love Him more, when dad has known and loved before them. That family problem, however complicated, is rare indeed, that will not give way to swift solution before the simple wisdom and prudent counsel of the Holy Gospel. The New Testament is the first handbook of the Christian Father.

But the words of the father are the very least tools of his teaching. What dad does speaks much louder than any word he says. Children are by nature imitative. They walk like their parents. They talk like them. They assume the same postures; they have the same reactions, the same scale of values as mother and dad. If they see dad at prayer in the family prayer corner; if they see in him a cheerful willingness to share mother's burdens; if they go with him to visit the sick; if dad, after a hard day's work kneels erect without support during the family evening prayer; if they find in their father a deep concern for the things of God, they are without a word taught weighty lessons of the Christian life. "Like father, like son" is no empty adage. Reverence witnessed in the father is piety begotten in the son. Sobriety practiced by the father is temperance born in the son. The Christian life lived by the father is Christ raised up in his son. He, then, is the best Christian father, who best shows forth Christ in his life. . . .

It is the father's task to school his family in the spirit of sacrifice so essential to the Christian calling. It is the father's privilege to whet youthful appetites, to inspire juvenile ideals to enkindle even to white heat young enthusiasm for the salvation of the world, for nations yet to be conquered for Christ. A father can so make his home fit for the greatest blessing that can come to his house: that God should find in his house instruments for the salvation of the world; that children of his loins should be called to share intimately the work of Christ as lay apostles, as religious missionaries, as, greater than all else, priests of the altar of God.

It is the part of the Christian father always to bear himself as becomes the natural leader of the family. Always hearing the wise counsel of his partner in Christ, constantly considering the welfare of the flock given into his care it is [the duty] of the father of the family to assume the initiative in all things that pertain to the welfare, both spiritual and temporal, of his wife and children. The father is the head of the family. But the family is not for the father, rather the father is for the family. . . .

In the midst of his family the Christian father is placed as an instrument of divine grace. He calls the family together for prayer. He leads in the family spiritual reading. He blesses his children with the powerful paternal blessing of the Christian Father. . . . When there are difficulties the Christian father is convinced with deep conviction that at every time and in every situation grace will be given to find the Christian solution to problems of his family.

Rich is the heritage and high the office of the father in the Christian home. To this we add, great is the responsibility of Christian fathers in our times. Only from their homes can we hope for a generation of young men and women who are dyed-in-the-wool Christian, steeped in the faith which alone is the "victory that overcometh the world." (I Jn. 5:4)

Teaching Children to Love Their Neighbor

EILEEN NUTTING

The hardest thing for the mother to get across to her children, I think, is love of neighbor, especially when that neighbor is a bossy big sister or a tormenting younger brother. The little folks love their parents, and they often love their next-door neighbors and the friends who come to visit, but they'll be darned if they will love the brothers and sisters of their own household—those pests who are forever in their hair, breaking toys, telling tales, causing trouble from dawn to dark. Yet to teach them to do what the second great commandment prescribes is next in importance to teaching them to know, love and serve God. It must be done, and, fears to the contrary, it *is* done, and usually very successfully.

In spite of the constant bickering that goes on among the children in most families, it is astonishing when one realizes the love that is growing there, too. And it is real love. You love your brother and sister in spite of the many failings you know they possess. Your friends are loved dearly, but close as you may be to them you seldom see them in the morning before they have had a cup of coffee. The early morning encounter takes place daily in the family. It is sandpaper against rough wood and tortures your nerves. Agony though it is, it serves a useful purpose. Right in the home, where all this construction should be done, the rough edges are rubbed off and the corners rounded. The children may think that they despise one another, but a short separation or a common foe often shows the depth of their love.

This is natural love. It is a mother's job to nurture it and supernaturalize it and help in making it grow to embrace all men. The method is example. If the child can say "Mother is kind," that is better than "Mother is smart," or "pretty," or "clever," or "a good cook." It is one of the nicest things a child can say about his mother, and it is often one of the hardest things to be. Just to speak kindly is an effort we find it hard to make, sometimes, merely for the family. Have you ever noticed a sudden change in your voice when you have been lecturing the children and then answer the phone? That "Hello" seems to come from another world. If we could always be polite at home!

The love of our neighbor cannot take holidays, nor exclude any one of God's people. We must show love for the clerks in the store, bus drivers, the children who come to play with ours. Negroes, Protestants, Jews, the driver of the "other car"—and in them all we must see Christ and show Christ to our children.

Love is shown in word and deed. The mother cannot fail to give the cup of cold water, for her own soul's salvation as well as for the training of her children. In fact, to get the idea across to the young fry, she had better make it a glass of iced lemonade, and then work on the toddlers to get them to give up half their bunch of grapes in love of their neighbor for love of Him. Then she has really done something.

After he has shared with his neighbor, have you ever noticed how a child will pray for that person? By that time the youngster feels that he has a vested interest, and he will go all out in his petition.

Teaching Honesty in the Home
THE MOST REV. EDWIN V. O'HARA

An ingenious Belgian writer has estimated that the average child in his first fifteen years of life has spent 1,000 hours in church, 9,000 hours in school and 50,000 waking hours at home; five times as many hours at home as in church and school combined. "For fifty families," he continues, "there are one pastor, two school teachers and a hundred parents, or thirty times more educators on the family staff than on the combined church and school staff." Multiplying the number of each staff by the number of hours during which they influence the children, we get the following amazing statement of the relative influence of these three agencies expressed in terms of teacher-hours:

For the church, one pastor face-to-face with the children for 1,000 hours—1,000 teacher-hours. .

For the school, two teachers face-to-face with the children for 9,000 hours—18,000 teacher-hours.

For the home, 100 parents face to face with the children for 50,000 hours—5,000,000 teacher hours [if both parents were home all the time].

It is not surprising that the influence of the home is far more enduring than that of church or school. And its influence would be vastly greater even than it now is if parents were better trained for their duties as educators. Much is being done to improve the professional training of pastors and schoolteachers. There is urgent need for the professional training of Christian parent-educators.

In considering the teaching of honesty in the home, we must as in all other teaching have regard to the age of the child. Honesty is to be inculcated, dishonesty is to be repudiated at all ages. Lowell wrote:

"In vain we call old motives fudge
And bend our conscience to our dealing;
The Ten Commandments do not budge
And stealing will continue stealing."

The principles are timeless, but in accordance with sound educational practices it is necessary to fit the instruction to the age of the child.

With the preschool child as with older children, truth in speech and regard for the property of others will depend more on example than precept. Fibbing, putting the blame on other children, monopolizing or injuring the toys of other children—these childish examples of dishonesty easily turn into habits that will endure into adult life unless parents are both watchful and firm in discouraging their earliest appearance.

In elementary school life the sacraments of Penance and the Holy Eucharist exert a profound influence and provide the most powerful aids for the development of high standards of honesty. During this period the child is peculiarly susceptible to scandal by seeing principles of honesty lauded in public but neglected or repudiated in family experience.

In the high school age, the hero worship which characterizes youth should lead the family to bring into the home circle neighbors of strict principles of honor and honesty, and to provide, in family reading, biographies of men and women who reflect the same qualities—above all, the lives of the saints.

Teaching Citizenship in the Home

J. FRANCIS MORONEY

There is no reason why the home and the family should not assume greater responsibility in the development of intelligent Christian citizenship, nor is there any reason why that task should be left entirely to the public or private school. . . . The difficulty is that with the increase in the complexities of modern life we have gradually lost sight of the importance of the home as the *first* school of citizenship. . . .

There is a part which the parent *must* play personally in the education of the child, and which he must not shirk or delegate to others if we are even to approximate the ideal of Christian teaching. And this program is bound up intimately with the education of the child for effective Christian citizenship. In fact the words "Christian citizenship" imply a recognition of certain values to which the public school is unable to give formal recognition. To the Christian, and especially to the Catholic, patriotism is not simply a matter of choice; it is a matter of conscience. Obedience to lawful secular authority is based upon the religious principle that all authority comes from God, and that in honoring and respecting those who have been placed over us we are honoring the Supreme Being from Whom all authority emanates. . . .

The parent, then, who insists upon obedience to superiors, respect for authority, deference to the rights of others, and who makes these virtues a part of the normal, accepted routine of the home, is not only discharging a moral obligation—he is also performing a patriotic duty.

But it is not enough to be satisfied with the development of these general virtues, which after all are but indirectly related to the subject of citizenship. There are countless opportunities in the well-ordered home directly to teach love of country, and directly to bring to the attention of the child some of the duties and responsibilities which membership in a democracy implies. For example, why is it not possible to guide more of the conversation in the family circle into channels which will develop interest in and discussion about topics relating to citizenship? There are literally hundreds of subjects which readily suggest themselves. The meaning and advantages of democracy, religious freedom, freedom of speech and of the press, the peculiar framework of our national and state governments, the reasons why we respect and reverence our Constitution, are but a few of the themes which need not be left to the schools but which can provide material for lively and instructive discussion of Christian citizenship in the home. . . .

Many beautifully illustrated juvenile books are now available to help tell the story of American democracy. The various patriotic holidays afford an excellent opportunity to read to the family group a bit of the history and romance connected with their observance. The simple ritual of putting up the flag on these days, in addition to instilling love and respect for the flag, can be made a lesson in citizenship and can help to impress youthful minds with the importance of the day.

Then again the practical operation of local government can furnish a rich field for investigation and study. I know a man who frequently takes his young son with him to the polls on election day and then enjoys answering the questions which are aroused by that practical lesson in one of the duties of citizenship.

These practical helps, however, are only secondary to the great lesson which the parent must teach by example. One of the most powerful influences upon the mind of the child is the attitude of the parents themselves toward their government. If parents adopt a cynical view of public institutions, if they are carping and destructive in their criticism of the machinery of government, if all public officials are indiscriminately labeled as dishonest politicians, it is not long before this frame of mind is absorbed by the child, and he begins life with a bias that makes him an easy prey to anti-social and subversive forces.

The world today is indeed in a sorry plight. What the years will bring we do not know; the outlook remains shrouded in uncertainty. For us it would appear that American democracy, with all its imperfections, offers the only material hope in a demented world. It is therefore our duty to teach our children to respect its principles and to honor its institutions. We have seen in some governments the fruits of a philosophy which denies to parents the right to say what kind of education their children shall receive. That philosophy finds repudiation in the natural law, in the teachings of the Church and in the decisions of our highest courts. Secure, then, in the knowledge that they live under a Constitution which protects them in the free exercise of their sacred parental rights, let Catholics take seriously their civic and religious duties in the education of their children, and make their homes real schools of Christian citizenship.

The Young Patriarchs

JOSEPH A. BREIG

A father is a patriarch. This may seem a startling statement, but it's an elementary truth. Each father is the founder of a family. For all he knows, that family may go on in unbroken line to the end of time. Each father, in this sense, is another Adam. He is the beginning of a new and unpredictable section of the human race. From his section new nations may grow. By his section continents may be civilized or recivilized in the future.

Each father is also, if he be a godly man, another Abraham. He is, or ought to be, the head of a great spiritual tribe. He should hand down benedictions from century to century. For the mercy of God is from generation to generation upon those who fear Him and love Him; and it may well be that a good father will walk about astonished for all eternity, stunned with the realization that he has helped save countless souls.

This is no mere flight of fancy. It only sounds like a flight of fancy because it is a much neglected fact. The fact is, to become personal about it, that five human beings, five immortal souls, have been handed over to a man named Brieg, and to his wife. They are to co-operate with God in the rearing of the five. Breig and his wife are to form the five so that they are children of God, and not children of the devil.

The plain fact is that these children came to the Breigs helpless and malleable. They came utterly dependent—dependent for their very lives. They were blank slates to be written upon; they were mirrors to reflect what they experienced. Later they would have minds and wills of their own; but by that time their characters, in considerable part, would have been formed.

What lies in the future for these children, God alone knows. But we know some of their capabilities. They are capable of becoming parents themselves; and grandparents and great-grandparents and so on into we know not what number of generations. They will probably not be rulers of nations. But in all likelihood they will be rulers of families; founders themselves of the little nations called homes. And to what nooks and crannies of the earth their influence may penetrate—and with it my influence and my wife's—we cannot guess.

But we can look backward and get some idea of what it means to be a father, the founder and the patriarch of a family. Before me now lies a book of some 1200 large pages. It is entitled, "Descendants of Jacob Hochstetler." Jacob Hochstetler was my I-don't-know-how-many-greats grandfather. He came to America from Switzerland in the early 1700's, when Philadelphia was a town of fewer than 10,000 persons. And more than 1100 of the 1200 pages in the book are devoted to a mere listing of the names of his descendants.

Who shall measure the influence of Jacob Hochstetler, a simple and illiterate, but profoundly good man, upon the history of the United States, and for that matter upon the history of the world? It may well be that he and his children and children's children, when all is said and done, will have had much more to do with the course of events through the centuries than all the Caesars and Napoleons and Hitlers and Stalins and Roosevelts. For in the long run the history of the world is written from the bottom up, not from the top down.

However that may be, it is a fact that each father and each mother hold in their hands incalculable power. One of their children, or one of their grandchildren or great-grandchildren, may be another St. Francis of Assisi or another St. Thérèse. Granted that that is unlikely; nevertheless the enormous weight of any man's descendants in the course of centuries may equal or surpass, for good or for ill, the influence of a St. Francis, or the influence of a Lenin.

We cannot know, of course, what is to come. But we may be sure that as we bend the twig of the future, the tree of all the tomorrows will be inclined. The task of a parent is not merely that of rearing two or three children, or a dozen, in the love of God and the love of fellow men. The task is to start countless generations along that magnificent way of life. What fathers and mothers actually are doing is forming in the hidden womb of the family, the future life of mankind. For this reason I say that every father is a patriarch; and every mother, if I may contrive a word for my purpose, a patriarchess. The word *matriarch* does not seem to serve here.

Now, this does not mean that a father and mother need be frightened. There is no good reason for them to go into agonies of scrupulosity because the powers which they hold in their hands are so great. Above all, they should not impose crushing burdens of responsibility for the future upon the formative and sensitive minds of their children. No; all that they are called upon to do is to rear a holy and happy family, and if possible a healthy family; and all the rest will take care of itself.

In this connection I would stress the word *happy*. Puritanism has so infected all of us that we tend to equate holiness with long-facedness and with self-conscious and posturing piety. Nothing could be farther from the truth. A family that is not happy is a family that is not holy. And a family that is holy is a family that is bound to be happy. What we too easily forget is that holiness is the natural state of the human being; the only state that really fits human nature. The odd thing about human nature is that it is never so completely natural as when it is lifted up to the supernatural.

The task, therefore, that confronts parents is simply that of perfecting the human nature of the children. In doing this, the father and mother perfect their own nature and fulfill their own vocation. And they perform for the entire human race a tremendous social function, for they add to the numberless nations called families one more family which, when the chips are down, will be found on the side of justice and love. They add one more stone to the structure of a decent civilization: a world in which men and women may live in accordance with their human rights.

All this can be done gently and with dignity. There need normally be no exhausting of the father and mother, and no badgering of the children. Discipline can be a lovable and almost invisible thing. The right kind of home should be a rollicking place, filled with laughter, relaxation, and good humor. This is one of the ten thousand paradoxes of life, that the best way to discharge the enormous responsibility of parenthood is to be lighthearted and gay about it; to be profoundly serious about the fundamental objective of rearing a holy family, but to know that the way to make the family holy is to make it childlike.

The Parents' Part in Sex Education

ALEXANDER A. SCHNEIDERS

Let us see this problem of sex education in its proper context. Let us realize that we are not dealing with a local difficulty which can be solved by quoting some pious excerpts from a ten-cent pamphlet. . . .

What, exactly, are the parents' responsibilities, and how should they go about working out these responsibilities? . . .

Undoubtedly, a great deal of the difficulty of this phase of the sex problem arises from the confusion in the minds of most parents as to the part they should play in the sex instruction. The majority of Catholic parents are aware of some responsibility in the matter. The Catholic press, the pulpit, the hierarchy are sending out constant reminders of parents' obligations to their children. . . . Let us ask ourselves very simply: what do we want our children to become as they reach adulthood? What do we hope for as regards their happiness and well-being?

Certainly, no right-thinking Catholic parent would permit the smallest obstacle to stand in the way of the child's happiness. All good parents strive to give their children all those things— education, good example, religion, health, and so on—that are necessary to wholesome living. Yet—and here is the crux of the difficulty—on some things many parents are willing to renege. When it comes to adequate sex adjustment, or the future marital happiness of their children, they want to abandon their responsibility. . . . They become irresponsive and completely incapable of meeting their responsibilities. . . .

Some parents are deathly afraid of sex, especially in relation to children. They have been conditioned to sex in a negative way for so long that they find it impossible to deal intelligently and objectively with the problems that arise in its wake. . . .

Then there are the parents who are ignorant of the *content* of sex instruction and its *methodology*. This ignorance makes them timid in the matter of their responsibilities to their children. . . .

There are some parents—quite a few in fact—who fail utterly to grasp the significance of proper orientation to sex experiences and practices. They wishfully believe that sex adjustment, like the variations in body temperature, will occur naturally in the course of events. They keep telling themselves that as long as Jane and Tommy go to church regularly, pray hard, and receive the Sacraments, the less they know about sex the better.

Well, there is one thing right about this attitude: their kids had better pray hard! These parents fail to realize that the various phases of human adjustment are inseparably linked together; and that human happiness in this life requires adjustment in all areas of human conduct and human relationships.

Finally, there are the parents who simply shirk their responsibilities. They are lazy, indolent, and unworthy of the great trust that God has given them. These parents are the most serious offenders. . . .

It is a wonderful privilege to play a leading role in this important drama of human maturation. It is a privilege to help children and youth effect the transition from sexual ignorance, superstition, and immaturity to an enlightened, wholesome maturity and adulthood. It is a privilege to help prepare this vessel of God in such a way that His graces will pour in and complete the adjustment that is begun by the parent with wholesome sex instruction. . . .

In the matter of content, the first issue that arises is the important difference between *sex information* and *sex instruction*. The first of these is a passive assimilation of what can be dangerous and disintegrating information. The well known gutter approach to sex knowledge belongs in this category. And parents must be wary of achieving nothing more than *informing* their children regarding sex.

Countless studies indicate conclusively that casual information, as against parental instruction, has damaging and sometimes lasting effects on adjustment and personality. . . .

Sex instruction is informative, and it is also integrative. Here the facts necessary to sex adjustment are brought into proper relationship with other facets of adjustment. They are integrated with attitudes, ideals, values, and goals. For example, sex information should be brought in line with the boy's attitudes and values regarding women, religious practices like Confession, the responsibilities of matrimony, the virtues of purity and the like. It is this approach that converts the empty reciting of facts into wholesome, personal instruction.

Regarding the problem of *what* children should be told, there is one principle that must be followed consistently: Children should be told what they *need to know* and what they are capable of assimilating, no more, no less.

What they are capable of assimilating is not easy to determine. Here the parent must exercise his own ingenuity and skill in sounding the youngster's capacity for understanding, and by careful observation and skillful questioning, determine the child's level of maturation.

Knowledge imparted at the wrong time can have a traumatic effect; but when in doubt, one should utilize the principle: "Better a year too early than an hour too late." Normally, if the child is not ready for a certain level of sex instruction, the information will be quickly forgotten.

Another principle that is useful in determining the content of sex instruction may be stated like this: Every child is entitled to know all the facts pertaining to both organic and psychosexual development by the time he has reached maturity. The chances are he will know them anyway, and parental instruction is the best means by which to learn them.

This knowledge should be imparted gradually to the youngster, in terms of the principles outlined earlier. The distinction between *organic* and *psychosexual* development is important here. By the former concept is meant only the structural and functional changes that begin at puberty, and which constitute the physical basis of sexual maturation. These facts the child should be acquainted with relatively early in the adolescent period.

More important are the facts regarding psychosexual development. This concept refers to the development of sexual excitement and desires, erotic night dreaming and daydreaming, and the gradual heterosexual orientation that marks the transition from childhood to adulthood. All of these facts and possibilities are grist for the instructor's mill. So, too, are the profound implications of these developments for the psychological, social and moral adjustments of the growing boy and girl.

It is actually these implications that the youngster needs to understand more than the facts themselves. In other words, the various facets of organic and psychosexual development must be brought into proper relation with other aspects of the youngster's development, including the social, the moral, and the religious.

One other aspect of the content of sex instruction requires emphasis. Children and youths need to know the essential facts regarding *sexual experiences and practices*. Included in this category are the data pertaining to normal experiences, such as desires, dreams, nocturnal emissions and involuntary erections; and also the facts regarding forbidden and undesirable practices such as petting and masturbation. . . . Parents should have the skill to deal with these problems as they arise, as well as the skill to impart the required information regarding such practices and problems. . . .

The first and one of the most essential conditions is a *wholesome, objective attitude* regarding sex and sex instruction on the part of the parents. There is nothing more damaging to adequate sex instruction than timidity, shame, embarrassment, or a general hyper-emotionalism regarding matters of sex. The attitude that sex is shameful, disgusting, immoral, and so on, makes it *impossible* for anyone to deal adequately with the problem. . . .

A second fundamental condition of adequate sex instruction is a *wholesome, receptive attitude on the part of children* receiving instruction. To the child or adolescent for whom anything relating to sex is tainted, sex instruction can be traumatic. Here the responsibilities of both parents and teachers are great. From the earliest years of childhood, the youngster must be gradually prepared for the developments and the information relating to sex life. Extreme care should be taken to avoid the inculcation of negative, damaging, or restrictive attitudes. . . .

The third condition of sex instruction is *wholesome parent-child relationships*. In the home where there is emotional warmth, affection, mutual trust, and strong ego-security, there exists a good groundwork for sex instruction. In this type of setting, it is easy for father or mother to broach the problems of sex whenever occasion demands. . . .

All of the foregoing statements regarding the contents and the conditions of sex instruction bear directly on the last phase of our discussion, namely, the *method* of instruction. Parental attitudes, parent-child relationships, and similar factors are much more important than how sex instruction is accomplished. But the relation between these factors and method should be emphasized; and we need to realize, too, the relative significance of methods themselves.

The question is often raised as to which parent—father or mother—should give the instruction. Usually, the answer is that the father should instruct the boy, and the mother the girl. The problem isn't solved that easily. If, for example, the father is emotionally immature; if his attitudes are restrictive and damaging; if there is negative or cross identification with the children; if he is sexually disturbed or maladjusted, then certainly he is *not* qualified to discuss the delicate questions of sex with his children. It may well be, in any given instance, that father or mother is better qualified to discuss the delicate questions of sex with his children. It may well be, in any given instance that father or mother is better qualified to impart *all* sex knowledge to *all* of the children. This is a problem that the parents have to work out for themselves.

The information given should be conveyed in a straightforward, matter-of-fact manner divested of all the excitable tones of emotional fervor, and free also of confusing analogy and circumlocution. This does not mean ribald frankness, or lustful conversation. All that is required is that the *necessary* information be imparted in a manner that the child can understand without either him or the parent getting excited about it. If this process can be aided by means of literature, mutual discussion, illustration, or in any other way, without damage to the relationships between parent and child, or to the success of the instruction, then certainly there is no gainsaying their use.

What Shall I Tell My Daughters?

PHYLLIS MCGINLEY

Mothers, even the wisest of them, are improvident creatures; they never really believe their children will grow up. It isn't that they do not plan. Their lives are feverish with planning, the paths behind them littered with discarded maps and charts and abandoned strategies. It is simply that parenthood is such a hand-to-mouth existence, such a series of skirmishes won (or lost), that they can only live, like soldiers in the field, from day to day.

Sufficient unto the hour is the crisis thereof. Babies must cut molars, kindergartners start off to school, little boys break windows, and little girls their hearts at dancing class. Each peril has to be faced as it is encountered—the first fib, the measles, the naughty word, the sprained ankle, and the explanation of sex. Puppies get run over, teachers are unjust, cronies turn out to be faithless; and every event is an emergency for which there can be no real preparation except love and common sense.

And then suddenly a mother looks about her and her children are children no longer. This is a curious moment, compounded in almost equal portions of exhiliration, panic, and surprise. In the ascent of her particular Everest, she has reached a sort of plateau, and there is triumph in that. But as she peers back at the trail by which she has come—at all the little peaks surmounted and chasms crossed—what a safe and pleasant climb it appears in retrospect!

How trivial seem those old anxieties—the tantrums and the tonsillectomies, the disorders and the disappointments, the bad grades and the poor postures and the braces on the teeth! Even the most desperate situation had this consolation—that however inadequate her hand, it was there to be reached for. She could interpose herself between the child and life.

Now that must change. Our daughters (for since I have only daughters, I must speak of the gender I know best) must climb the rest of the way very nearly unaccompanied, and it wrings the heart. For perhaps they have not quite recovered from adolescence. They are still unsure of themselves. They still keep diaries, which they lock away in secret drawers. They worry about their complexions and are touchy about their friends and take a gentle suggestion as a personal affront. But they have driving licenses and a clothes allowance; and the boys they bring home are growing up to their ears and speak condescendingly to adults in manly voices. Next year or the year after will bring college or a job. It will also bring either love or its facsimile.

What then shall I, what shall any mother, give them for an amulet against the dangerous journey they must take alone? For we know, unfashionable as it may be to say so, that the dangers are real. Thousands of textbooks; editorials in the press; papers read to learned societies; a whole new profession of consultants on the matter, often attached to the schools—all these, plus the conversation of the young themselves, attest their genuineness.

Surely no one would be naïve enough to think that little biological chats about conception and bodily structure are sufficient. Our daughters have known for a long time just how babies are born, and have accepted, we hope, their theoretical knowledge of sex gravely and sweetly. But the tides of spring run strong. Home ties are breaking off, and to the confusion of new voices and circumstances and the competition for popularity will be added the pulse of their own blood. Curiosity, even, will have its urgent pull.

Admitted that illicit sexual adventure is a peril, at least for what used to be called "marriageable girls," what memorable word can we teach them that they can repeat like an incantation if the tide should become a threatening flood?

I have talked this over with friends and psychologists. I have read the brochures and the textbooks. I have also thought about the problem deeply, and I know what I, for one, shall do. It's a very iconoclastic thing; it has not been mentioned at all in any of the dozens of pamphlets and tomes I have dipped into. But it seems sanest. I shall remind my daughters simply that there is such a thing as right and such a thing as wrong. I shall commit the dreadful heresy of talking about sin.

Now sin has always been an ugly word, but it has been made so in a new sense over the last half century. It has been made not only ugly but passé. People are no longer sinful, they are only immature or underprivileged or frightened or, more particularly, sick. And I think it has no doubt been helpful to some unfortunates to find themselves so considered. But my daughters and yours are fairly brave and certainly privileged and more mature than we might have hoped; and if their souls had been sick, we should have known it before this. *My* children would believe themselves mortally insulted to have their misdemeanors classified as illnesses. In our household we have never been afraid of sin as a proper noun.

In fact, although until now we have never used the word in connection with matters of sex, we have found it a subject of fruitful discussion. We think it is sinful to slander our neighbors. We believe that stealing and cheating and bearing false witness are sins. We think dishonest politicians are sinners. Once, when intolerance raised its unattractive head, we disposed of it readily. We refused to repeat all the windy arguments that have become the standard clichés; we just said that anti-Semitism, like every other artificial bias against one's fellow man, is a sin. And that—as nearly as is humanly possible—was that.

Oddly enough I find little opposition to this last stand among the schoolbook coterie. If they decline to mention sin in connection with prejudice, they do consent to speak of "erroneous social thinking." But not once, in any text, did I come across a reference to either right or wrong in regard to the great act of love. Most of the books naturally deplore sexual experiment. They use all the commonplace arguments. They point out the physical dangers, the emotional involvement, the inconveniences and distresses of furtive passion.

And while some writers I find inane to the point of vulgarity (one author even suggested coy things to say to "break off a petting session"), others have set down superbly reasoned appeals for chastity. But how strong is reason against a tidal wave? I think conscience proves a superior shelter. My daughters shall be told that there exist a moral law and an ancient commandment and that they do wrong to flout them.

And now against my critics (who will be many if they are well-versed in the gospel that has its ultimate evangelist in Dr. Kinsey) I should like to argue the wholesomeness of treating extramarital relations as sinful. For that is what I do consider such teaching—wholesome and even effective.

To begin with, sin implies goodness, and the young love goodness with all their hearts. We all know what idealists they are, how fiercely they react against injustice and cruelty, how they hate hypocrisy and cant. To take away their delight in virtue, to tell them that they must withstand temptations because temptations are merely urges toward immature behavior, is to give them stones when they pant for bread. It is to weaken the muscles of their characters.

In the second place, it is confusing. I think we have all argued too much with our children in this generation. It has been drummed into our ears that we must explain the reasons behind every taboo, and we in turn have drummed these reasons into their ears until they are nearly deafened. I remember my older daughter, when she was small, once listening quietly to my careful dissertation why some action was not to be tolerated. Finally she burst out, "Oh, Mother, why don't you just tell me not to for once and stop explaining!" Just so. It is simpler to treat sex morally than reasonably. Moreover, believing in sin is a kind of tactful armor. A girl might find, in a given situation, that it was better to tell a young man that he was doing wrong than that he was being a social dunce. His self-esteem would suffer less.

"But how about guilt?" ask my opponents. "When the young believe in sin, they must necessarily feel guilty if they commit it. Is not that destructive?"

From my fallible viewpoint, I do not think so. For sin implies forgiveness. One who has done a wrong can be sorry and recover. If he is generous enough, he can even forgive himself. But how does one go about forgiving oneself for a lapse in taste or a gaucherie? We have all committed sins in our lives, meannesses and angers and lies. But most of us have forgotten them easily. What we find hard to forget or to forgive are the silly things we have said, the times we have been awkward and doltish. It is one of my articles of psychological faith that a girl (and perhaps the same thing applies to a boy) would find life less broken apart after a misguided love affair if she could feel that she had been sinful rather than a fool. And I hope that all our daughters are sure enough of parental love not to let a sense of guilt destroy them in silence.

Now all this does not mean that because I am, like Coolidge's minister, against sin, I am also against sex or that my girls will get that impression. On the contrary, they will believe, I hope, that it is one of the moving graces of the world, far too magnificent a gift to be carelessly handled. We three women in our house are proud of being women. We feel a little sorry for men, who can never bear children or be wives. Puberty was something welcomed by my daughters with delight. So when I mention the moral standard, they will understand that it is for the sake of protecting this magnificence that mankind has slowly, strugglingly, been building for several thousand years. Fashions in morals fluctuate. Puritan rigor gives way to Restoration license, and that in turn is drowned in Victorian severity. It is possible that much of our own permissive nonsense will be frowned on by the generation now growing up. But right and wrong do not really alter, nor do their consequences. And of this my daughters must be aware.

So what in the end shall I tell my daughters about chastity before marriage? Of *course*, I shall be sensible and point out the ordinary social penalties attached to any other conduct. I shall touch on the possible pregnancy, the untidiness, and the heartbreak. But I shall also say that love is never merely a biological act but one of the few miracles left on earth, and that to use it cheaply is a sin.

In fact that is what I have already told them.

A Catholic Approach to Dating

ED WILLOCK

In our times, we have developed a reflex action set off by the term "old-fashioned." Our response is "Throw it out!" It does not necessarily follow that we always find something *better* to replace the old thing. More often than not, we find ourselves unequipped to handle situations that used to be handled according to customs we have thrown out. I can think of no other situation where this is more true than in the practice of "dating." All of the old-fashioned customs surrounding courting have been discarded. This puts parents and their juveniles in a sweet dilemma as to how this time-honored practice should best be conducted.

As things stand, courting puts too much strain upon the individual parent. Even a Solomon would be hard put to come up with precise answers to precise situations: "Why can't I go out with Johnny? I know he's a non-Catholic, but after all, I'm not going to marry him!"

"Why can't I go on a date? I'm 14. Other kids date when they are in grammar school."

"Do you think I'm old enough to go steady? At my age (16) it's hard to have to hunt around for a different girl every Saturday night!"

"Do you think I should stop dating Judy? Her parents are afraid to let her out, so we have to sit in a dark room all evening while they watch television."

"Can I take the car tonight, Dad? We have a double date and I don't like to go in Al's car. He drinks too much and drives like a cowboy."

A parent with teen-agers cannot but long for the "good old days" when dating was strictly for grownups, when kids did not drive cars, when a teen-aged girl was always at home "after dark," when a kiss meant a promise of marriage, when boy-friends and girl-friends were chosen from among one's own neighbors, or even the long-forgotten custom of unmarried women never being without a chaperone.

Don't misunderstand me! I am *not* arguing for the revival of old-fashioned customs. I am only complaining that we really haven't any new customs to replace them. At present, anything goes. There simply are no customs! Things would be much easier for us parents if the modern world presented us with a set of customs we could evaluate. At least we would have something to work from!

From my own experience in this matter, I find there is currently no customary time at which teen-agers should get home from a date. There is no approximate age set when youngsters should start dating. It is not a question of criticizing the narrowness or the broadness of the limits. There are no limits! *That* is our problem.

When I say problem, I feel very strongly that it is a far greater problem for our youngsters than for their parents. It is difficult for youngsters to protect themselves against a danger, the nature of which they do not know. The danger in dating, courting, and hasty marriages cannot be learned by hearsay. *That* is why courting customs are so important!

We have no choice but to re-evaluate the whole question of courtship. This is what all Catholic parents are being forced to do. It is far from being a merely academic question. Two facts are completely clear: Christianity is here to stay, and courting is here to stay. Therefore, courting should be a Christian practice.

The biggest difficulty in trying to establish a set of customs surrounding sexual behavior is today's complete bewilderment about the matter of sex. The person of Catholic mind, in this matter, finds himself squeezed between two sentimentalists: the Prude and the Libertine. These two groups constitute the bulk of the population, and neither have a recognizable *theory* about sex. All they have is *strong reactions* to it. . . .

The Catholic theory of sex, based upon a knowledge of human nature, incorporates such factors as these: sexual intercourse is exclusively a marital function; any misuse or abuse of sexual privileges and appetites is a threat to the institution of marriage;

all behavior between the sexes should be prescribed by customs that will safeguard the virginity of the unmarried and the fidelity of the married. . . .

We hold that there is a purpose and a cause-and-effect relationship between all practices that are sexual in nature. The ultimate purpose of marriage is to beget children. The ultimate purpose of engagement is to get married. The ultimate purpose of courtship or dating is to find a partner for marriage. This is the chain of cause and effect.

Consequently, dating should be recognized as a preparation for engagement, engagement as a preparation for marriage and marriage as a preparation for parenthood.

Against the background of these notions, certain courtship customs suggest themselves.

It is hard for young people to realize that very few people ever intend or desire to get married when they start dating. Yet, in 99 cases out of 100, dating leads to marriage. In retrospect, we parents can see this fact *plainly*. Young folks can't see it *at all*.

A young boy or girl must learn to trust their parent's judgment concerning the likelihood of dating ending up in marriage, and act accordingly. When you date, you must face the fact that marriage might be the ultimate result. A second or third date makes the likelihood even greater.

This likelihood should not be put in the category of "danger of an accident" such as one must realistically face whenever one takes a car on the highway. This would be a perverse attitude toward dating. Marriage is an *expected*, *normal* consequence of dating. Any youngster, who will not face this fact, is simply too young to be dating!

At first, it sounds altogether innocent and charming for a boy or girl to say about their dates, "Who's thinking about marriage? Don't worry, Mommy, we're just having fun!" Parents who have their eyes fixed on the danger of a hasty, premature marriage may actually sigh with relief when hearing this childish remark. This is unfortunate, because hasty marriages are probably the least of all dangers risked in habitual dating.

Habitual dating puts the Catholic youth into a whirl of practices that are utterly irresponsible. Some of these "practices" are known as "running around," "petting," "going steady" and "having a ball." These are "practices" as distinct from "customs." A custom springs from a theory of life. It is a widely thought-out way of doing things. A practice is a *habit fallen* into by people who don't particularly know what they are doing.

"Running around" is the habit of endlessly taking part in boy-girl affairs, night after night and week after week. It is dangerous in that it is without purpose; the head is left at home while the heart and glands are allowed to romp, playfully. At any one point on this merry-go-round, everything might be quite innocent and coca-colaish. A boy or girl may even go through years of this without any apparent "trouble." The thing that happens inevitably is that the youth who "runs around" is squandering the best years of his life! . . .

People irresponsibly remark, "Enjoy your youth while you have it!" Actually, young folks who playfully squander their teen-years, usually spend the rest of their life regretting it. If you don't work at becoming a competent adult during your teens, it is unlikely you will ever be competent or adult. The energy and enthusiasm that makes a person "run around" is the same stuff of which genius and sanctity are made.

"Petting" is a happy, carefree, childish playing with adult things. "Petting," properly understood, is a preliminary to sexual intercourse and (for that reason) belongs to marriage.

"Going steady" is a childish playing at marriage. No one should expect a girl friend or boy friend to *"be their property."* It is convenient to have one's own escort for dancing, dining, skating, chatting, etc.; but it is an unfair childish advantage to take of a person's misplaced affections.

What both youth and their parents must keep in mind is this: courting is not for children. It is a situation, once begun, over which parents have no control and, therefore, no responsibility apart from advisory. Youth should be made aware of two facts. First, that they are doing something adult in which they must make the decisions and live with the consequences; secondly, that they should look for advice from parents at every stage of development.

The ideal situation is when the parents meet, know and discuss their youngsters' girl-friends and boy-friends, as a regular part of family routine. In this way parents are in daily touch with what is going on. This ideal situation is only possible where an intimate affection already exists between parents and children. . . .

It is advisable that parents "trust" their children during the courting stage. Parents *often* transfer their own uncertainties to a youth just at the time when the youth must make his first adult decisions. Young people tend to be cocky or shy in order to compensate for their lack of experience. A parent must see through this sham and yet generate a sense of trust to lend courage to the newly-adult.

There is a basis for this trust. Young people have natural safeguards against indiscretions, a sense of shame and self-containment. We can also presume they have graces sufficient to their temptations. In many ways, they are better equipped for prudent courtship than are the middle-aged.

Furthermore, there is the idealism of youth that the middle-aged are inclined to underestimate. I would say that a proper nurturing of this youthful idealism is the key to successful courtship. Young people have, generally, a far greater *capacity for greatness* than older people. Young people are considerably more "serious" than their elders. All the *"toujours gaie"* and practiced cynicisms of youth are shells of protection behind which they hide their serious idealism. Perhaps at no other time in life is it so easy to desire sanctity or great personal achievement! Elders, who have permitted their idealism to languish, are often taken in by the contrived gaiety of youths, attributing an empty-headedness to heads that are very full. . . .

It is possible for youth to *aspire* to holy Matrimony! They are able to look upon family, children, home and parenthood as something *great!* If *we* parents have lost our idealism, let's not rob them of theirs!

It is because of this youthful idealism, which is so precious and a more than adequate antidote to the poisonous secularism surrounding us, that the growing custom of Solemn Engagement should be encouraged. If engagements are made public and festive religious occasions, as can very well be done, a new monument on the road to marriage can be built in what is now a desert of purposeless dating and running around.

Young people looking for a marriage partner can aim at the Solemn Engagement. The Solemn Engagement can be followed by a preparation for marriage course. The solemnly-engaged couples in a parish could become a nucleus around which all boy-girl affairs can be built. Here we have a skeleton frame for a whole new set of courting customs which will be clothed with idealism, festivity and an awareness of the sacredness of marriage. . . .

Until this group of customs can become regular parish routine, our youths will have to fight to retain their virtue and their idealism while being inundated by a sea of "running around," "petting" and other irresponsibilities.

Mothers-in-Law and Others-in-Law

THE REV. MARIO L. DITTAMI, O.CARM.

Who hasn't chuckled at one time or another over a "mother-in-law joke?" And what battle between young husband and bride doesn't finally come around to that highly amusing line, "You leave my family out of this!"

The simple, pathetic fact is that it's pretty hard to leave the in-laws entirely out of the marriage scene. There are sound psychological reasons for this, and it behooves us to understand them as fully as possible so that we may regard them as tolerantly as possible.

To start with, society has much to say to us about the "obligation of parents." This is quite as it should be, for when two people bring a child into the world, they receive into their hands an immortal soul to mold and shape. Parents have the absolute responsibility of watching over their child and of training him so that eventually he may take his proper place in adult society.

On the other hand, the child has an obligation, too. He is obliged by the terms of the Fourth Commandment to obey his parents under pain of sin. . . .

A parent may be prosecuted in court for dodging his responsibility to a child. He may be charged with non-support, or with contributing to the delinquency of a minor.

BUT—that situation of authority on the one hand and submission on the other usually ends the day a child reaches the age of twenty-one. . . .

Yet the fact remains that a child of twenty-one is not a child at all. He is free, and if his dad continues to give him money to see him through college, it should be understood that this is entirely voluntary on the dad's part.

By the same token, the dad no longer has the right to give orders and expect complete obedience. Of course, if a son (or daughter) continues to live at home after twenty-one, he (or she) must obey the rules of the household laid down by the parents. After all, any house guest must do the same thing.

For a father to say that a girl of twenty-one may not smoke is foolish. She may smoke if she chooses. For mother to object because son, aged twenty-one, drinks beer is equally foolish.

This may sound like subversive propaganda to some parents, but actually it is solid theology. . . .

All find it difficult to let their children go, to let the little birds fly out of the nest and admit that the little birds can do a better piece of flying then even than the old birds can do. It is psychologically hard to admit that someone else is as good as or better than you are yourself.

And so it is that dad feels this or that boy isn't good enough for daughter, not able to fill dad's old place in her life.

So it is that mother thinks this girl isn't good enough to pick out the drapes that are going into her son's new house.

So it is, psychologically, that both dad and mother find it almost impossible to keep hands off and mind their own business in connection with the new marriage venture that has come to the family. And, basically, so it is that we have what we call "in-law trouble." . . .

Once we understand the basis of in-law trouble, we have the whole problem just about two-thirds whipped.

For example, suppose that the husband comes home from his office or shop dead tired. The day has been warm and all he can think about is a cold can of beer and perhaps forty winks before dinner in the hammock in his own, pleasant back yard.

But he arrives at his door-step—and who should be standing right there behind the wife but the mother-in-law.

"Hello, Herbert," she says a little grimly. And then, almost before he can set his course for the icebox . . . "Herbert, when my husband was alive, he *prided* himself on how he kept up our yard . . . Why, he wouldn't have let a week go by without mowing the lawn . . ." And so on and so forth.

Now everyone knows how the husband is going to react to this. Herbert must make a choice. He must decide to say substantially one of two things:

(1) "Mom, you're absolutely right. I ought to get out there and cut the grass, and I will just as soon as I get my strength back. About Saturday, I should think." Or . . .

(2) "Aah, shaddup, ya big buttinski!"

Line Number 2 has several things in its favor. It's short, snappy, and to the point. It requires the husband to think practically not at all, and it honestly reflects his feelings.

But if he's the least bit smart, the husband never will say it. He will have himself so well in hand, and he will have learned so thoroughly the very things we were discussing a few minutes ago, that he will begin almost automatically to think something like this:

"It's true that I don't like my mother-in-law any too well. She gives me a bad time. But then, I realize that a lot of people think she's very nice—mainly because they don't have to see her as much or know her as well as I do. She does give me a bad time—but it isn't because she's really a bad sort, but rather because she bears me a peculiar relationship.

"That is, she remembers the days when she used to be all the world to my wife. My wife depended upon her for everything, did everything she said, thought just as she thought. And now I've come along to take her place in my wife's affections. That's galling to her, quite naturally. She feels as if her own daughter had said to her, 'I've found someone I like better than you, someone who in a lot of respects *is* better than you.'

"Mother-in-law is hurt and stung by that. She wants to prove that, actually, she's better than I am. So she nails me for not cutting the grass. Psychologically, what she's saying is this, '*You* don't cut the grass, but if I were the man of this house the grass would be cut. So that makes me better than you.'

"So, since that's really what's going on in her mind, I must remember that it isn't that she cares whether the grass is cut or not. Rather she's crushed because I stole her girl from her, and looking at it that way, I can see she has a point. In these circumstances, the best way for me to handle the situation is to say something that will indicate I admire and agree with her and not that I think she's a meddlesome old woman. All she really wants is for me to be nice to her—not nice just now, but always nice so that she can truly feel she has gained a son and not that she has lost a daughter."

If hubby can remember all that in a flash, and if he can act upon it, a wonderful thing will happen. He'll find, next week or next month, that the mother-in-law has become a fan of his. She'll actually be taking his part in arguments with the wife instead of interfering the other way around.

All this, of course, is just as true when you apply it in the other direction. If the husband's mother tries to tell the wife how to run the house, it isn't really that she cares how the house is run. It's just that she's trying, psychologically, to put over the point that she knows how to run a house better than the wife. It'll take patience on the wife's part to let her get away with this, but the wife will be wise if she's able to apply a little tact, based on her own understanding of what's really wrong with her troublesome in-law.

Let's get another thing straight now. It should be understood that the person closest to a man is his wife. And the person closest to a woman is her husband. Husband and wife are closer than child and parents. And if parents attempt to make little of their child's spouse, it is most definitely up to the child not to stand for it.

Suppose the mother-in-law starts picking on the husband about not mowing the lawn. It will help a lot if the wife promptly says, "Now, look here, Mom, Herb's tired. It's a hard job to cut the grass after the kind of day he puts in at the plant, and I'm not going to hear of any lawn mowing around here this evening!" That kind of attitude, stated *politely* but firmly, will probably end the discussion at once.

Incidentally, it would be very pleasant indeed if all in-laws could understand their own relationship to a marriage. In an extreme case, husband and wife might even try to sit down in a calm moment and explain it to them.

Parents interfere almost without realizing it. They interfere because, in a subtle way, it builds them up and make them feel bigger than the person who came and stole a loved one from their home.

Parents tend to tone down the faults of their own offspring and magnify the faults of their own offspring's spouse. But the application of just a little common sense should make it clear to them that their own offspring has faults, and that even though he has to put up with faults in his mate, it's equally true that she is putting up with the faults she finds in him.

Parents tend to go on "protecting" their children. This, too, makes them feel important. It's as if everybody admitted that the kids aren't as smart or as tough or as experienced as the older folks. And meanwhile the parents make this seem right by telling themselves that "my kids aren't going to suffer the things I had to go through."

I even knew of a mother who didn't want her daughter to have babies because of the pain involved. So she went down to the drugstore and bought some kind of contraceptive for daughter. She told herself that she was helping and protecting daughter— and not, of course, that she was helping daughter to commit sin.

Another point: Never take your spouse to live with your parents unless there is some *truly* urgent circumstance that makes it unavoidable. And if you do it, realize that you are providing an occasion for the older folks to indulge their very natural desire to meddle.

Even if it means leaving three vacant rooms at dad's place and going to live in a one-room kitchenette—do it. It won't hurt you. Don't even live in an apartment building owned by your folks. It will only cause trouble. I'm not guessing about this.

To put the shoe on the other foot, don't bring the folks to live with you if you can help it. And don't impose on the folks. Don't regard them merely as free baby-sitters. Let husband and wife be infallibly courteous and kind and understanding in connection with all the in-laws on the fringe of the marriage—but let it all be done at a distance of at least a couple of miles.

In other words, honor and respect your parents. If you have married, you realize more deeply what your mother and father have done for you. Respect them for it. Honor them. Offer them little tokens of love and consideration. Visit them and invite them to your home. Give them presents now and then. BUT DON'T REMAIN TIED TO THEIR APRON STRINGS.

At the same time, don't for a moment think it is proper for you to be too aloof at a time of need. If, for example, the wife's mother is a widow with no means of support, the wife should join with her brothers and sisters to provide for mother. And the husband should go along without complaining and without acting as if he were doing something heroic and noble. His wife's obligations are his obligations, and it is just his routine, day-to-day duty to cooperate fully with the wife in whatever is reasonable for his mother-in-law's comfort.

Now let's cover another point. No two people ever lived together as man and wife without doing their share of fighting. I imagine Adam and Eve quarreled about who was responsible for getting them thrown out of the garden. Because, in marriage, there always is a kind of competition, a game to see who can heap blame on the other. And when these inevitable causes of war come up in your marriage, don't—I beg of you—go to your own father and mother to do your complaining.

They naturally are prejudiced in your favor and will take your side. It may not be the just side, but they'll take it. Isn't that why you'd go to them in the first place?

But their willingness to take your side will only serve to convince you all the more of the justice of your own position. And such a reconviction will only strengthen you in your refusal to go "half way" to see your mate's point of view.

If you have to talk, go to an intelligent friend, or to your pastor, or to your doctor or lawyer. But never go to your folks. It's so easy for you to gain *their* support—and your mate will only resent the fact that you took the trouble of digging up such easy backing. Besides, going to your folks merely provides them with an occasion to start meddling in your marriage—something they have no business doing anyhow.

And finally, let's end this discussion by reemphasizing one vital point.

Once a girl marries, the one closest to her is her husband, not her parents.

Once a man marries, his wife is closer to him than his folks.

Husband and wife are partners for life. They are each other's *alter ego*. They must stick together, work together, face issues together.

And their in-laws will admire them for doing it.

Four

THE FAMILY

Wives, be subject to your husbands, as is becoming in the Lord.

Husbands, love your wives and do not be bitter towards them.

Children, obey your parents in all things, for that is pleasing in the Lord.

Fathers, do not provoke your children to anger, that they may not be discouraged.

ST. PAUL TO THE COLOSSIANS 3: 18-21

Notable Statements on the Family by Pius XII

Its Natural Rights

There would be danger lest the primary and essential cell of society, the family, with its well-being and its growth, should come to be considered from the narrow standpoint of national power, and lest it be forgotten that man and the family are by nature anterior to the state, and that the Creator had given to both of them powers and rights and has assigned them a mission and a charge that correspond to undeniable natural requirements.

Its Significance

The family is the foundation of society. Just as the human body is made up of living cells which are not merely placed in juxtaposition, but which constitute an organic whole by their intimate and constant relationships, so also society is formed, not of a conglomeration of individuals, scattered beings, appearing one instant only to vanish the next, but rather of the economic community and moral solidarity of the families, which, handing down from generation to generation the precious heritage of the common ideal, of a common civilization, of a common religious faith, assures the cohesion and continuity of social bonds. St. Augustine noted this fifteen centuries ago when he wrote that the family should be the first element and, as it were, a little cell of the city.

Its Function

The family is sacred. It is the cradle not only of children but also of the nation—of its force and its glory. Do not let the family be alienated or diverted from the high purpose assigned to it by God. God wills that husband and wife, in loyal fulfillment of their duties to one another and to the family, should in the home transmit to the next generation the torch of corporeal life, and with it spiritual and moral life, Christian life; that within the family, under the care of their parents, there should grow up men of straight character, of upright behavior, to become valuable, unspoiled members of the human race, manly in good or bad fortune, obedient to those who command them and to God. That is the will of the Creator.

Its Mission

In promoting this participation by the laity in the apostolate, which is so important in our times, the family has a special mission, for it is the spirit of the family that exercises the most powerful influence on that of the rising generation. As long as the sacred flame of the Faith burns on the domestic hearth, and the parents forge and fashion the lives of their children in accordance with this Faith, youth will be ever ready to acknowledge the royal prerogatives of the Redeemer, and to oppose those who wish to exclude Him from society or wrongly to usurp His rights.

When churches are closed, when the Image of the Crucified is taken from the schools, the family remains the providential and, in a certain sense, impregnable refuge of Christian life.

Its Equality

The whole education of your children would be ruined were they to discover in their parents—and their eyes are sharp enough to see—any signs of favoritism, undue preferences or antipathies in regard to any of them. For your own good and for the good of the family it must be clear that, whether you use measured severity or give encouragement and caresses, you have an equal love for all, a love which makes no distinction save for the correction of evil or for the encouragement of good. Have you not received them all equally from God?

The Christian Family

KARL ADAM

The Christian Family differs specifically from every other family, even though, from the ethical viewpoint, the latter be entirely above reproach, and even exemplary. As a social structure the Christian Family is something completely new in the world—something which cannot evolve from purely natural forces. It belongs to an entirely different order of being. It is supernatural; and it is such precisely because its foundation, the marriage bond, is supernatural. Christian marriage is a sacrament.

The Inspiration of Christ at Home

THE VERY REV. IGNATIUS SMITH, O.P.

Intelligent and constructive piety sends thinking men and women to Christ when the problems of the home are under discussion. They recognize that the most important institution of society from prehistoric times to the present day is the home. . . . They turn with increasing eagerness to the teachings and the example of Christ.

The most arresting fact in the life of the Divine Christ is that He selected an humble home in which to live. By His divine power He might have commandeered one of the palaces of the Caesars, flung in magnificent array along the Mediterranean. He might have taken up residence in one of the mountain recesses of Palestine or among the hermits in the desert. But He chose to live in a home at Nazareth and there to pass His babyhood, His boyhood and the toiling days of His manhood. To know that

Christ selected the home on which to place divine sanction and eternal approval is of inestimable consolation to those who spend even the smallest human effort to make and to keep together a home. A warning it is to those who are tinkering with home peace and domestic happiness to know that they are undermining a pillar of society that was ornamented by the living presence of the Son of God. . . .

Picture a little square house of brick or stone covered with sun dried clay and whitewashed. A long courtyard in front. A bake oven in the corner and all surrounded by a wall of loose stones. Close by is the carpenter shop where Joseph worked and where Jesus learned His trade. Step inside the house. Just a few rooms. A scarcity of furniture. A table; a few stools; rugs; mats and cushions. A little oil lamp burns in the corner and the hearth is in the center of the room. There is a closet for the linen and a mortar for the grain. The house is overcrowded, for, besides, Jesus, Mary and Joseph, you find there the widowed sister Mary, with her children, the cousins of Jesus, sometimes called the brothers and sisters of the Lord. There are no comforts, no luxuries; there is deep concern about daily bread. This worry is written on the face of Joseph through whose labor the family is supported. Such is the home Jesus chose to live in and to make happy. . . .

The home at Nazareth was blest by the careful attention, not part-time attention, of a loving mother. Mary was uncomplaining in her labors; unselfish in her sacrifices; glorying in her responsibilities to her home and to her child; alert in the protection of her partnership with her spouse and with her God; careful in the instruction and example she gave her son. From the notes struck by the life of such a mother, there rises, even today, the melody and harmony of a truly happy home. The home in which Jesus lived was a sanctuary of love where love of Mary for Joseph, of Joseph for Mary, love of parents for Jesus and of the child for His parents was ennobled and elevated by a mutual love of God and a recognition of the place of God the Father in the affairs of the family.

In such a home Jesus learned the lessons of obedience and religion by which He advanced in wisdom and grace before God and before men. You can picture Him running errands for Mary; you can visualize Him sweeping the carpenter shop for Joseph. You can imagine Jesus manifesting more and more those attractive habits which in His public life made Him the unforgettable ideal of all time. Kindly, merciful, considerate of the needs of all, self-sacrificing and eager in the tasks of the school to which He was sent. Keen in learning the law and the scriptures at the synagogue. . . .

This devotion of Jesus to His home and to His parents has written into the ideals of the race an imperishable standard inspiring mankind for nineteen hundred years to imitate Him in devotion to their homes and in their mutual efforts to make every home successful and happy. . . .

Wherever the spirit of Christianity has breathed upon the life of a people their institutions have been transformed. This is never so evident as in the effect of the example of Christ on the home life of heathen and pagan people. Before the home life of pagan Rome was elevated by the teachings of Christ and the memory of His example the father of the family was a tyrant with the right of life and death over his children and with almost equal power over his wife. Children were neglected, exposed to the elements that would destroy them, thrown to dogs to be devoured or suddenly murdered, when unwanted, at the whim of the father. The wife was a chattel, she had no place in the councils of the home, she had no voice in the government of the family, she had no say in the education of the children. The family institution was a citadel of tyranny and fear. . . . But as soon as Jesus becomes a part of the family the home is regenerated. Nineteen hundred years of facts stand behind the truth of this statement. And whether paganism be old or new here is the achievement that is accomplished.

Marriage becomes a permanent institution and an enduring union between a man and a woman who have become not merely husband and wife but father and mother as well. Womanhood shares the dignity and respect shown to Mary the mother of Jesus by Christ and by His followers. The human body is regarded as touched by God and as the temple of the Divine spirit. The offspring is regarded not as an unwelcome and unwanted intruder but as a son of God and an heir of Jesus Christ, in whose name father and mother exercise trusteeship. Between parents there is mutual affection and devotion, sympathy unfailing, patience, if not peace, broadmindedness and tolerance of mutual faults. Over their children they are watchful even as Mary and Joseph were, and careful to instruct, by word and example, not only in the things of this world but in the things of God as well. Children render unto them obedience, affection, attention, love and service because those tributes were given by Christ to His parents in His home. Thus the pagan citadel of fear and tyranny under the magic touch of Christ in the home becomes a sanctuary of love and affectionate government; the parents become the partners of God and the ministers of Christ. The pagan house of misery and chaos becomes, under the magic wand of Christ, a home of happiness and peace. Such is the miraculous elevation of the home by Christ from the degradation of paganism to the sublimity of Christianity.

The Christian Family

CATHOLIC BISHOPS OF THE UNITED STATES

(1949)

Perhaps the most evident and devastating effect of the disregard of supernatural faith in human society is to be found in what it has done to family life. The world which discounts supernatural faith in God's revelation, praises family life, declares its place and function essential to human well-being, and speaks with high sentiment of the sacredness of the home. Yet by countless acts and agencies it moves steadily to disrupt family life and to destroy the home. It approves and facilitates divorce as a cure for domestic ills. It accepts multiple marriages which usually mean a hopeless entanglement of the infelicities of a plurality of broken homes. It sponsors planned parenthood by use of unnatural and morally degrading means, thus infusing poison into the heart of family life by destroying in husband and wife the self-respect and mutual reverence on which alone are built enduring love and patient fidelity. . . . Its social legislation in point of suitable housing, decent material facilities, security in income and prospects, is slow, fumbling, and inadequate. An unbelieving world professing recognition of the essential value of family life, actually discounts that value and moves to destroy what it claims to cherish.

All this amounts to a calculated attack upon family life. . . .

In the view of faith the family is first, first of all a divine institution. A divine institution is not within man's control to abrogate or alter. It is God's own work. Attack upon it is even humanly speaking disastrous. It strikes tragically at the even balance of right human relations, and ends in calamitious disorder.

Faith merely confirms reason in holding that husband and wife constitute conjugal society. When their union is blessed with offspring this society becomes a family. It is a divinely founded natural society. It is prior, in existence and in its nature, to every other human society, to every state or nation. It is the basic social unit. It has its own native rights which no civil power can take away or unduly limit. To serve and protect the family and its life, states are formed and governments established. . . .

Family life encircles the child with no mere casual set of surroundings. It is his constant school; it is his realm, his world. Even through his adolescence he returns to it as to the moorings of his soul. Family life, far beyond any other external influence, moulds lastingly the tastes, the temperaments, the attitudes, the personality of the child. No human social influence can compare with the family in power to form and to direct the individual lives of men. . . .

It is the family that produces the citizen. No nation can be greater than its families. In vain does the world that disregards the injunction of God loosen family ties and break up family life then look to state schools to produce good citizens. At its best the school is only a strong aid to the home. Good citizens must first be good persons. . . . And virtue is the basis of good citizenship. The state which weakens the family inflicts deep injury upon itself. Any attack of the state on family life is suicidal. . . .

To exist in full effectiveness, family life must have permanence. This permanence depends chiefly upon the permanence of marriage. Strictly requisite is marriage that is monogamous and indissoluble: the marriage of one man with one woman in divorceless union that is broken only by the death of one of the spouses. . . . Any marriage which looks to dissolution or divorce, even as a possibility, cannot give to children the security they need; cannot surround children with the enduring atmosphere of home; cannot breathe into children the spirit of true family life. Nor can such a marriage give to husband and wife the complete reliance on each other which is requisite for their peace and happiness under the exacting conditions of marital duty.

Further, family life must have freedom. There must be no undue intervening of the civil power in the domain of the husband and wife. This requirement involves two points of obligation. Freedom implies that rights be respected. The state must respect the rights of the family. It must not therefore fail to provide opportunities for the adequate housing of families, for the requisite schooling of children, for the use of common benefits supplied through the taxing of citizens. On the other hand, the state must not oppress the family. It must not discount parental authority by invading the home and legislating upon matters which are of strictly domestic concern. It must be neither arbitrary nor tyrannous. It must not usurp the right which belongs to parents, of educating their children. On this score, the part of the state is to furnish opportunity for schooling, and to see that parents are not recreant in making use of the opportunity on behalf of their children. The state cannot force a child to attend this school or that; it cannot prescribe courses of study that may involve intellectual or moral dangers for pupils. Nor can the state make discrimination among families, distributing common benefits to some and withholding them from others.

To the Church belongs the pre-eminent right to guide the child's spiritual and moral formation; to the parents belong the natural right to govern and supervise the child's nurture and general education; in society is vested the right to transmit, generally by means of schools, the cultural heritage of successive generations.

The function of the state is to assist these three agencies to discharge harmoniously their responsibilities in the best interest of the public welfare. The state must ever keep in mind that children belong to their parents before they belong to the state. . . .

Again, the family to exercise its good influence in full effectiveness, needs a just measure of economic security. When, in a wealthy and prospering nation, diligent and willing parents are forced to live in grinding poverty; when parents have no opportunity of owning their own home; when the aid of government is extended to those who raise crops or build machines but not to those who rear children, there exists a condition of inequity and even of injustice. . . .

Finally, the family needs religion. It requires the high morality and the unvarying standards of duty which only the spirit of religion can supply to family life. It needs the strong quality of staunch loyalty to God and to His commandments, to His Church and her precepts. It needs the filial piety which has its source and support in piety towards God. It needs prayer and the example of prayerfulness. . . .

The family needs to gather again around its hearth and rekindle there the fires of religious fervor. The home must again become a shrine of fidelity, a place where God is the unseen Host.

Love When Divinely Protected

THE REV. BEDE JARRETT, O.P.

It is perfectly clear from any study of human nature that the whole tendency of individuals, especially when thrown into each other's company, is to separation: the ideas of two tend on the whole to spring apart: the very fact that the other person holds a view is reason sufficient for holding its opposite. Especially is this likely to happen where two are facing each other at all times of day, in moments of irritability, in all moods and tempers. The very likeness in taste or temperament or habit is bound to appear at times when it should not, and to produce friction that will lead to serious trouble unless it is treated with a tact which is rare to find and still rarer to find continuously. The effect of a family, which should prove a bond by linking the parents together in a mutual love of at least a third person, in fact, turns sometimes to the other result and produces such divergence of views on education, etc., as to produce, rather than peace, ultimate estrangement. Of course, the answer to all this is, that it supposes the absence of love, whereas the idea of marriage is based on love, and apart from love has no significance. Once let love come in, and then the things that might prove a source of difference result on the whole in a deeper affection. Difference itself becomes a bond of union; the two souls become complementary to one another; each supplies what is lacking to the other. This is true. It is obvious that love does bridge over the chasm and holds souls together. But is not this, too, part of the danger? For though love unites as can nothing else, so long as love is there, what is to happen at those times when love is least powerful? When human charms cease to appeal or by their satisfaction have extinguished all desire? Love is strong while it lasts; but who shall guarantee love lasting?

It is just here that the sacrament of marriage enters into its place in the stream of Catholic tradition. It brings to love the safeguard of a divine protection. It wards off the approach of dullness and boredom by illuminating the whole of family life with the outpouring of love divine. The Spirit of God in virtue of the Passion of Christ sets in the soul the power to hold on in spite of every difficulty. It adds to love the wisdom and discernment to allow to each that freshness and spontaneity that is required for the full tale of love. When pleasure in such a life might make men forget the responsibilities of their high calling, it is the infusion of grace that brings back the vision of earlier days. It is the sacrament that makes the father and mother realize that they have duties to perform to their race, and holds them to the labor and travail whence is born the joy of the world. Abolish this, and in how many cases would not the result be the end of the family, often the end of the national existence? . . . The married state is itself a high calling from God. The duties therein incurred are of divine origin, blessed by God, and safeguarded by the grace that this attracts; they have become the living symbols of God's union with man. Mutual acceptance means one single law of faithfulness for both, which no amount of custom or tradition can be allowed to impair. Thus does the blood of Christ make holy a calling that is the exact reproduction of the central fact of the Christian revelation, for it takes God to make a family.

Woman: Peacemaker and Homemaker

THE REV. WALTER FARRELL, O.P.

Mary was a wise woman. The Catholic woman, who is her child, is a wise woman, must be a wise woman, for she is essentially a homemaker as Mary was.

Long before marriage becomes a personal problem, and indeed all through life if she never marries, the Catholic woman must make a home in the house of her soul. She is a Martha to the sacramental Christ, with this difference: it is not a passing visit for which she must prepare. The Lord abides in her; she must offer Him a permanent, peaceful haven of complete understanding, generous love, sacrifice, and all the things that go into the make-up of a home.

Leaving aside the supernatural for a moment, and concentrating on the purely human, it is an unquestionable fact that home is made or unmade by the woman who is its mistress. We are sorry for the widow left to rear her children alone; but we can, with no unkindliness, limit our pity to the woman herself. But in the case of the widower, we can well be uneasy, also, about burnt meals, broken china, lumpy beds, and originally dressed children. In other words, a womanless house has little of home about it, even physically speaking. Nor does that house fare much better where the woman at its head leaves the home to servants, to spare moments, or simply to itself. Such a house may lack nothing of the material, but still it fails to be a home, for what is lacking is fundamental.

When we remember that peace is of the essence of home, we understand that a home is neither made nor unmade by the solidity of its walls, its palatial furnishings and efficient servants. And that intangible but mighty thing which is peace *is* of the essence of home. Surely the house of a woman's soul that is befouled by sin is no home for Christ, it is no haven for the woman herself; there is a civil war going on there and both Christ and the woman are refugees. This is no longer a home but a place to run away from. In the domestic sphere, bickering parents, sullen, rebellious children, self-centered members of a family who can think only of their own rights, all of these destroy home as effectively as a high-powered bomb. Or, taking it on the positive side, that home must be a place of peace, for it is a place where we can rest, a source of strength, a kind of spiritual hospital where our wounds are bound up and our weary souls comforted. Rest, strength, and comfort are not to be sought amid bursting shells and the rattle of machine guns.

But if there is to be peace in the home there must be order there, for order is a fundamental condition of peace. Nor is this merely a matter of picking up clothes and dusting in corners. It is not a mere matter of avoiding slovenliness, though that minimum of order certainly enters into the question. It is much more fundamentally a matter of long goals plainly seen and persistently aimed at; goals that are savored by the mind, that nestle close to the heart and color the judgments of all family activities.

Consequently a woman who finds other things more interesting than the goals of the family, demolishes the home by neglecting its ends; she makes impossible the serene order that must run through the activities of the household if there is to be peace. Her house now harbors chaos in place of order, and war in place of peace; whatever the funeral hush that haunts its rooms, the perfect service it boasts, the deluxe hospitality it offers to an unceasing parade of guests. For in this household, first things are not put first; they are put out. This insistence on the primacy of first things—long, far, hard things—is at the very root of order and so of peace. Thus it is that, on a purely natural basis, the primary place given to the consideration of the children, their health, their growth, their education, their future, gives an almost automatic peace, for it gives an almost automatic order. . . .

There is a literal and beautiful truth in the reward promised in the seventh beatitude: "Blessed are the peacemakers: for they shall be called the children of God." It makes children of parents, and home as wide as the world; which is as it should be. For the Catholic woman is a peacemaker because she is a homemaker. She will be sought, even instinctively, in all the family's search for peace: for physical peace when the children depend utterly upon her in their hurts and sicknesses, for intellectual peace in the midst of the doubts and problems of her husband and her children, for the emotional peace that only love and sympathy can give. Her joy in the homemaking is only another witness to the effects of wisdom at work; for it is wisdom's happy task to turn labor to rest, and bitterness to sweetness.

In the concrete, this means that the closer a woman gets to the last things, the divine things, the better homemaker she is, for the wiser she is. But how to get closer to those divine things? St. Augustine's dictum is still true: we advance toward God, not by steps of the body but by steps of the heart. And Mary's practice is the primary requisite for the taking of those steps; she pondered these divine things in her heart. The parallel, in the natural order, of the Virgin Mother's first step in homemaking is seen in the mother's pondering the things of others, of children, of husband; and it has analogous results, a measure of peace because of its measure of wisdom.

But this is looking at a little world in the light of a partial end, not of an eternal enduring end. It will give a little peace, a kind of home, a degree of order; but not that foretaste of our heavenly home and eternal peace that must be the characteristic of a Christian home.

It is essential to women, then, that they ponder divine things, that is, that they read, meditate, give their hearts a taste of the serenity of quiet prayer. It is not mere chance that women show such a quick appetite for frequent Communion, for daily Mass, that they are often the motive power in the family getting to the mission, and so on. These things hit the very heart of their homes, and women are quick to realize their importance, panic stricken at any evidence of neglect of divine things by the family.

In a family of twelve, where does a woman find time for such reading, meditation, quiet prayer? This is the difficulty naturally brought up by a pagan world which does not understand that this thoughtfulness of wisdom is not so much a matter of a quiet day as of a quiet heart; not so much a matter of closed eyes as of eyes wide open; of using the routine of family life for plunges into the heart of things divine.

With her mind fixed to the last things, the divine things, a woman's little world is seen in the light of the divine; not in the light of social advancement, financial position, conquests of the children, personal convenience, and all the other false beacons that lure the modern home to destruction. The light that illumines the long future of her family is a divine light, the goal of real happiness for herself and her family, the light of the eternal home of which her home is a miniature.

The enemies of the home are the enemies of wisdom, those things that pull the mind and heart of woman away from proximity to divine things, that make it impossible for her to ponder these divine things and, of course, impossible to judge by them. Such things, for example, as the overwhelming interest in earthly things that infest the heart of the mother who has no time for her home. Or, by way of corollary, there is the sluggish lack of appreciation of things spiritual, the jaded appetite's distaste for the things of God; the inevitable enemy that dogs the footsteps of the pagan mother whose eyes fail at the earthly horizon. And then there is sin. The immediate and complete opposition between our very notion of a mother and of a slave of sin is nature's revulsion from the burlesque of homemaking by one who is completely lacking in wisdom, who has made a shambles of her own life, who knows nothing of peace. Vice and the Catholic woman must be strangers, at least they can never be intimate friends; for there is no such thing as a vicious homemaker and the Catholic woman is essentially a homemaker.

Mary was the perfect mother, the ideal of all homemakers, because she was the seat of wisdom; that is, because she was so very close to God, because everything that affected that family circle was seen in the light of the divine goal. There is no other prescription for homemaking, which means there is no other prescription for a Catholic woman's life. Wisdom alone gives order, and tranquil order is peace; without peace, home cannot exist.

The Emancipation of Domesticity

G. K. CHESTERTON

There is only one way in the world to preserve that high levity and that more leisurely outlook which fulfills the old vision of universalism. That is, to permit the existence of a partly protected half of humanity; a half which the harassing industrial demand troubles indeed, but only troubles indirectly. In other words, there must be in every center of humanity one human being upon a larger plan, one who does not "give her best," but gives her all.

Our old analogy of the fire remains the most workable one. The fire need not blaze like electricity nor boil like boiling water; its point is that it blazes more like water and warms more than light. The wife is like the fire, or to put things in their proper proportion, the fire is like the wife. Like the fire, the woman is expected to cook: not to excel in cooking, but to cook; to cook better than her husband who is earning the coke by lecturing on botany or breaking stones. Like the fire, woman is expected to tell tales to the children, not original and artistic tales, but tales—better tales than would probably be told by a first-class cook. Like the fire, the woman is expected to illuminate and ventilate, not by the most startling revelations or the wildest winds of thought, but better than a man can do it after breaking stones or lecturing. But she cannot be expected to endure anything like this universal duty if she is also to endure the direct cruelty of competitive or bureaucratic toil. Woman must be a cook, but not a competitive cook; a schoolmistress, but not a competitive schoolmistress; a house-decorator, but not a competitive house-decorator; a dressmaker, but not a competitive dressmaker. She should have not one trade but twenty hobbies; she, unlike the man, may develop all her second bests. This is what has been really aimed at from the first in what is called the seclusion, or even the oppression, of women. Women were not kept at home in order to keep them narrow; on the contrary, they were kept at home in order to keep them broad. The world outside the home was one mass of narrowness, a maze of cramped paths, a madhouse of monomaniacs. It was only by partly limiting and protecting the woman that she was enabled to play at five or six professions and so come almost as near to God as the child when he plays at a hundred trades. But the woman's professions, unlike the child's, were all truly and almost terribly fruitful; so tragically real that nothing but her universality and balance prevented them being merely morbid. . . .

The shortest way of summarizing the position is to say that woman stands for the idea of Sanity; that intellectual home to which the mind must return after every excursion on extravagance. The mind that finds its way to wild places is the poet's; but the mind that never finds its way back is the lunatic's. There must in every machine be a part that moves and a part that stands still; there must be in everything that changes a part that is unchangeable. And many of the phenomena which moderns hastily condemn are really parts of this position of the woman as the center and pillar of health. Much of what is called her subservience, and even her pliability, is merely the subservience and pliability of a universal remedy; she varies as the medicines vary, with the disease. She has to be an optimist to the morbid husband, a salutary pessimist to the happy-go-lucky husband. She has to prevent the Quixote from being put upon, and the bully from putting on others. . . .

Woman always varies, and that is exactly why we always trust her. To correct every adventure and extravagance with its antidote in common-sense is not (as the moderns seem to think) to be in the position of a spy or a slave. It is to be in the position of Aristotle or (at the lowest) Herbert Spencer, to be a universal morality, a complete system of thought. The slave flatters; the complete moralist rebukes. . . .

It is not difficult to see why the line of cleavage has followed the line of sex, or why the female became the emblem of the universal and the male of the special and superior. Two gigantic facts of nature fixed it thus: first, that the woman who frequently fulfilled her functions literally could not be specially prominent in experiment and adventure; and second, that the same natural operation surrounded her with very young children, who require to be taught not so much anything as everything. Babies need not to be taught a trade, but to be introduced to a world. To put the matter shortly, woman is generally shut up in a house with a human being when he asks all the questions that there are, and some that there aren't. It would be odd if she retained any of the narrowness of a specialist. Now if anyone says that this duty of general enlightenment (even when freed from modern rules and hours, and exercised more spontaneously by a more protected person) is in itself too exacting and oppressive, I can understand the view. I can only answer that our race has thought it worth while to cast this burden on women in order to keep commonsense in the world. But when people begin to talk about this domestic duty as not merely difficult but trivial and dreary, I simply give up the question. For I cannot with the utmost energy of imagination conceive what they mean. When domesticity, for instance, is called drudgery, all the difficulty arises from a double meaning in the word. If drudgery means only dreadfully hard work, I admit the woman drudges in the home, as a man might drudge at the Cathedral of Amiens or drudge behind a gun at Trafalgar. But if it means that the hard work is more heavy because it is trifling, colorless and of small import to the soul, then I say, I give it up; I do not know what the word means. To be Queen Elizabeth within a definite area, deciding sales, banquets, labors and holidays; to be Whitely within a certain area, providing toys, boots, sheets, cakes, and books, to be Aristotle within a certain area, teaching morals, manners, theology, and hygiene; I can understand how this might exhaust the mind, but I cannot imagine how it could narrow it. How can it be a large career to tell other people's children about the Rule of Three, and a small career to tell one's own children about the universe? How can it be broad to be the same thing to everyone, and narrow to be everything to someone? No; a woman's function is laborious, but because it is gigantic, not because it is minute. I will pity Mrs. Jones for the hugeness of her task; I will never pity her for its smallness.

Economic Principles for the Christian Family

SISTER MARY ANSELM O'BRIEN, C.S.J.

In these materialistic times, all too many Christian families become saturated with modern secularism, and, consequently, come to think of success in terms of material possessions. . . .

That many families will have economic problems is inevitable; however, it is not at all inevitable that money matters must destroy family life. The fact is that there are three ways to handle family finance, and two of them are undesirable. One of the wrong methods is for a family to try to amass enough money to supply all the wants of all its members. The second is for parents to shirk their duty by limiting the size of the family so that the few survivors may have all the gadgets they wish. The third, and only correct answer to the problem of family economics, is to adopt a Christian standard of living and to control material desires, so that married life can be lived as God, the Author of life, intends. This means recognizing with Sigrid Undset that "no other belief can give the people of our day the courage to live according to nature and to accept the children which God gives them; only this, to believe that every child has a soul which is worth more than the entire visible created world."

Particularly is this true of those young people who have had everything their hearts desired and who feel that they should begin married life with a standard of living which it took a quarter of a century for their parents to achieve. For too many families today, the problem is not freedom from want, but freedom from wanting everything. Among the things which a really successful marriage requires are these: God's grace, time, and material goods. An all-consuming love of the last of these can absorb so much time and energy in the quest for position, wealth, and security that dependence on God is wholly overlooked, and His sacramental graces are rejected. In terms of the things which really count, like peace of mind and family unity, poorness in spirit will pay dividends far more precious than a late model car, a TV set, or a country club membership, and, in addition, there is that great reward promised in the first beatitude to the poor in spirit: theirs is the kingdom of heaven.

To put these ideas on a workable day-by-day plan, it is not enough merely to warn people to avoid materialism or to buy only necessities. The first warning is too abstract; the second is inadequate to cover the dozens of borderline items which are neither absolute necessities nor outright luxuries. For a down-to-earth guide for the use of material goods, the best we have seen is one derived from the economic views of Saint Thomas Aquinas by Dom Virgil Michel, O.S.B., who makes a very logical division of material goods into:

1. Absolute necessities: the basic foods, clothing, and shelter necessary for life.
2. Conditional necessities: items made necessary by time and place and one's state in life. In this unusual class of goods, a family will be able to govern expenses only by considering whether the item in question will contribute to a more wholesome family life in its particular circumstances.
3. Luxuries: these are items without which a family can get along very well, particularly when acquiring them takes time and effort which should go into family living.

In accordance with this guide, a family should first provide the absolute necessities, by which I mean nourishing, not fancy foods: adequate, but not pretentious housing; and clothing for service, not merely for display. Next arises the question of those conditioned necessities which will best contribute to comfortable, happy living. Only when the family has obtained its absolute and conditioned necessities will it look toward luxuries.

In this matter of conditioned necessities we find the real test of a family's detachment. Will goods be selected honestly in terms of the everlasting nature and purpose of marriage, or will some luxury item be rationalized into the class of essentials? For example, a car is frequently a necessity because of a man's work or his place of residence. For other families, however, a car is a luxury and should be purchased only after the home has been made cheerful and attractive so that the children will seek their recreation within the family circle rather than habitually attending commercial places of amusement which are too often both expensive and morally dangerous. A good example of a genuine conditioned necessity is the tools which a father needs to support his family. Another may be a reasonable amount of home appliances to relieve mother of unnecessary drudgery. Here we have a concrete example of how the Thomistic division of goods takes into account the particular time and place. Things have changed considerably since grandma raised a family in spite of the inconveniences of outdoor plumbing and a wood range, and yet she did not have to contend with city traffic, bubble gum, and other problems which the modern mother must face every day. Grandma was able to hire a girl to help with jobs which can never be done by machine. Today's mother must do these things unassisted, because, at present, it is almost impossible to hire girls to help in the home. When a family purchases a washing or sewing machine which will save both money and a mother's time and energy for child care and other matters which require her personal attention, we have a good illustration of material things being used for a proper end.

And thus we may see that the idea of detachment, based on the first beatitude and on the division of goods according to Aquinas, is not a mere theoretical notion, but a very practical guide for the handling of family finance. Such guidance is badly needed today in this age of materialism, when constant over-emphasis on the possession of goods pushes into the background the more important but less tangible spiritual values. When these are given their proper place, there is no conflict between the all-important Christian standard of living and the very desirable American standard. In fact, they should go hand in hand, using modern comforts and conveniences to conserve time and energy for family activities and the development of individual talents. A gradually rising standard of living is a proper goal for any family so long as possessions are sought as means and not ends, and so long as expenditures do not get ahead of income. The trouble is that high pressure salesmanship, so prevalent today, induces people to persist in buying new things so rapidly that they go far into debt, or consume so much time and effort in making money that they sacrifice higher human aims to material progress.

We Didn't Pray Alone

EILEEN FARRELL

All *our* night prayers seldom go off so peacefully. "Joseph kneel up!" "Eily, kneel down!" "Slower, John!" "Boys, stop kicking!" And so forth.

Nor are the children the sole offenders. Even the head disciplinarian has been known to get the giggles at prayer time, to "break up" as they say in the theatre. But this, I have heard, happens in other families too. Sometimes even in seminaries. It is a peril of the regular common prayer of common people. Or perhaps one of the blessings in disguise, because it is a sure cure for pomposity.

We really want to pray. We need to pray. We like to pray. Now and then we think we may have prayed well. More often we don't. But we keep trying, sustained by the knowledge that He who made us out of nothing understands our nothingness. Sustained also by the conviction that (though there might be more tranquility if each child recited prayers in the cloister of his own bedside) praying together is part of living together. . . .

Tonight we said the night prayers of the Church, condensed and simplified for people like us. . . .

Tonight we wound up, as usual, with the Serra prayer for vocations. Also there was a prayer in honor of St. Thomas on his feast day. And all of this, which may sound like nothing short of a Holy Hour, took well under ten minutes.

We pray for the physical and spiritual health of those closest to us in the bond of charity (not hesitating to say such things as, "Please make us more patient, more gentle"). We pray for our own departed, for those of the parish and those of the neighborhood, Protestant, Jewish, Catholic alike.

We remember the victims of disaster, the cold and hungry, and homeless, the persecuted and dispossessed. We pray for peace.

Well, that's what the petitions are like. They vary from night to night. Whoever leads the decade offers the petitions, so there is quite a bit of free wheeling. In any case it takes no more than a minute or two. Another minute or two goes into thanksgivings. For warmth and food and a downy bed, for a beautiful day, for one another and love, for the faith, for God's grace, for chastisements (can't say this comes without prompting) for the prayers answered the way we hoped, and for those answered in ways unsuspected by us.

Such is our general pattern in verbalizing our love to God at the end of the day. If the words are empty, that is to say, if we haven't been loving Him in our thoughts and works since morning prayers, we know it. . . .

Tonight when we said our prayers, there was no poet to romanticize the two fair, two dark, and one bald head drooping in prayer. As a matter of fact, the heads were pretty steady. We had one of our better evenings. A neutral observer might have thought it an acceptable ritual. Only the eyes of faith could have perceived what was really going on in those few minutes that we knelt to bless the Lord our God.

We didn't pray alone. We were joined by families we know and families we don't know, north, south, east and west. The Sign of the Cross put us side by side with them.

We didn't pray alone. We were praying with Monsignor Maguire, our pastor, and our parish curates, with Cardinal Stritch, our bishop, with all the bishops on earth and their flocks, with Pius XII, our Holy Father. With a Columbian missionary in Binalbagan, a White Father in Uganda, a Cistercian in Dallas, a Dominican in Dubuque, a Passionist in Buenos Aires, a Sulpician in Louisville. With the Sisters of Mercy who teach our children, with Daughters of Charity, Poor Clares, Little Sisters of the Poor.

We prayed with our parents and grandparents, with aunts and uncles, brothers, sisters, cousins, friends, and every faithful Christian who has gone before us into eternity. With our son's sons, with Christians not yet made, who will follow us in life, in death, in resurrection.

The five of us, saying our poor prayers, prayed alongside Peter and Paul and all the apostles, the popes, the martyrs and confessors and doctors and virgins and widows; alongside our patron saints and our favorite saints—Vincent, Therese, Patrick, Thomas, Catherine, Bernadette, Ruth, Blessed Martin, Adam, David.

We knelt with St. Joseph. We knelt with our Blessed Lady.

A flight of fancy? Oh, no. This very morning at Mass we calmly said, not once, but over and over, that we were doing exactly that. Listen: "In communion with . . . *the glorious Virgin Mary* . . . the Blessed *Apostles* and *Martyrs* . . ." and "This oblation of our service and that of *Thy whole family* . . ." and "We Thy servants, and likewise *Thy whole household,* make this peace-offering," and "We Thy servants and with us all *Thy holy people,* offer . . . the Holy Bread of eternal life and the Chalice of everlasting salvation."

We even said we wanted to unite with the angels in prayer: "The heavens and the heavenly hosts, and the blessed seraphim join together in celebrating their joy. With whom we pray Thee join our voices also, while we say with lowly praise . . . holy, holy, holy. . . ."

We didn't pray alone. In those few minutes tonight, we were with men and saints and angels. But above all we were with Jesus, through whom and with whom and in whom all prayer rises to God.

It was Christ within us and ourselves in the Body of Christ who said prayers here tonight, whether any of us thought about it or not. We were gathered in His name. He was here as He said He would be.

Where is the poet who can sing the wonder of a Christian family at prayer? Of the lowly prayer of one very imperfect little human family, made part of the great prayer of God's whole household, and turned to flame by Christ the Lord.

More Miracles at Cana

JOHN C. KNOTT

On the day of their wedding the Church makes to a couple a promise She makes to no one else in the Church. She assures them that this marriage is supposed to be to them "the source of the greatest measure of earthly happiness that may be allotted to man."

This is a promise She does not make to a priest at the time of his ordination. Nor does She give it to a nun at the time of her vows. But to a married couple entering into their vocation of love-service to God and to each other the Church with Her usual realism does state that this couple is supposed to be happy.

The newly-wed reaction to this is—"Why, of course. What else? Why do you think we are getting married except to be happy."

The older married couple inclined to be cynical because of punctured dreams and the necessity of facing the unattractive reality of present sacrifices is liable to mutter—"Don't be too sure, kids. This seems to be part of the old come-on. We had the same dream when we were young, but in time you have to get realistic."

Many married couples give the interested observer the impression that their main object in life now is how to be happy—although married. . . .

One of the hidden sadnesses about so many modern Catholic marriages is that so many good couples are living just a life of duty. The vision of a life of love together they had as an engaged couple has been lost somewhere. The problems arising from the adjustment of two different personalities to a common way of life and love, the strain of rearing children in a confused society, the insecurity of modern living despite the abundance of material things, the countless pressures, little and big, against leading a Christian family life all operate contrary to the advice of Christ to be "glad and lighthearted." They make the promise of the Church to the bride and groom seem unrealistic and of the pie-in-the-sky variety.

For a married couple to recapture today the vision of love they once had and to find in their marriage the source of the greatest measure of earthly happiness possible would seem to demand a miracle. Despite the song title that The Age of Miracles is not Past, most people seem to think otherwise, at least as far as their personal lives are concerned. Yet the fact of history and the evidence of the present would disprove the seeming contradiction in a God Who would give to a young couple the vision of love and deny them at a later date the means of achieving it.

The fact of history is the miracle at Cana in Galilee performed by the Son of God. Although it occurred 2,000 years ago the scene is a familiar one. A new bride and groom are at their wedding reception surrounded by rejoicing relatives, friends and neighbors. Like all newly-weds they were celebrating many firsts as man and wife—their first kiss, their first toast, their first meal and, even so soon, their first problem. The word came that they were running short of wine. Not an important problem one would think today. But to an Oriental such an event would be a minor calamity reflecting as it did on his hospitality.

Fortunately for this unnamed couple "the mother of Jesus was there. Jesus Himself . . . had also been invited." At her intercession He changed the water into wine.

That was the obvious miracle and it happened to a couple in another time and another place. Of more lasting import to the modern couple is the belief that it was then that Christ instituted the Sacrament of Matrimony. Certainly by His presence and His action He evidenced for all time His interest in the practicalities of marriage.

The evidence of the present would indicate that "miracles" in another sense of the word, miracles of grace and love, are happening still to other couples in a time other than the beginning of the Christian era and in a place different than Cana of Galilee. The time is now; the place is America; the intercession is by Our Lady of Cana; the grace is by her Divine Son; the instrument of grace is the Cana Conference Movement with the stewards and drawers of water being the priests, physicians, couples and others engaged in the work.

The "miracles" happening are not as dramatic as the changing of water into wine. In fact, after more than ten years of serving coffee at Cana Conferences, coffee beans, or at least jars of instant powder, are still a necessity. But anything that affects or changes lives, as Cana today has done, does have drama attached to it.

There was a couple who told a priest Cana Director two years after a Cana Conference—"Father, we thought we were as happy as any couple could be two years ago, but since that Conference we have touched depths of happiness that sometimes scare us."

The wife mentioned that since the Conference so many little things had taken on such new meaning. The dish cloth, the mop, the dust-rag, the pots and pans, all the household tools were now instruments of love by which she gave herself in love of her husband and children and through which God poured out His love to her. . . .

Another husband, after attending a Cana Conference ruefully admitted that despite being married for over ten years this was the first time he had ever looked at marriage. Seeing his role as a husband and father as something far wider and deeper in its extension than that of a bread-winner and money maker was a bit humbling and at the same time challenging. He discovered the biggest gift he could give to his wife and children was the gift of himself. Money and the things money could buy had their importance. Yet far more essential to his wife was having a husband who was not only an economic man, but a man standing in the place of God to her, complementing and perfecting her and in turn being completed by her. . . .

Years of experience in Cana work confirm the conviction that with God there is no such thing as a coincidence. It is just God's grace answering a need. Each couple seems to get something different even from the same Conference. The man who said the big thing he received from Cana was a new attitude toward money was speaking for himself, yet if, as someone has said, 67% of the trouble in marriage is caused by money perhaps he was not alone in the help he received from the Conferences.

It is not money itself that causes problems, nor having too

little of it (the common complaint), nor having too much of it (a complaint rarely heard). It is the attitude toward money that determines whether it will be a divisive wedge or a unifying force in a given marriage. A family budget will work only if it is based on the well understood and carefully thought out distinction between needs and wants. . . .

There is a tremendous relief for a couple in being released from the pressure of wants and the constant pursuit of money to satisfy these wants. It also gives an opportunity for the Providence of God to operate. As one veteran husband of five years' service advised a group of newlyweds who were overly concerned with money, bills, paying for children, the insecurity of the future and the like—

"Listen," he said, "when Mary Lou and I were married we had no money. But after five years we have picked up three children, a house and a dog. And we still have no money."

Even if Cana did nothing but give to modern couples, married or about to be, a realistic Christian attitude toward sex, it would have served a great cause. The Catholic woman, by reason of inheritance and education, is liable to look on sex as being dirty, shameful and sinful or at least unwomanly and not respectable. Her gift of herself is then colored by an air of guilt, of sin or at least of reluctance. The husband more readily susceptible by nature to the American error that sex is primarily a physical thing with some emotional overtones ignores the human and personal elements and gives inadequately because he gives incompletely.

Sex understood from a Christian viewpoint has almost "miraculous" effects on the lives of married people. To see sex as a work of God's creation and, therefore, good and to accept it as something sacred because it is concerned with either the giving or the completing of life does much to dispel fears. Cana makes people think about sex and not just talk about it or joke about it or drool over—to paraphrase Frank Sheed. . . .

St. John closed his Gospel with the intriguing verse—"There is much else besides that Jesus did; if all of it were put in writing, I do not think the world itself would contain the books which would have to be written." (John XXI, 25)

Although it may seem so, it is not presumptuous to close the good tidings of Cana with the same thought. The effects Cana has had on the lives of people today are beyond calculation, let alone description. They are found in the hearts, the minds, the souls, the bodies, the lives of families everywhere. They are known only to the mind of the Savior.

To those who have not yet tasted "this water, which has now been turned into wine" (John II, 9) by Cana, Philip's invitation to Nathaniel might be extended "Come and see."

Wanted: Married Saints!

JOHN C. CORT

Just last week a priest friend told me that I should read an article he had found in an obscure theological magazine. It was entitled, "Can a Layman Be a Saint?"

The very fact that the theologians are still asking such questions is enough to prove how new and strange the idea remains, nearly two thousand years after Christ.

Pursuing the subject further, I just went downstairs to the kitchen and asked my wife to name a few lay saints. My wife is a very smart woman.

"Thomas More," she said without much hesitation. (We have a picture of him in the living room.) There was a pause. "Elizabeth of Hungary." (Four of our children were born in St. Elizabeth's Hospital.) Longer pause. "Was John Fisher a layman?"

"No," I said coldly. "He was a cardinal."

At this point she made a break for the religious calendar. "No you don't!" I insisted. "I want to know how many you can give me by yourself."

"I couldn't give you half a dozen, darling," she said, returning to the sink, "and I think it's a disgrace."

"What's a disgrace—the fact that there are so few or the fact that you can't remember them?"

"Both," she said. . . .

The list grows smaller if you lop off the unmarried saints. . . . Then if you lop off the martyrs, kings, queens and princesses, the list grows even smaller and about all you have left is St. Frances of Rome. Even she was "a noble Roman lady" and presumably had plenty of servants to protect her from her three children and make it possible for her to retire to her chamber periodically for prayer and contemplation.

What I am looking for is some poor slob who wasn't much of anybody, worked at an ordinary job, went home at night to his wife and six kids, and did the ordinary things a husband and father does, but did them so well that all the neighbors, after his death, realized he was a saint and started praying to him so hard that miracles began to take place. Before his death most of them probably thought he was a little foolish.

Or maybe it was the poor fellow's wife who worked like a dog keeping the house and the kids and her temper in order, who not only conquered the kids but also herself, and died beloved by all in the full odor of sanctity. Or maybe, which is best of all, it was both of them who became saints, not in spite of the fact that they were married, as most of our married saints seem to have been, but precisely *because* they were married. Perhaps there are such people in the hagiographies, but I can't find them.

Why is it that the married state should be considered such an unlikely place to look for saints?

Sanctity involves love—love of God and love of neighbor—in a heroic degree. And where is such love any more possible than in the married state?

If heroism is the overcoming of extraordinary trials and tribulations, then where are you going to find more extraordinary trials and tribulations than in the married state?

Can one devise a more harrowing experience than taking care of four or five small children for even a few hours on end? My wife takes care of eight all day, every day, all year round, with hardly a hand lifted by her lazy, no-good husband. She is tempted to blow her top a dozen times a day, tempted to the limit of human endurance. When she doesn't, is anything more heroic than that?

Let's face it: if there is no state where heroic love is any more possible than in the married state, we have to admit that it is certainly more probable in the religious state.

Why? To be perfectly blunt about it, it is my opinion that to pursue sanctity in the religious state is to do it the easy way. The priest or religious has part of the job done for him by the very nature of his vocation. He is required by that vocation to devote so much time each day to prayer and the Mass. He is forbidden to assume the responsibilities, distractions, and time-consuming chores that go with matrimony. The whole emphasis of his life is on religion and the love of God. He has a chance to train himself for heroism. For years he attended a seminary and studies how to go about it.

The married man, on the other hand, is thrown into his vocation without special training at all. And by the time he stops bouncing he is either dead or so discouraged that he only wants to be left alone. Ditto for his poor wife.

All this being so, it is remarkable that there has been so little written or done to assist the married couple in pursuit of that goal to which we are all called, namely, to love God with our whole heart, our whole soul, our whole mind, and our whole strength, and our neighbor as ourself. . . .

Fortunately, the Holy Father has been doing a few things that will make sanctity a little easier for married people. He has introduced the evening Mass and changed the rules for the Eucharistic Fast. Already the man of the house can eat his breakfast, go to work, and then attend Mass and receive Holy Communion during his lunch hour at an in-town church. Soon, it is to be hoped the woman of the household, unable to get out for Mass before the old man leaves for work, will be able to make it in the evening after he comes home.

For without the Mass and Holy Communion, without the spiritual nourishment that comes from feeding on the Body of Christ, sanctity surely is next to impossible.

What else can be done? The temptation, of course, is for the married man or woman to think of sanctity in terms of behaving as much as possible like a priest or religious—that is, going to Mass and other religious exercises, getting off in a corner by oneself to pray and read and contemplate, etc. Some of that is certainly necessary.

But if that alone is going to be the goal, then the married person will never make it. Until the children grow up and leave home, there just isn't the opportunity, and by that time it's too late to start.

The only hope is for the married couple to seek their religious life with and through each other and their children. Family prayer is a must, and it need not be limited to once a day. . . .

Bible-reading in the evening is an excellent idea. . . .

After the children are asleep, there comes the opportunity for more advanced spiritual reading and discussion between man and wife. It seems to me that some of this, on a regular basis, is essential. And I would add, some prayers together. *Compline* in English is an excellent exercise to finish off the day.

The longer I live, and the more I struggle with this problem, unsuccessfully, the more I believe that the single most important factor for married people in pursuit of the spiritual life is the ability to turn off the television set, put aside the paper, the book, or the magazine, and start for bed early enough in the evening.

For several reasons: the most appropriate time to do your spiritual reading and say your prayers together is the last thing before you go to sleep. If you wait until it's too late, then the odds are that you're going to fall asleep while you're reading and praying. Secondly, if you don't get to bed early, you're not going to be able to get to Mass or to get in some mental prayer. . . .

Some day I believe there will be religious orders for married people. It's coming. Already it is possible for them to be Oblates of St. Benedict or members of various Third Orders. But with all due respect for these great institutions, they are not designed primarily for the needs of married people. They are adjuncts to great religious orders which are designed for celibates. . . .

Of course only God knows how many married saints there have been. Perhaps when and if we get to heaven we may find that some of the brightest jewels in His crown are obscure husbands and wives, fathers and mothers, that nobody paid any attention to here on earth.

Still, judging only from the evidence available to us, it appears that sanctity is a rare commodity in the married state and that the average man and wife regard it as either impossible or not-to-be-expected.

I suppose the true saint will go ahead by himself anyway, without waiting for any such organization to be formed. And with God all things are possible. But as for the rest of us poor slobs—we need help.

A Plea for the Family

MAISIE WARD

Reading any daily newspaper you feel how deeply imperiled is that ancient institution the Family: plans for education of the child, for his feeding, his playing, the care of his health and his teeth, his whole vocational equipment and training as a citizen, are more and more independent of, separated from, the family unit. Not by totalitarian rulers only but by all governments the pressure is increasing towards treating the child as belonging to the State and reducing to vanishing point the responsibility (to say nothing of the authority) of the parent. And parents seem very ready to co-operate with the State in this matter: accepting the State school and its outlook, rejoicing in the fact that the child's play hours too are handled in groups of his fellow-scholars, that almost all his waking day is outside their ken.

"It's lonely for him at home," the parents of one child very truly remark. And small families are the order of the day, divorce the remedy applied when husband and wife cannot live happily a life which they have almost emptied of the great purpose which should keep them together.

And yet . . . and yet . . . Have you ever made a long journey by plane, train or boat and fallen into casual conversation with the man in the next seat on the plane or the neighbor assigned to you in the ship's dining room? And how long was it before he pulled out his wallet and showed you pictures of his wife and children? Love of family is one of the deepest natural feelings: Père Loew has told us out of his wide experience as a priest working among the workers of Marseilles that not even the brutalizing conditions of life, overcrowding to a point of horror, insufficient food, inescapable filth can altogether destroy a man's love for the baby his wife has borne him. The family is the primary unit of natural society, and nature is hard to kill.

There are other things you can read today—more in periodicals than in the daily press—straws some of them, indications that the wind is shifting its direction a little, others more serious pointers, but all pointing the same way. There are magazine stories of children in anguish for fear their parents intend to divorce, of girls or boys growing up totally unable to adjust to life because of the broken homes in which they had first awakened to it.

Some of these stories are doubtless fiction, but these fictions are the mirror of the fact. . . .

Social workers are increasingly bidding us fix our eyes on these facts. During the blitzing of London they noted that children evacuated to the country away both from the bombing and from their parents suffered far more from nerves and unhappiness than did those who remained with their families, slept in shelters and shared all their dangers and miseries.

In Chicago a number of young divorcees have discovered the fallacy of Chesterton's ironic ending for the modern fairy story, "They were divorced and lived happily ever after," and have formed themselves into a group to work against divorce. Calling themselves "Divorcees Anonymous," they offer to meet and talk with women who intend to break up their marriages, that they may tell them of their own experience, and persuade them at least to wait. One or two divorce court judges accepted this offer, and at the end of a year the group was able to say that it had mended fifty marriages which had appeared hopeless.

In these new discoveries of old truths: that children need their parents, that husband and wife need one another, that the family is of nature's ordering, human beings are going along an old road of establishing truth by seeing the results of denying it. . . .

It was a weakness of nineteenth-century social and religious work that it always grouped the objects of its attention by age and sex. Today we still see this in the structure of our parishes: men's clubs, women's clubs, boys' clubs, girls' clubs. Children of Mary, Knights of Columbus, Men's Communion Day, Children's Mass. The family has been split today, not only by its enemies the Communists but by its friends the Catholics. Not intentionally of course. Taught by the Church to prize family life, we never dreamed that by following the common pattern of our age we might be weakening it. Our eyes were fixed upon certain objectives: the children must learn their doctrine, they must go to a Catholic school: we were willing to pay, to make sacrifices for this end. So much the better if the school in turn took off our hands these other problems of their worship and of their leisure hours—in a good Catholic atmosphere. It was far better equipped than we were to teach, to guide, and likewise to amuse. And so, bit by bit, we parents let go our responsibilities, and in so doing, loosened if we did not lose, the structure of family life. . . .

Somehow we must get back to conceiving the family, not the individual, as the unit. It is too easy for the State to absorb the individual; it is too easy for propaganda, for waves of enthusiasm, to sweep off their feet masses of the young. For the young are naturally conformist: they like to dress alike, to do the same things, to think the same thoughts as all around them. Hence it is always too easy for either Communism or any other ideology to sway them in masses. The absolutely necessary counterweight must be found in the family, in the balance it gives between generations, in its possession of treasures of wisdom and tradition lost in the impersonal school and in the paternalistic State.

But until Catholics themselves return to a full realization of what this means, the Catholic family will do but little. In France, the Young Christian Workers began a splendid apostolate. But when the first generation married and became parents they soon learnt that to continue the techniques they had been using got them nowhere: they must re-think the problem, they must re-group: the unit must now become the family. In such countries as Poland and Hungary where the old traditional pattern of Christian living had been kept, not reflected upon perhaps but simply followed generation after generation, the only chance for Totalitarianism was to break that pattern by breaking up the families. Read the tragic stories of the deportations: fathers and mothers separated, their children torn from them. . . .

There are, as we have seen, indications today that the pagan world around us is discovering that its road to social experiment has been to some extent a road of error: that an effort must be made to restore the stability of society through stable families. Even more is there among Catholics a drive toward re-discovering the fullness and richness of the supernatural community, through exploring all that is contained in the Christian idea of marriage and family life. Family-life study groups, Cana conferences, retreats for married couples, the Catholic Rural Life Movement, the Christian Family Movement, the Liturgical Revival are all increasingly centered on the family. . . .

The restoration of the Christian family can never be done by any family alone: they cannot lift themselves by their own bootstraps. The whole Catholic body must become aware of this problem.

Index of Authors with Sources

ADAM, KARL (1876)
   Holy Matrimony (pamphlet), 243
ANONYMOUS
   Blessing of Nuptial Bed, quoted by E. C. Messenger in *Two in One Flesh*, 59
   Pledge to Christian Marriage, quoted by John A. O'Brien in *Happy Marriage*, 99
   Priest's Customary Address from *The Rites for Marriage and the Nuptial Mass*, 105
   A Wife's Prayer, *The Ave Maria* (May 25, 1957), 159
   Code of Canon Law, quoted by A. H. Clemens in *Marriage and the Family*, 169
   An Ancient Legend, traditional, 170
   A Mother's Prayer, *The Ave Maria* (July 6, 1957), 182
AQUINAS, ST. THOMAS (ca. 1225-1274)
   Summa Theologica, Third Part (Supplement, Q. 41, art. 1), 65
   Summa Theologica, 3a.xxix.2, in *St. Thomas Aquinas Philosophical Texts*, ed. Thomas Gilby, O. P., 68
   Summa Theologica, III Supplement, Q. 41, art. 4, quoted by E. C. Messenger in *Two in One Flesh*, 116
   Summa Theologica, Part 2, Second Part, Q. 151, art. 1, 118
   Summa Theologica, quoted by Fulton J. Sheen in *The Philosophy of Religion*, 127
   Summa Theologica, Q. 94, art. 6, in Modern Library ed. of Aquinas, ed. by Pegis, 128
AUGUSTINE, ST. (354-430)
   De Genesi ad litteram, Lib. lx, cap. 7, n. 12, *Patres Latini*, xxx, 187

BREIG, JOSEPH A. (contemporary U.S.A.)
   A Halo for Father, 173, 213
BROWNE, MICHAEL J. (1895-   )
   The Sacred Roman Rota, 75

CARREL, ALEXIS (1873-1944)
   Man the Unknown, 85
CATHOLIC BISHOPS OF THE UNITED STATES
   N.C.W.C. pamphlet, 193, 246
CERVANTES, LUCIUS F. (contemporary U.S.A.)
   Marriage and the Family: A Text for Moderns (with C. C. Zimmerman), 77, 80
CHESTERTON, GILBERT KEITH (1874-1936)
   What's Wrong with the World, 255
CHRYSOSTOM, ST. JOHN (ca. 347-407)
   "Homilie on First Corinthians," *Select Library of Nicene and Post-Nicene Fathers* (Vol. 12), 27
   "Homilie on Colossians," *Select Library of Nicene and Post-Nicene Fathers* (Vol. 13), 50
   "Homilies 20 on Ephesians," *The Nicene and Post-Nicene Fathers* (Vol. 13), 141
   "Homilie on Titus," *Select Library of Nicene and Post-Nicene Fathers* (Vol. 13), 155
   "Homilies 12 on Colossians," *The Nicean and Post-Nicean Fathers* (Vol. 13), 165
   "Homilie III on St. John," *The Nicean and Post-Nicean Fathers* (Vol. 14), 192
CLEMENS, ALPHONSE H. (contemporary U.S.A.)
   Marriage and the Family, 20
CORT, JOHN C. (contemporary U.S.A.)
   Grail, The (August, 1957), 268
COUNCIL OF GANGRA SYNODICAL LETTER
   The Nicene and Post-Nicene Fathers (Series 2, Vol. 14), 66
COUNCIL OF TRENT
   Catechism of the Council of Trent for Parish Priests, trans. John A. McHugh, O.P. and Charles J. Callan, O.P. (Part II, ch. 8), 48
   Quoted by E. C. Messenger in *Two in One Flesh*, 71
CUTHBERT, FATHER (1866-1939)
   Catholic Ideals in Social Life, 86

DAVIS, THURSTON (contemporary U.S.A.)
   Statement prepared for Maisie Ward and published in her *Be Not Solicitous*, 128

INDEX OF AUTHORS WITH SOURCES 281

DEVAS, FRANCIS (contemporary)
  The Law of Love, ed. Philip Caraman, S.J., 59, 91
DIMNET, ERNEST (1866-1955)
  What We Live By, 40
DITTAMI, MARIO L. (contemporary U.S.A.)
  I Thee Wed, 231
DOLAN, ALBERT HAROLD (1892-   )
  Happiness in Marriage, 164
DOYLE, CHARLES HUGO (contemporary U.S.A.)
  Grail, The (September, 1957), 110

FARRELL, EILEEN (contemporary U.S.A.)
  Grail, The (September, 1956), 261
FARRELL, WALTER (1902-1950)
  The Looking Glass, 251
FRANCIS DE SALES, ST. (1567-1622)
  Introduction to the Devout Life, 125

GANNON, PATRICK JOSEPH (1879-   )
  Holy Matrimony, 53
GEISSLER, EUGENE (contemporary U.S.A.)
  Grail, The (December, 1956), 175
GREGORY THE GREAT, POPE ST. (544-604)
  "The Book of Pastoral Rule," *The Nicene and Post-Nicene Fathers* (Series 2, Vol. 12), 156

HOPE, WINGFIELD (contemporary Great Britain)
  Life Together, 103

JARRETT, BEDE (1881-1934)
  Meditations for Layfolks, 249

KINSELLA, LEO J. (contemporary U.S.A.)
  The Wife Desired, 161
KNOTT, JOHN C. (contemporary U.S.A.)
  Columbia (June, 1957), 264

LACORDAIRE, JEAN-BAPTISTE HENRI (1802-1861)
  Conferences of, 32, 36, 181
  Thoughts and Teachings of, 46, 171

LECLERCQ, JACQUES (1891-   )
  Marriage, A Great Sacrament, 67
LEO XIII, POPE (Gioacchino Pecci) (1810-1903)
  Arcanum divinae sapientiae (1880), 61
  Rerum novarum (1891), 172
  Noblissima Gallorum gens (1884), 190
LORD, DANIEL ALOYSIUS (1885-1955)
  Love's All That Matters, 43

McGINLEY, PHYLLIS (contemporary U.S.A.)
  Good Housekeeping, August, 1954, 221
MACKEN, FORREST (contemporary U.S.A.)
  Ave Maria, The (November 16, 1957), 145
McNABB, VINCENT (1863-1943)
  The Wayside: A Priest's Gleanings, 51
MARITAIN, JACQUES (1882-   )
  Reflections on America, 33
MAURIAC, FRANCOIS (1885-   )
  The Woman of the Pharisees, 35
MILLER, DONALD F. (contemporary U.S.A.)
  For Wives and Husbands Only, 131, 136, 159
MONTJAMOT, R. DE (contemporary France)
  Marriage is Holy, ed. Caffarel, 93
MORE, ST. THOMAS (1478-1535)
  Quoted in *The Father, The Head of the Home* (1956 Proceedings of National Catholic Conference on Family Life, N.C.W.C.), 196
MORONEY, J. FRANCIS (contemporary U.S.A.)
  The Parent-Educator (New Series, Vol. 5), Confraternity of Christian Doctrine, 210

NEW TESTAMENT
  St. John, 167
  St. Paul to the Colossians, 239
NUTTING, EILEEN (contemporary U.S.A.)
  It's A Woman's World, 207

INDEX OF AUTHORS WITH SOURCES 283

O'BRIEN, SISTER MARY ANSELM (contemporary U.S.A.)
The Mother, the Heart of the Home (1953 Proceedings of National Catholic Conference on Family Life, N.C.W.C.), 258
ODENWALD, ROBERT P. (contemporary U.S.A.)
The Father, The Head of the Home (1956 Proceedings of National Catholic Conference on Family Life, N.C.W.C.), 177
The Child and Problems of Today (Symposium sponsored by Family Life Bureau, N.C.W.C., 1952), 197
O'HARA, EDWIN VINCENT (1881-1955)
The Parent-Educator (New Series, Vol. 4), Confraternity of Christian Doctrine, 209
OLD TESTAMENT
Genesis, 25
Canticle of Canticles, 101
Tobias, 108

PASCAL, BLAISE (1623-1662)
"On the Passion of Love" in *Miscellaneous Writings*, 31
PATMORE, COVENTRY (1823-1896)
Religio Poetae, 29
PIUS XI, POPE (Ambrogio Domiano Achille Ratti) (1857-1939)
Casti connubii (1930), 9, 47, 49, 69, 70, 72, 54, 126, 142, 144
Divini illius Magistri (1929), 188, 189
Ad Catholici sacerdotii (1935), 192
PIUS XII, POPE (Eugenio Pacelli) (1876-   )
"The Sacraments" in *The Unwearied Advocate*, II, 50
Catholic Mind, The, xiv, 79; xlviii, 137; and two paragraphs added from *Address to National Congress of the Family Front* and *Address to Association of Large Families*, 134
The Holy Father Speaks to Newlyweds, ed. Schmeideler, 107, 122, 190, 191, 241
Address to the Italian Midwives, 1951, 122, 129
Address to Newlyweds (1942), 158
Christmas Message (1949), 172
Address to Women of Catholic Action (Nov., 1941), 183, 242
The Modern State (1950), 190
Summi pontificatus (1939), 191, 241, 242
Address to Women's Apostolate (1949)

Education and the Modern Environment (1948), 191
Address to Newlyweds (1940)
Plea to Warring Nations (May, 1942), 242

PLUS, RAOUL (1882-   )
  Christ in the Home, 37
  Priest's Customary Address *The Rites for Marriage and the Nuptial Mass*

SCHNEIDERS, ALEXANDER A. (contemporary U.S.A.)
  The Child and Problems of Today (Symposium sponsored by Family Life Bureau, N.C.W.C., 1952), 216
SHEED, FRANCIS JOSEPH (1897-   )
  Society and Sanity 108, 112
SHEEN, FULTON JOHN (1895-   )
  Three to Get Married, 138
SMITH, GREGORY (contemporary U.S.A.)
  The Father, The Head of the Home (1956 Proceedings of National Catholic Conference on Family Life, N.C.W.C.), 205
SMITH, HENRY IGNATIUS (1886-   )
  Radio Address, "Catholic Hour" (April 10, 1932), 243

TERESA GERTRUDE, SISTER M. (contemporary U.S.A.)
  The Child and Problems of Today (Symposium sponsored by Family Life Bureau, N.C.W.C., 1952), 201
THOMAS, JOHN L. (contemporary U.S.A.)
  Grail, The (March, 1956), 202
THOMPSON, FRANCIS (1859-1907)
  In *Modern Catholic Prose*, ed. Theodore Maynard, 44

ULLATHORNE, WILLIAM BERNARD (1806-1889)
  Endowment of Man, 30

VANN, GERALD (1906-   )
  The Heart of Man, 118
  Eve and the Gryphon, 150

WARD, MAISIE (contemporary U.S.A.)
  Be Not Solicitous, 272

WAYNE, T. G. (pen-name for "a professor of theology and a doctor of Catholic philosophy," *ca.* 1936)
Morals and Marriage, 38
WILLOCK, EDWARD (contemporary U.S.A.)
Ave Maria, The (April 20, 1957), 226